Arts, Culture and the
Making of Global Cities

Arts, Culture and the Making of Global Cities

Creating New Urban Landscapes in Asia

Lily Kong
National University of Singapore

Ching Chia-ho
National Taipei University, Taiwan

Chou Tsu-Lung
National Taipei University, Taiwan

Edward Elgar
PUBLISHING

Cheltenham, UK • Northampton, MA, USA

Published by
Edward Elgar Publishing Limited
The Lypiatts
15 Lansdown Road
Cheltenham
Glos GL50 2JA
UK

Edward Elgar Publishing, Inc.
William Pratt House
9 Dewey Court
Northampton
Massachusetts 01060
USA

A catalogue record for this book
is available from the British Library

Library of Congress Control Number: 2014952134

This book is available electronically in the **Elgar**online
Economics subject collection
DOI 10.4337/9781784715847

ISBN 978 1 84980 176 8 (cased)
ISBN 978 1 78471 584 7 (eBook)

Typeset by Servis Filmsetting Ltd, Stockport, Cheshire
Printed and bound in Great Britain by T.J. International Ltd, Padstow

Contents

Tables

Acknowledgements

The National University of Singapore and the Ministry of Science and Technology (Taiwan) funded the research from which this book was written (HSS-0702-P15; NSC98-2410-H-305-053 and NSC99-2410-H-305-064, respectively).

Some of the material in the book has been extracted or modified from:

Chou, Tsu-Lung (2012), 'Creative space, cultural industry clusters, and participation of the state in Beijing', *Eurasian Geography and Economics*, **53** (2), 197–215.

Kong, Lily (2000), 'Cultural policy in Singapore: negotiating economic and socio-cultural agendas', *Geoforum*, **31** (4), Special Issue on Culture Industries and Cultural Policy, 409–24.

Kong, Lily (2007), 'Cultural icons and urban development in Asia: economic imperative, national identity and global city status', *Political Geography*, **26** (4), 383–404.

Kong, Lily (2009), 'The making of sustainable creative/cultural space: cultural indigeneity, social inclusion and environmental sustainability', *Geographical Review*, **99** (1), 1–22.

Kong, Lily (2009), 'Beyond networks and relations: towards rethinking creative cluster theory', in Lily Kong and Justin O'Connor (eds), *Creative Economies, Creative Cities: Asian-European Perspectives*, Dordrecht, the Netherlands: Springer, pp. 61–75.

Kong, Lily (2011), 'Sustainable cultural spaces in the global city: cultural clusters in heritage sites, Hong Kong and Singapore', in Gary Bridge and Sophie Watson (eds), *The New Blackwell Companion to the City*, Malden, MA: Wiley-Blackwell, pp. 452–62.

1. Arts spaces, new urban landscapes and global cultural cities

This book is about cities 'going global' and the cultural and urban strategies adopted towards that end. While global cities have most commonly been characterized as key sites of capital transactions and accumulation, as command centres of intensive and extensive economic activity and as networked nodes, with multiple and recurrent global flows of people, goods, services, ideas and images, the quest for global city status also increasingly rests on the production and consumption of culture and the arts, so that global cities might well be characterized as 'global cultural cities'. This book examines the ambitions and projects relating to arts, culture and creative production undertaken in five major cities in Asia, namely, Beijing, Shanghai, Hong Kong, Taipei and Singapore; it analyses the similarities and differences in their strategies, and their relative successes and failures. In so doing, we hope to contribute to a range of literatures on global cities, urban imaging, urban boosterism, urban rejuvenation, cultural mega-projects and cultural/creative industries and clusters.

This introductory chapter provides the theoretical context and larger empirical backdrop within which subsequent individual chapters are to be read. In particular, we introduce the reader to the literature on global cities, highlighting the ways in which global cities have typically been characterized and the manner in which competition among global cities has been studied. We then elaborate on the ways in which new urban landscapes are very much a part of many urban boosterism strategies, and we introduce the key literature that has examined such new urban landscapes, usually in the form of mega-projects. Often, these are economic projects that entail the development of a mix of retail, industrial, leisure, residential, infrastructural and/or other facilities on large tracts of land, but, increasingly, attention has also been given to the cultural production of space and place, often in monumental proportions, as a means of attracting and sustaining global human and economic flows. We examine the literatures on these cultural icons and their role in urban imaging strategies, in the process highlighting the shift in thinking whereby culture and creativity became important considerations in city competition. Following this, we introduce some of the literature on another dimension of urban

1

landscape change that has occurred around arts and cultural activities, namely, the growth of cultural/creative clusters within which cultural/creative workers engage in cultural/creative production and, often, where cultural consumption takes place. These are typically disused industrial spaces that are transformed, sometimes organically and sometimes via government-led action. Much of this literature draws from cluster theories that are formulated through observation and study of businesses and traditional industries (see, for example, the works of Michael Porter and an even earlier tradition evidenced in Alfred Marshallian ideas), highlighting the agglomeration effects on cultural/creative workers. A critical reading of these literatures helpfully sets the stage for analysing similar, though not identical, urban landscape developments and cultural changes in Asia in subsequent chapters. Much of the existing relevant literatures come from the Western world. In addressing the range of phenomena in the five selected cities in Asia, we hope to seize the opportunity to rethink some of these phenomena.

Finally, this chapter provides an overview of the book chapters and, in so doing, briefly introduces the cities that form the focus of the book.

GLOBAL CITIES AS ECONOMIC PHENOMENON

When the concept of global cities first emerged, the criteria for identifying a 'global city' were largely confined to the nature and level of economic activity of these cities, such as whether the city served as a key location for banking and financial institutions, transnational corporation headquarters or producer services (Hymer, 1972; Paul, 2004; Reed, 1981; Sassen, 1991). Much of the literature reflected this bias, characterizing global cities as 'staging points for global capital formations and flows and nodes of global governance' (Paul, 2004, p. 592). Global cities specialize in global services and are sites 'where truly global services cluster', often serving as hubs of global supply chains that accommodate the headquarters of multinational firms (Sally, 2014). Global cities follow a market logic – they must be open to trade, foreign capital and migrant workers, with regulatory environments conducive for business. They have also been described as places where 'business – in finance, the professions, transport and communications – is done in several languages and currencies, and across several time zones and jurisdictions' (Sally, 2014).

Reflecting the economic bias in most studies of global cities, numerous indices have been devised to measure the relative competitive position of these cities. These indices not only provided a method of measurement but were also complicit in instigating competitive behaviour. John Friedmann, for example, established the notion of a structured hierarchy of global cities (or world cities[1]) – a 'hierarchy of spatial articulations' – in which cities can be arranged according to the economic power they command (Friedmann, 1995, p. 23). He provided a means for visualizing a ranked ordering of major cities, based on the nature of their integration with the world economy (Table 1.1) (Friedmann, 1986). Friedmann examined the hierarchy of global cities in two categories – core countries and semi-peripheral countries[2] – assigning cities in each category with the rank of primary or secondary. Global cities of first/primary rank in core countries were identified as London and Paris, and also included Frankfurt, where the West German economy was centred, Zürich, as a leading money market and the Europort of Rotterdam. Singapore and São Paulo ranked highly for semi-peripheral countries. Selection criteria included whether the city serves as a major financial centre, key manufacturing centre and major transportation hub; whether it houses headquarters for transnational corporations and international institutions, with consideration also paid to population size and whether the city's business services sector was growing quickly. Not all criteria were used in every case, but several criteria had to be met before a city could qualify as a global city of a certain rank (Friedmann, 1986, 1995). Given the state of world development during the years in which Friedmann's world city hypothesis was published – first in 1986, then reproduced in Knox and Taylor's 1995 book *World Cities in a World-System* – his hierarchical ranking did not include cities from countries like India and China since, at that point in time, India and China were only weakly integrated with the world market economy.

Cities of secondary rank in Friedmann's world city hierarchy included cities like Brussels, Milan and Vienna, but Friedmann notes that the list of secondary cities was meant to be only suggestive. He made two observations regarding secondary cities. First, for core countries, secondary cities are usually smaller and more specialized than cities of first/primary rank. Second, for semi-peripheral countries, most secondary cities identified are capital cities (Friedmann, 1986). Above all, he pointed out that intense competition among cities and the volatile world economy meant this hierarchy did not remain stable. Cities are constantly fighting among themselves for more power and control. 'Competitive *angst*,' he wrote, 'is built into world city politics'. With the competitive position of cities continuously changing, any hierarchical ranking can only remain relevant for a relatively short period of time (Friedmann, 1995, p. 23). The implication was also that cities of secondary rank have a chance to achieve global city status.

Likewise, Peter Taylor's (2000) hierarchy of world cities sought to identify cities with the highest 'world city-ness values'. His framework further demonstrates the hegemonic economic criteria. Even while he

Table 1.1   Friedmann's world city hierarchy

Core countries		Semi-peripheral countries	
Primary	Secondary	Primary	Secondary
London* I	Brussels* III		
Paris* II	Milan III		
Rotterdam III	Vienna* III		
Frankfurt III	Madrid* III		
Zürich III			Johannesburg III
New York I	Toronto III	São Paulo I	Buenos Aires* I
Chicago II	Miami III		Rio de Janeiro I
Los Angeles I	Houston III		Caracas* III
	San Francisco III		Mexico City* I
Tokyo* I	Sydney III	Singapore* III	Hong Kong II
			Taipei* III
			Manila* II
			Bangkok* II
			Seoul* II

Note: * National capital; population size categories (recent estimates, referring to metro-region): I 10–20 million, II 5–10 million, III 1–5 million.

acknowledged John Friedmann's widely used hierarchy of world cities, he was nevertheless disappointed by the lack of methodological clarity. Taylor wrote that 'in his [Friedmann's] original list, we are told "selection criteria include" which implies an incomplete enumeration, followed by a collection of functions (for example, corporate headquarters), processes (for example, growth of business services) and measures (for example, population size). How these are combined is not made clear.' In establishing his own order of world cities, Taylor identified three levels of cities – alpha (the highest), beta and gamma. He looked at four key service sectors – banking/finance, accountancy, law and advertising – and identified cities that serve as prime, major and minor centres for each of these sectors. A score of 3, 2 and 1 was assigned to cities for being prime, major and minor centres in the different sectors, respectively. The scores for each city were summed up and the cities arranged according to their total scores, with the highest score being 12. World cities were identified as those that scored four and above. The world cities were then divided into alpha, beta and gamma cities, with alpha cities having the highest 'world city-ness values' and gamma cities the lowest. Alpha cities in Taylor's model included London, Paris, New York, Tokyo, Frankfurt, Hong Kong and Singapore. Beta cities included San Francisco, Sydney, Toronto and

Table 1.2   Taylor's ordering of world cities

	World city-ness value
A. Alpha world cities London, Paris, New York, Tokyo	12
Chicago, Frankfurt, Hong Kong, Los Angeles, Milan, Singapore	10
B. Beta world cities San Francisco, Sydney, Toronto, Zürich	9
Brussels, Madrid, Mexico City, São Paulo	8
Moscow, Seoul	7
C. Gamma world cities Amsterdam, Boston, Caracas, Dallas, Düsseldorf, Geneva, Houston, Jakarta, Johannesburg, Melbourne, Osaka, Prague, Santiago, Taipei, Washington	6
Bangkok, Beijing, Montreal, Rome, Shanghai, Stockholm, Warsaw	5
Atlanta, Barcelona, Berlin, Buenos Aires, Budapest, Copenhagen, Hamburg, Istanbul, Kuala Lumpur, Manila, Miami, Minneapolis, Munich	4

Zürich (Beaverstock et al., 1999; Taylor, 2000, pp. 12–15). A full list of Taylor's alpha, beta and gamma world cities is shown in Table 1.2.

CULTURE IN/OF GLOBAL CITIES

While early global city studies focused on economic criteria and neglected cultural character, since the late 1990s, academic and policy attention has broadened to consider the place of culture in/of global cities. One body of literature highlights the culture of global cities. Among the most notable is the dynamic transcultural character of such cities. Yeoh (1999), for example, observes that global cities are 'sites of transnational cultural mixing'. Similarly, Hall (2000, p. 646) views global cities as sites where transnational flows of various peoples from various cultural backgrounds occur, bringing in creativity that continually renews the city. He observes that the global city is an 'absorptive, continuously changing terrain that incorporates new cultural elements whenever it can' (Hall, quoted in Sassen, 2000, p. 176). As Jacobs (1996, p. 4) believes, the cultural energy from such transnational urban encounters may be leveraged by cities for economic regeneration. Such transcultural encounters bring with them challenges as well: global cities must address inequality and related social issues. The inequality gap in global cities tends to be wider as skilled, educated workers enjoy a larger share of the returns to capital than those lacking in skills. In cities like Hong Kong and Singapore, people have become more sensitive to growing income inequality, more opposed to large-scale immigration and increasingly expect the government to provide more affordable housing, healthcare coverage, pensions and social security (Sally, 2014).

Of particular concern to us in this book is culture in global cities. Competition to become a global city has 'intensified around the production and consumption of culture and the arts, often taking the form of the construction of mega-projects and hallmark events, the development of a cultural industries sector and an upsurge of urban image-making and branding activities' (Yeoh, 2005, p. 945). Cultural development has thus become indispensable to any strategy of global city building (Bryan et al., 2000; Leyshon, 2001; Scott, 1997, 1999, 2000a), and cities striving for global city status do so on the basis of integrating cultural and economic activity. This is manifest in the production and consumption of the arts, architecture, fashion and design, media, food and entertainment (Yeoh, 2005, p. 946). Municipal authorities are increasingly formulating their cultural policy to include the building of high-profile urban flagship projects, production-based strategies such as channelling more resources towards nurturing the cultural industries and consumption-based strategies through urban imaging and place marketing (Kong, 2000b; Watkins and Herbert, 2003; Yeoh, 2005, p. 946). Increasingly, cities hoping to become global cities recognize that they cannot rely on economics alone, but must also become global cultural cities. As Hall (2000, p. 640) observes, many cities believe creating a new urban image requires culture as the 'magic' ingredient that boosts the attractiveness of a city to mobile capital and mobile professional workers.

As competition among cities for global city status intensifies, more and more cities are turning to the accumulation of cultural capital as an essential part of their strategy. Such cultural assets take the form of cultural facilities and cultural spaces, leading to a new wave of cultural space construction, resulting in new urban landscapes. One key strategy that cities have adopted is the building of top-quality cultural facilities (such as museums, concert halls, grand theatres or art galleries), considered by many cities as essential to achieving and maintaining their global city status (De Frantz, 2005). This line of thinking is further strengthened when the most imageable and prototypical global cities are remembered by their cultural infrastructures. The most obvious examples include the Louvre and Pompidou Centre in Paris, the Tate Gallery and British Museum in

London and so forth. Cities in Asia striving for global city status have recognized what such cultural infrastructure adds to their project of 'going global' and have, in recent years, adopted the strategy of creating new urban landscapes through the making of cultural infrastructure, often impressive for their size and scale and their architectural distinctiveness.

The development of cultural mega-projects and icons began with the emergence of cultural policy as an urban regeneration strategy, particularly in the 1980s among Western European cities. During this period, declining cities such as Glasgow and Sheffield – which were struggling to find sources of economic growth as the sectors they had formerly relied on were becoming obsolete – turned to developing large-scale cultural projects to serve as 'symbols of rebirth, renewed confidence and dynamism' (Bianchini, 1993b, p. 15). Frankfurt in Germany pursued its global city aspirations by launching a major project to enhance the city's cultural status. It pumped approximately one billion[3] deutsch marks into constructing high-quality cultural buildings, developing 13 new museums along the River Main and transforming a run-down opera house into a concert hall. More evidence of its increasing emphasis on cultural policy was reflected by the fact that government spending on cultural policy increased from 6 per cent of municipal expenditure in 1970 to 11 per cent in 1990. Paris, under President François Mitterrand, embarked on a series of extensive cultural projects to build its status as the future 'economic and cultural capital of Europe'. It created cultural and architectural icons such as the Louvre Pyramid, the Musée d'Orsay, the Opéra de la Bastille, as well as the Institut du Monde Arabe (Arab World Institute) and Museum of Science and Technology. Similarly, Rotterdam in the Netherlands overhauled its image from that of an industrial centre through cultural projects, such as a new museum of architecture (the Netherlands Architecture Institute) and by developing itself as a site for international film and jazz festivals (Bianchini, 1993b, pp. 16–17). Flagship projects undertaken in the United Kingdom were also crucial in urban imaging. Birmingham's mega-project, for example, was based on urban design strategy and public art policies, and involved building a new concert hall for the city's symphony orchestra, reusing the city's canal system, enhancing the distinctive features of its urban districts, and recreating the city as a site for arts festivals and as a relocation site for London-based arts organizations (Bianchini, 1993b, p. 18; Bianchini et al., 1992). Such cultural flagship projects and icons indeed helped cities to create positive urban images, attract economic investment, develop their tourism sector and enhance their competitiveness (Bianchini, 1993b).

Building top-quality cultural facilities enables cities to host world-class cultural activities or performances, and is regarded as an essential element of the strategy to attract high-end artists/performers and cultural elites from around the globe as a means for the city to develop and maintain its competitive advantage (De Frantz, 2005; Kong, 2007; Landry and Wood, 2003). Cultural infrastructure is also justified as fulfilling other functions in city development. It is argued that cultural infrastructure offers artists or cultural workers a creative environment and platform for interaction and physical spaces for citizens to enrich their cultural life. Cultural infrastructure is said to cultivate local artists by developing their linkages to global counterparts. In addition, it is believed that the development of creative industries – such as music, film, visual arts and fashion design – is promoted through the availability of cultural infrastructure. Further, cultural infrastructure can serve to beautify the city through the creation of symbolic icons and images. This can help the city enhance its attraction and bolster its tourism industry. The development of cultural infrastructure can also increase a city's global visibility through the enlisting of renowned architects to design unique, world-class cultural monuments. It is through all these connections that the city can offer its citizens a more diversified and richer cultural life, and thus solidify its cultural development and identity.

The physical fabric of cultural infrastructure/facilities is more tangible than the invisible or non-physical aspect of cultural development; building huge cultural infrastructures has become the prevailing strategy in many Asian cities. These kinds of projects are seen to be an essential part of national development. However, such projects require a huge amount of resources for construction and operation. The state is highly involved and plays an important role in planning, building, organizing and managing the use of these facilities. However, despite the amount of academic and policy attention that the strategy of building cultural mega-facilities has received, voices of dissent against such a strategy are routinely heard.

Critics assert that the competition for culture tourists biases a city's cultural policy towards the commercialization and marketing of its cultural assets. Even if commercialization per se is above reproach, it could turn pernicious on account of its potential to marginalize local participation in the cultural enterprise, truncate other functions of a cultural policy and dilute the city's local flavour. Badly managed, the strategy of constructing showpiece facilities can contribute to and coincide with the depletion of local cultural assets in the long run (Lee, K-S., 2011). This anxiety is justified by pointing out, first, that while these mega-facilities consume large amounts of public resources, their benefits accrue only to a small group of individuals or particular communities. Second, a commitment to these projects diminishes the resources available for the construction of numerous, spatially dispersed, smaller-scale facilities, which are considered better able to function as spaces for socialization and cultural education. Further, once the facilities are operational, they mark a shift in resource allocation towards organizing large-scale cultural festivals directed at attracting tourists and external performing arts groups. Consequently, while local cultural activity and local artists suffer in general, a significant burden of this resource squeeze is incident on minority cultural groups (Bianchini et al., 1992; Lee, K.-S., 2007). If this trend towards the marginalization of local culture persists, there is a real risk, in the longer term, of what Evans (2003) calls the 'brand decay of the city'.

We draw attention to the critiques that two important scholars have presented. First, Andy Pratt has drawn attention to the need for urban regeneration to reflect a city's unique culture/heritage, which necessarily means developing 'place-bound' strategies. Using the example of the Guggenheim museums, Pratt (2004a, p. 2) observes that culture-based urban rejuvenation projects do not necessarily provide a city with a unique advantage when they consist simply of installing a Guggenheim museum as part of that museum's international franchise. As other Guggenheim museums are found in various countries across the world, the cultural monument is far from being an exclusive, one-of-a-kind asset. Pratt also cautions that 'this trend to sell cities using public money is a socially regressive form of taxation; it is also politically divisive', since promoting elite culture will likely alienate a significant proportion of the electorate (Pratt, 2000a, 2008, p. 112; Zukin, 1995).

Similarly, Allen Scott is wary of embracing elaborate urban rejuvenation projects with uncritical optimism. He notes the growing multitude of programmes driving cities' investment in cultural facilities and emphasizing more culture-intensive forms of production (Scott, 2004) – in cities like Hong Kong, Sydney, Osaka and Singapore but also in places like the Ruhr region in Germany, where heavy-manufacturing infrastructure was recycled to accommodate cultural projects and services production; the Northern Quarter of Manchester; the Cultural Industries Quarter of Sheffield; and the Westergasfabriek in Amsterdam, a former gasworks site converted into a cultural venue (Gnad, 2000; Scott, 2006). This trend of reinventing urban landscapes and engaging in place marketing, which is intertwined with creative city theory, has seen some successes in achieving the desired goals of enhancing the image/prestige of a city, elevating a city's global reputation and its attractiveness to investors and highly skilled labour. Nonetheless, Scott points out such strategies are 'greatly constrained as to both their range of applications and their likely economic results' (Scott, 2004, pp. 464–5) and that, in many other instances, the actual returns on major investment in urban amenities turned out to be much lower than expected. He warns against indiscriminately adopting and applying generic models to individual cities (Scott, 2014, p. 9). Essentially, urban development policies should be designed to suit a specific place and period, as simply implementing a borrowed policy or model does not guarantee the desired outcome (Scott, 2006, p. 12). Scott's view is that urban imaging projects which rely on cultural/heritage and place marketing 'need to be put in due perspective, especially by comparison with an alternative (or, rather, complementary) set of approaches that has more recently started to come into focus'. The alternative he refers to here is a policy focused less on urban reimaging and the selling of places and more on the export of local cultural products to markets across the world (Scott, 2004, pp. 464–5).

Like Pratt and Scott, other scholars have raised questions about the viability of the strategy of constructing cultural mega-facilities. Empirical enumerations of the costs and benefits of such projects remain scarce. Studies comparing the actual and expected performance of these venues are lacking as are cross-sectional comparisons between cities with such facilities (Hamnett and Shoval, 2003). This is a surprising oversight given the consensus that, especially in developing countries, the real challenges come after the facility becomes operational. Supporting the operation and management of the cultural facilities generates a continuous appetite for resources. Evans (2005) identifies how the economic mandate for such projects may be jeopardized when visitor and income targets fall short and delegitimize the continued commitment of resources for their operation. In this light, the need for empirical studies that focus on the post-construction phase of cultural facilities to identify their impact on multiple scales is urgent.

Despite the lack of thorough investigation into the post-construction impact of cultural infrastructure, the strategy of building such cultural mega-facilities continues to be adopted, as we shall demonstrate through our focus on five Asian cities. However, though investing in cultural mega-projects has shifted culture to the forefront of strategies for improving a city's image and its competitive positioning, there is recognition that hardware alone is insufficient. To attract investors and high net worth, skilled global workers and migrants to their cities, city governments have recognized the need to offer an exciting and vibrant cultural life, to which cultural monuments and icons play a role, but which entails more than that. Cities have therefore adopted consumption-based strategies that take the form of urban imaging and place marketing, building a global image and attracting flows of global elites and tourists (Landry and Wood, 2003; Strom, 2002; Zukin, 1995). One approach has been to host hallmark events, ranging from the Olympics (Beijing) to the World Expo (Shanghai), as well as major cultural events, such as Tresors (Singapore), art biennales (Taipei, Beijing, Shanghai, Singapore) and architecture biennials (Hong Kong). Hall (1993, p. 891) cites the example of Barcelona, where, since hosting the 1992 Olympics and using the Olympic Village as a site for urban renewal, the city has launched other urban rejuvenation projects such as the Forum-Besòs project, centred around an Arts Forum (EUKN, 2006). The Arts Forum – a cultural fiesta comprising art exhibitions, concerts, dance and theatre performances – near the River Besòs served as the impetus for transforming and investing in new urban infrastructure in the area (EUKN, 2006; Riding, 2004). Furthermore, effort has been made – though with much more difficulty – to develop a lively local arts and cultural scene in order to provide a diverse cultural life for the city's residents (Goldsmith and O'Regan, 2004; Watkins and Herbert, 2003). The urban imaging strategies that cities undertake, both in the form of elaborate and monumental mega-projects and mega-events to create positive images and the perception of global status, are 'in their essence the pursuit of an ideal, a vision of the city's identity as much as its levels of capital investment, employment or income' (Paul, 2004, p. 574). While an important topic in itself, the study of mega-events must be left to another book; we have chosen to focus in this book on cultural spaces in urban landscapes.

Apart from the production of cultural mega-structures and the hosting of mega-events, initiatives have been introduced to grow (culture-based) creative industries. As mentioned earlier, this is a production-based strategy and is closely associated with urban landscape change, as subscription to the normative theory of clustering leads to the development of creative clusters or creative parks, as they are sometimes termed. We return to this in the next section.

We draw attention to one final point before turning to cultural creative industries and the spaces they occupy. Departing from the obviously economic criteria of Friedmann and Taylor, in recognition of the growing role of creativity in the economy and its potential in boosting a city's competitiveness, Richard Florida has developed an index for measuring the creativity of a city. Florida is best known for his concept of the creative class, in which he posits that in order for economies to grow and compete they need to attract the so-called creative class of workers to leverage creative energy for their development, as he believes human creativity is the ultimate economic resource (Florida, 2005). His theory of economic growth, as articulated in his book *The Rise of the Creative Class* (Florida, 2005), has attracted considerable controversy, with critics charging that his creative class theory is elitist and questioning the soundness of his methodology and data (Clark, 2004; Glaeser, 2004). Nevertheless, the Creativity Index developed by Florida remains a method by which competition among cities has been studied (see, for example, CCPR, 2005). It is intended to serve as an indicator of a city's overall standing in the creative economy, by measuring the creative capabilities of a particular place. The Creativity Index is a composite indicator made up of four equally weighted factors: (1) a Creative Class Index; (2) a High Tech Index; (3) an Innovation Index; and (4) a Gay Index (Florida, 2002b, p. 6, 2005, pp. 332–4). The Creative Class Index shows the percentage of creative workers in the workforce. The High Tech Index acts as a measure for high-technology industry, while the Innovation Index is a measure of patented innovations per capita. Finally, the Gay Index is a measure of the representation of gay people in a region relative to the country as a whole, and serves as a gauge for diversity or as a proxy for the city's openness to diverse people and ideas (Florida, 2002b, p. 16, 2005, pp. 332–4). Cities are ranked according to their overall Creativity Index score, providing an indication of their competitive position. Although not explicitly about global cities, Florida's Creativity Index provides another yardstick by which cities compete.

THE SPACES OF CULTURAL CREATIVE INDUSTRIES[4]

Cities in Europe and other parts of the world have subscribed to the idea that cultural or creative industries form the basis for economic regeneration (Hall, 2000, p. 640) and increased competitiveness. These ideas have 'travelled' to Asia (J. Wang, 2004), albeit unevenly (Kong et al., 2006). The normative script is characterized as follows. To compete in the new creative economy, cities should seek to implement particular initiatives: encourage creative industry clusters; incubate learning and knowledge economies; maximize networks with other successful places and companies; value and reward innovation; and aggressively campaign to attract the 'creative class' as residents (Gibson and Kong, 2005). In this book, our focus is particularly on the adoption of creative industry clusters as an urban strategy.

'Clusters', or the co-location of specialized industries, are not new. The phenomenon has been acknowledged since 1890, with the writings of Alfred Marshall, who noted the 'concentration of specialised industries in particular localities' (Martin and Sunley, 2003). Since then and in more recent years especially, a number of authors have attempted to develop conceptualizations of such concentrations.

Most of the literature has focused on industrial or business clusters, which have drawn the attention of many policy-makers seeking to promote national, regional and local competitiveness, innovation and growth. Drawing particularly on the work of Porter (1998, 2000), the following refrain has developed about the benefits of clustering: it delivers higher rates of innovation because it allows rapid perception of new buyer needs; it concentrates knowledge and information; it facilitates ongoing relationships with other institutions including universities; it allows for rapid assimilation of new technological possibilities; and it provides richer insights into new management practices (Simmie, 2004, p. 1096). Much attention has also been paid to the transaction cost advantages and increasing returns to scale that arise from clustering, as well as less measurable benefits such as the building up of social capital (Fukuyama, 1995), tacit knowledge and informal networks, and the 'cafeteria effect' (Konstadakopulos, 2000). This adds to the explosion of literature acknowledging how inter-firm learning is facilitated with concentrations of firms, institutions and labour; how interactions between different agencies, including government agencies, are enhanced; and how understanding of client needs are sharpened (see, for example, Amin and Thrift, 1994; Cooke, 2002b; Grabher, 1993; Scott, 1996, 2001; Scheff, 2001; Storper, 1997).

How might all of this be relevant to cultural/creative clusters? It is a question that deserves to be asked, but which has been elided once too often. The cultural/creative cluster is too often conflated with business and industrial clusters, and subjected to the same economic analysis and policy response as other industries. This is unsatisfactory, as many creative clusters are 'de facto cultural quarters with assorted cultural consumption and not for profit activities' (Evans et al., 2005, p. 26), thus meriting evaluation through a different lens. The relevance and supposed benefits of applying cluster logic to the cultural/creative industries may be described as follows. Cluster logic posits that concentrations of related activities produce 'creative milieux' (Hall, 2000) or 'creative fields' (Scott, 1999, 2006) in which exist structures that encourage learning and innovation, and social relations that exhibit trust, mutuality and cooperation. These institutions and networks are socially constructed and culturally defined, as well as deeply embedded in local contexts. Cultural and artistic communities located in physical propinquity are thus 'not just foci of cultural labour in the narrow sense, but are also vortexes of social reproduction in which critical cultural competencies are generated and circulated' (Scott, 1999, p. 809). They attract other talented individuals, who migrate to join these communities. These communities are 'collectivities' whose members are engaged in 'mutually complementary and socially coordinated careers' and are 'repositories of an accumulated cultural capital' (Scott, 1999, p. 809). Institutional infrastructure such as schools, training and apprenticeship programmes, workers' organizations and industry associations serve to sustain cultural capital within the community. These features serve as an overarching order, the 'industrial atmosphere' that Marshall (1919, cited in Scott, 1999, p. 809) referred to almost a century ago.

In addition to coordination, cultural communities that group together benefit from sharing codified as well as tacit knowledge. The latter implies that knowledge is embedded locally, thus cultural producers need to be 'inside' the circuit of knowledge. Consequently, the cultural sector relies on a network of creative producers. Collective learning and transfer of knowledge arise from such frequent interactions within a cluster (Bassett et al., 2002, pp. 172–3; Capello, 1999). Further, with 'insiders' knowledge and immersion in the local scene', the 'vital innovations and mutations' take place and the 'creative work gets done' (O'Connor, 2004, p. 136). Such work involves the transformation of signs, the creation of 'a style, a look, a sound' by local culture, made possible because the city (and the cluster) has acted as a 'crucible' (O'Connor, 2004, p. 134). Such place-focused cultural work results in cultural products often becoming associated with particular locales; the consequent 'reputation effect' becomes the source of location-specific monopoly rents (Scott, 1999, p. 810).

Efforts to improve our conceptual understanding of cultural/creative clusters have drawn attention to the following additional distinguishing dimensions. The first is an acknowledgement that location is not only about a physical coordinate, or indeed about relative location – that is, location in relation to other activities. Instead, it is about 'the particular traditions, conventions and skills that exist in any given urban area [that] help to infuse local products with an exclusive aura that can be imitated by firms in other places but never completely reproduced' (Scott, 2006, p. 10). Location is thus about the unique character of a place that shapes the nature of the cultural product. Where a cultural cluster exists matters because it moulds the specific identity and character of the cultural product, whether it be music, art or poetry.

The second distinguishing quality of cultural/creative clusters is the fact that cultural producers need to be 'inside' the circuit of knowledge where 'insiders' knowledge and immersion in the local scene produce the vital innovations and mutations' (O'Connor, 2004, p. 136), because the unique 'style . . . look . . . sound' of 'local culture' cannot be transmitted formally as codified knowledge. The (re)production of a cultural product is dependent on such a nuanced and tacit understanding of the qualities of a place and the character of a product.

The promise of clusters has led to enthusiastic development in numerous cities, including those we study in this book. Cities have taken to redesignating existing spaces to perform cultural functions and recycling urban spaces as creative clusters, in the hope of boosting their cultural and artistic capacity. Examples are old urban spaces that have been converted into working space for artists and, in some instances, industrial parks for the concentration of creative works and cultural entrepreneurs (Grodach and Loukaitou-Sideris, 2007; Hitters and Richards, 2002). Potts and Keane (2011) documented the 'several distinct, although overlapping stages' of the formation of cultural/creative clusters in China, which was led by various city governments. A first wave comprised spaces dedicated to industrial design, antiques, animation and sculpture. A second involved artist zones and cultural districts, followed by media content clusters (especially animation). Stand-alone cinema, television and animation production centres followed and, finally, the incubator model emerged, 'often with a purported emphasis on R&D, and often with the declared intention of making science parks more "creative"' (Potts and Keane, 2011)

While the above demonstrates that there have been efforts to conceptualize and categorize clusters, including cultural/creative clusters (for example, Bassett et al., 2002; Evans et al., 2005; Flew, 2005; Mommaas, 2004; see also Kong, 2012b), conceptual models are often built on theoretical logics not always grounded in in-depth ethnographic analysis of empirical phenomena, let alone in different parts of the world and under different circumstances where different logics may prevail. Zukin's (1982, 1989) well-known work on the concentration of artists living in lofts in downtown as well as midtown Manhattan and Brooklyn remains one of the most memorable and richly detailed works that deserves to be emulated. As she details, the movement into and settlement of cultural/creative workers in Manhattan, New York City, stimulated the transformation of the former industrial area into a vibrant artistic district. Until the end of the 1960s, Lower Manhattan's urban landscape consisted mainly of manufacturing compounds and stores, along with ethnic neighbourhoods and some newer office buildings. Garment factories, printing plants, small manufacturers of mechanical and consumer goods, distributors and suppliers occupied the area. Towards one end of Lower Manhattan stood a group of nineteenth-century, multi-storey loft buildings with large, open spaces on each floor formerly used by manufacturing firms (Zukin, 1982, pp. 259–60). Due to changes in production processes that required even more floor space, these manufacturing firms had relocated from the lofts to larger premises elsewhere. The general feel evoked by the remaining loft buildings was one of urban decay; both vacancy rates and rents there remained low. However, from around 1961, artists began to move into these lofts in downtown Manhattan as well as midtown Manhattan and Brooklyn, as part of New York City's growth as a world art capital

(Zukin, 1982, pp. 260, 263; 1989). Artists were attracted to the lofts not only because of the low rent but the expanse of floor and window space, which made them suitable as live-in studios. The high ceilings were particularly useful for exhibiting large works of art (Zukin, 1989, p. 2). More and more lofts were soon converted into studios for artists and musicians, home offices for writers or used to house new service-sector cottage industries such as fashion design (Zukin, 1982, p. 257). Loft buildings became 'artists' quarters' where artists held exhibitions; they drew art dealers, museum curators and collectors (Zukin, 1989, pp. 2, 4). The urban environment thus began developing into a place for arts and cultural activities, and a site for cultural production and consumption. Visitors to the area were impressed by the stylish lofts done up by artists, and the public began to pay increasing notice. By around 1970, lofts had been transformed into a symbol of 'bourgeois chic', attracting large numbers of middle- and upper-middle-class people who began to move in and live in lofts (Zukin, 1989, p. 2). Zukin surmises that loft housing attracted those in search of the unconventional: 'closet hippies' seeking 'marginal chic'. The idea of residing in post-industrial spaces perhaps appealed to people's sense of art and history, space and time. Artists' living habits had become 'a cultural model for the middle class' (Zukin, 1989, pp. 14–15). Some of the new middle-class residents paid architects and designers to carry out major renovations to their lofts. As this urban resurgence continued and more lofts became converted for residential use, investors and professional real estate developers began to take notice and get involved. The real estate market in lofts grew further (Zukin, 1989, pp. 2–3). Over time, loft buildings and the manufacturing districts where they were located were transformed into residential and commercial spaces. Stylish loft residences and boutiques of cultural consumption burgeoned in areas formerly monopolized by factories or warehouses (Zukin, 1982, pp. 256–7). Although Zukin's study of New York lofts was not focused on the dynamics within the cluster, which so much of the literature has tended to valorize, it succeeded in demonstrating how urban landscape transformation can be driven by arts and culture, and the role of arts/culture in enabling social and economic change (Zukin, 1982).

While Zukin's work has long been in circulation, and the phenomenon she describes and analyses is well known, the empirical case in other contexts needs to be carefully made. Rather than assuming that the relationships and processes in Manhattan and Brooklyn, or those in Porter's business clusters and Marshall's industrial clusters, will be replicated elsewhere, there needs to be detailed empirical and ethnographic work conducted of other places and experiences in order to draw up more robust theory about clustering and urban change. As Martin and Sunley (2003,

p. 28) observed, the empirical case for clustering remains unclear; 'explanation of causality and determination' has become 'overly stretched, thin and fractured'. Even though Martin and Sunley were mostly focused in their critique on the economic benefits of clustering, their concern to have sound empirical evidence of causality is pertinent here in relation to cultural and creative workers and groups, though they sometimes (or often) differ in being non-profit groups; the questions asked about the value of physical proximity must thus be focused on other kinds of benefits. Today, there remains a severe shortage of micro-level analyses of cultural/creative clusters at ground level, and theory built up from there. This book is motivated in part by a desire to contribute to the micro-level understanding of specific sites in the hope of contributing towards a more refined and robust theory of cultural/creative clusters.

METHODOLOGY

Before we introduce the cities that form the subject of analysis in this book, we add a short note on our methodology. The material for this book is drawn from detailed ethnographic fieldwork conducted by the three authors mainly over a four-year period from 2007 to 2010. Interviews were conducted with a total of 226 individuals across the five cities (35 in Beijing, 55 in Shanghai, 51 in Hong Kong, 51 in Singapore and 37 in Taipei). Among those interviewed were arts practitioners (visual artists, theatre practitioners, gallery curators, exhibition organizers, designers and so forth), gallery owners, café owners, local scholars, arts educators, officials in various government agencies (such as urban planning departments and art councils), and cultural facility and cultural cluster managers. During the fieldwork period, we made numerous visits to all the cultural monuments and creative clusters covered in this study, including the studios, galleries, cafés and other facilities within. We were participant observers, studying, *inter alia*, visitor rates, audience make-up and programming (often, performances and exhibitions). We also relied on various other sources of information, including the local newspapers in each of the cities, magazines, online reports, policy documents and significant speeches by government leaders. In sum, we believe that the rich ethnographic detail afforded by painstaking fieldwork, set within the broader contexts of the economic, political and cultural changes in these cities, as drawn from primary and secondary documentary analysis, will provide many new insights into the arts spaces and new urban landscapes of the five (aspiring) global cities. The empirical material thus collected will also contribute to a better understanding, if not reformulation, of various theories.

ORGANIZATION OF THE BOOK

Following this introductory chapter, the book comprises ten substantive chapters divided into two parts. Part I examines the construction of cultural mega-facilities, the hopes invested in them and the challenges faced in their construction and subsequent consumption. The five chapters in this part, each focusing on one city, tell a story of global city aspirations, the use of a cultural (infrastructure) strategy and the urban change that is attendant on such a strategy. Part II focuses on the same five cities, this time addressing a different kind of arts space, that of clusters, sometimes organically evolved, other times state-implemented and yet other times business-led. Through the reuse of old factories and schools, new urban landscapes emerge that contribute in varying degrees to the cultural and creative lives of the cities. Following the ten substantive chapters, the final chapter summarizes observations and draws together lessons learned in order to refine and sharpen theoretical understandings of arts spaces, new urban landscapes and global cities.

We have chosen to focus the first of the book's substantive chapters on Beijing because, in one sense, it may be described as a city of monuments. From the Forbidden City to the Summer Palace, from the Great Hall of the People to Chairman Mao's Mausoleum, this city with its ancient history is full of mega-structures that speak of the grandeur and political power of another time. Chapter 2 contextualizes the development of one of the latest cultural infrastructure projects – the National Grand Theatre – by tracing the ideological and policy shifts that have shaped the production of cultural space in Beijing, highlighting the early use of cultural space as a tool for nation-building, the more recent treatment of culture and space as capital in the period of Reform and Opening Up and the still more recent period of building Beijing into a global city. The chapter focuses particularly on the discourse and reality surrounding the construction of the National Grand Theatre in Beijing's cultural landscape. Three sets of questions are addressed. First, the genesis of and motivation behind the construction, as well as the building strategy and process, are examined. Second, the construction of a new urban cultural space and the changes wrought foreground diverse issues such as architectural design, public project safety, the changing city image and so forth. The ways in which these issues were debated, the public discourse generated and the insights gained of the relationship between the state and public participation are all examined. Third, since completion in 2008, the National Grand Theatre has been subject to multiple interpretations; the different rewritings and rereadings of the new cultural landscape by various communities within Beijing are analysed.

Following this chapter on Beijing is, unsurprisingly, a chapter on Shanghai (Chapter 3), a city that has long felt a sense of rivalry with the national capital, desirous as it is to gain primary position within the national imaginary and, simultaneously, the world stage. In its efforts to pursue global city status, Shanghai has devoted significant resources to develop its cultural infrastructure in order to support 'global' cultural activities as well as flows of global elites, tourists and investments. This cultural emphasis is also intended to assist local cultural development, to solidify civic identity and to promote the cultural sophistication of its citizenry. By examining two of the most significant cultural projects in recent years, namely, the Shanghai Grand Theatre (SGT) and the Oriental Art Center (OAC), this chapter examines the ways in which cultural infrastructure projects have been used to promote the city's global status, as well as what these cultural infrastructure projects mean to various groups in Shanghai. In particular, the chapter introduces the top-quality facilities at these cultural mega-projects that have managed to attract a range of global cultural activities, thus promoting Shanghai's city image and cultivating a sense of pride. SGT and OAC have also attracted 'high class' audiences from nearby provinces and international tourists, promoting Shanghai's status as a cultural centre in the Yangzi Delta region in southeastern China, and even in China and the Asia-Pacific region. However, due to Shanghai's ambition to be a global city and the high costs of operating top-quality facilities, SGT and OAC seem to cater exclusively to tourists and local elites. Lacking are efforts to draw in local residents as audiences and strategies to support local art groups that develop local cultural contents. While it is relatively easy to build cultural infrastructure in the short run, fostering art and cultural appreciation needs long-term planning and development. The growth of an art-appreciating population, the maturation of local artists and the availability of space for local art-workers are requisites for economic development based on cultural industries. Thus, while investments in 'high culture' facilities have the potential to enrich cultural life, the promotion of local cultural development is necessary for cultivating the artistic and cultural sensibilities of the resident population.

Unlike in Beijing and Shanghai, where major cultural infrastructure construction has transformed the urban landscape, in Hong Kong, the large cultural infrastructure project is still being constructed. Chapter 4 focuses on 'Asia's world city' and how it sought to get an iconic project off the ground – taking more than a decade and a half. The idea of a cultural district in West Kowloon was first mooted in 1996 after the Hong Kong Tourist Association released the results of a survey it had conducted, in which 1.3 million of the tourists polled expressed an interest in arts and cultural and entertainment events. The association thus proposed that more large-scale performance venues be developed. The plans of the early 1990s were for the land at West Kowloon to include a park, for commercial and residential development and government or community uses, but in 1998, informed by the tourist association's research and ideas, the then-Chief Executive, Tung Chee Hwa, announced the government's plan for a new performance venue in West Kowloon. In 1999, it was specified that the 40-hectare site in West Kowloon would facilitate the development of an integrated arts, cultural and entertainment district. Since the announcements of over a decade ago, there have been many twists and turns in the plans for the West Kowloon Cultural District, as it has come to be called. The chapter analyses the many public responses to the plans, the ways in which civil society organized itself in opposition to what they saw to be a property development under the guise of an arts and cultural hub and the official efforts to respond to the public and interest group protests. The economic imperatives were thought to get in the way of real cultural and artistic development; the (*de jure*) democratic openness of Hong Kong society enabled the participation of many individuals and civil society groups. The result is that Hong Kong's answer to the many new cultural monuments being established in rival cities in Asia still remains to be completed after more than a decade and a half.

Singapore and Hong Kong are often compared with each other – the next chapter on Singapore (Chapter 5) allows for the situation of the two benchmarked cities to be analysed side by side. Singapore, as with the other cities examined in this book, has global aspirations to be in the superleague of cities. Indeed, some argue that it can already claim global city status, as a linchpin of the new global capitalism. At the same time, this city-state is ceaselessly engaged in the project of nation-building and the construction of national identity. In all of this, a cultural focus has been acknowledged as an important component of the city-state's overall strategies; the development of new cultural monuments has, in turn, been a part of the cultural strategy. At the same time, the cultural strategy is an economic one, recognizing the potential of the cultural industry to generate income and contribute to the city's economic growth. Cultural ambitions in Singapore are expressed in terms of a desire to be a 'Renaissance city' and a 'global city for the arts'. In terms of major cultural infrastructure, the Esplanade – Theatres on the Bay and the renovated and extended National Museum are among the major enhancements to the hardware supporting the performing and visual arts in the city. Yet, while acknowledging that global cities have world-class cultural infrastructure, the arts community in Singapore has argued that providing the 'hardware' (infrastructure and facilities) without concomitant attention to the 'software' (creative development) has a regressive effect on the development of local/indigenous arts. For members of the arts community, the development of large cultural infrastructure attracts large exhibitions and performances, but leaves little room for local communities to develop their own art forms. While a global flavour is apparent, so too is the absence of well-developed indigenous arts. The local arts community thus sees Singapore as 'a kind of emporium for the arts', offering yet another retail space, which they fear will stymie the blossoming of local styles and the maturing of national identities. No global city is worth its salt if it does not have a strong base of indigenous works that express local flavours, showcase local idioms and styles and develop national identities. The chapter thus focuses on Singapore's evolution in the successful provision of cultural infrastructure next to its search for a local voice and local styles.

Of all the cities examined in this volume, Taipei is the one city that has perhaps had the most troubles economically and politically in recent years. In that sense, its energies have been absorbed; the ambition of being a global city with its concomitant projects and strategies has perhaps seemed less urgent and pronounced. The idea of developing a major arts and cultural facility came late to Taipei, in 2004. Chapter 6 – the last chapter in Part I – begins by setting out the political and economic contexts in Taipei and the ways in which they have influenced the evolution of cultural infrastructure developments in the city. It then analyses the impacts of such infrastructural developments on Taipei's cultural workers, particularly artists, and on the cultural life of its citizens. It explores the dynamics of global–local cultural interactions and the influences of such dynamics on Taipei's urban landscape. As the capital city, Taipei is the main site of Taiwanese cultural infrastructure investments, such as the National Palace Museum, the Sun Yat-sen Memorial Hall, the National Theater and Concert Hall. All these facilities have had their political functions since 1949. On the one hand, these facilities helped the Republic of China (ROC) government declare to the world that Taipei still had legitimacy in Chinese cultural production. On the other hand, they were used to implement ideological education in order to unite the people against communism. The situation changed in the early 1990s, when the government rescinded martial law and implemented democratic processes. Accordingly, many assembly halls previously used for political functions were released for cultural and art performance use. This change has restructured Taipei's cultural landscape significantly. It now offers space for the development of the performing arts as well as provides its citizens with more diversity in the arts. Since the late 1990s, due to globalization and competition from other cities, the state has recognized the ability of special cultural assets to offer competitive advantage and secure its global city status. Decision-makers thus planned to construct new cultural infrastructure aimed at accumulating Taipei's cultural assets and promoting civic cultural life. In the development of Taipei's new central business district (CBD), Xinyi Center, the state succeeded in mobilizing private resources to build the Novel Hall for Performing Arts. At the same time, in acknowledgement of the enlarging audiences for the performing arts and of the competition from other cities in the Asia-Pacific region, many domestic performance groups and artists called on the state to construct a new concert and theatre hall to support performances, particularly international, high-end performances. In 2004, the central government proposed a construction plan for building the largest theatre in Taiwan, the Taipei New Grand Theatre, in the new Banqiao CBD of Taipei County. Due to the huge financial investment needed, the state sought to mobilize private developers' resources once again but the plans received support from neither the state nor the cultural community. The failure of the plan stimulated the newly elected Taipei mayor to put up plans for another facility instead – the Taipei Performing Arts Centre – with investment from the city. Taipei's situation offers different insights from that of the other cities examined in this book. Here, cultural life is active, with a large number of performing arts groups, including some internationally acclaimed ones. Yet, the construction of cultural infrastructure has not caught up with the quite mature cultural and performing arts scene and the level of cultural appreciation of the citizens. This is not because of a lack of vision; rather, the inability to implement the state's plans can be attributed to political disputes and unstable administrative arrangements.

The chapters in Part II consider another dimension in the evolution of global cultural cities. This is the use of old urban landscapes in new ways as part of the artistic and creative life and the cultural/creative economy of the cities, particularly in the form of cultural clusters.

Chapter 7 returns to an analysis of the situation in Beijing, beginning with an investigation of the policy discourse and practice for the development of cultural creative industries, addressing both organically evolved clusters and the state-led cluster strategy for cultural creative industries and their impacts on the development of cultural creative work. This is the context of a specific analysis of the space now nationally and internationally known as '798' or 'Dashanzi'. The original organic development of the cluster in former factory space was facilitated by low rents at the turn of the century, which attracted artists from Beijing, other parts of China and overseas. We examine the conditions that supported the development of the arts cluster and the growth of a nascent, socially embedded cultural network. Subsequently, as the government and the Seven Star Group began to be interested in its development, conflicts emerged; we examine the multiple and complex relations between artistic networks and state interventions. The chapter makes the point that much cultural space construction in Beijing is a state-sponsored effort, as is the approach to creative cultural clusters, emphasizing physical infrastructure construction while neglecting the construction of artistic networks and institutions. The 798 case presents evidence that the state attempts to establish and predetermine a developmental path, rather than promote the indigenous growth of artistic creative networks. The result of state interventions was the lack of a conducive environment that supports organic and indigenous development of cultural space.

We then turn to Shanghai in Chapter 8. As with numerous other cities in Asia, Shanghai has sought to promote its creative industries as part of its urban competition strategy, through which it seeks to maintain its global status and functions. One of the key approaches adopted is the revitalization of vacated industrial premises through the establishment of 'creative clusters' or 'creative precincts/parks' to house artists and other creative workers. Since 2006, the city government has approved over 100 creative parks. This chapter examines the driving force behind the development of creative clusters in Shanghai and documents the ways in which the urban landscape is changing as a consequence. It also explores how vacated premises are used to assist artists and develop Shanghai's creative industries. It then evaluates the effects of the development of these creative clusters on the city's cultural and spatial development. The chapter uses three cases to examine the evolution of Shanghai's creative clusters and the interactions and dynamics among different key actors. These clusters are M50 at Moganshan Road, Tianzifang at Taikang Road and 1933 at Hongkou District. M50 and Tianzifang are first-generation projects in Shanghai's development of creative clusters, while 1933 is a newly developed cluster. M50 and Tianzifang have undergone a more organic evolution than 1933, supporting creative industries with cheap space for artists. Tianzifang in particular has been the site of significant interaction with the community immediately surrounding it, thus contributing socially. From a cultural perspective, M50 and Tianzifang are also clusters that have 'real content', having attracted some top artists in Shanghai. Galleries in these two clusters mostly exhibit Chinese contemporary artists' works rather than foreign artists' work. They thus contribute to the longer-term sustainability of Chinese art and culture, although they also face many issues in their current and future development. In contrast, the state has intervened to a large extent in the development of 1933. Originally slated to become the essential place for leading design and innovation work, it was to have cultural, educational, entertainment and food and beverage businesses located on its premises. However, its space is mainly for consumption rather than artistic creation. After a period of slow development, it has now witnessed the opening of many shops, restaurants, wine bars, clothing outlets and other consumption spaces. Despite the support of the government of Hongkou District, the project has not become a space of creative production.

In Chapter 9, we turn to Hong Kong, the cityscape of which is usually associated with modern, high-rise, gleaming structures and towering skyscrapers. But Hong Kong also has its fair share of old factories, depots, warehouses and such, associated with its more industrial face. In this chapter, some of the transforming urban landscapes of Hong Kong are introduced as emergent spaces for the arts. These cultural clusters are found in industrial estates, factory spaces and old depots. We focus on two different clusters of arts activities in Hong Kong – one that exists amid functioning factories and another that occupies a former quarantine depot for cattle. Through these cases, we analyse the differences between organically evolved clusters and those with a high degree of government management. The first of the two clusters is in the Fotan industrial estate in the New Territories, where units had become available at highly affordable rent and sale prices post 1997, when many factories relocated to China, a situation exacerbated in 2003 when severe acute respiratory syndrome (SARS) struck and affected the Hong Kong economy particularly negatively. Art students from the nearby Chinese University of Hong Kong and other visual artists as well as some performing artists, architects, designers and others in the creative industry began to rent and buy units in the factory spaces, particularly from 2000/2001. Occupying units scattered across floors in the high-rise factories as well as across factory buildings, the largely young artists have found the organically evolved cluster a positive environment for their art, even though the factory buildings are old, even dirty and smelly, and still used for industrial purposes as diverse as food processing, furniture-making and warehousing. The value of such an environment, particularly as a site of artistic production, is examined and set against a second cluster, the Cattle Depot Artists Village, a heritage site leased by the government to a small group of performing and visual artists since 2001. While appreciating the space that they have, the groups occupying Cattle Depot are clearly frustrated by the restrictions and constraints imposed on them by government authorities, as well as the lack of coordination across government units. The combined efforts to organize themselves are examined and the key strategy of turning the government-sanctioned private space into an artistically vibrant public space is analysed.

The idea of reusing old factory space for artistic purposes is similarly evident in Taipei (Chapter 10). Here, the failures and marginal successes of the 'cultural parks' developed out of abandoned factories draw attention to the real needs of the artistic community, as opposed to those based on the received wisdom about the value of clustering and reuse of industrial space. One essential characteristic of cultural/creative clusters that emerges is that spatial proximity is not a necessary condition for artists or creative workers in their production process. Their 'production' sites are by no means limited or fixed to a specific locus, for example, within the premises of cultural parks. More importantly, creative workers need a place that has abundant cultural assets, alongside an environment that is able to support and stimulate them. On the one hand, artists need affordable working space (studios) for carrying out their creative work (production space). On the other hand, they need a place to display their products, to interact with other creative workers and to collect or obtain related information in their field. All these activities require a space that can attract a mass population to come to see and purchase their artworks or creative products. This is the exhibition and consumption space, which should be in a convenient location, with a comfortable environment. These essential differences between the spatial needs of cultural creative production and those of cultural consumption give rise to different kinds of urban landscapes for the arts. This chapter focuses on three case studies to analyse how Taipei reuses its old urban space to support the arts and its related cultural industry. The three cases in question are Huashan Park, Chienkuo Beer Factory and Sungshan Cigarette Factory. Huashan Park originally housed wine factories and warehouses, but was abandoned in 1997. Artists moved in and held an international arts festival there. At the same time, the premises provided space for artists to carry out their creative work. We trace the growing government involvement in its development, with several concomitant shifts: the involvement of private sector management; the increasing profit-making imperatives; the transformation of a cultural production space into an exhibition and consumption space; and the shifting scale of focus, from an emphasis on international events to its role in national life. The second site is the Chienkuo Beer Factory, the earliest brewery in Taiwan, founded in 1919. Through an analysis of the changing fates of the factory space, we demonstrate the role of local cultural organizations, the trade unions associated with the brewery workers, and the surrounding community in shaping its current role in the urban and cultural life in Taipei, including its preservation from demolition and its redevelopment as a cultural park. The last site is the Sungshan Cigarette Factory, located in the city centre. Since it stopped production in 1998, there have been many disputes over the use of the facility. The city government's proposals to convert the site to a cultural park and a stadium have met with opposition from residents and environmental organizations. At the same time, the city government failed to contract out the development and operation of the cultural park due to the risk of uncertainty in its operation and the high costs of repair and maintenance of historical buildings. Its plan to use the site for exhibitions, performances and public interactions, as well as to offer affordable spaces to creative workers, has not attracted any willing developers. The cases in Taipei that we analyse in this chapter highlight the fact that the main contributions of the government in the development of the creative industry are in offering vacated public space to creative workers and establishing a liberal environment to stimulate their creative activities. To intervene too much in urban landscape change or to set too many goals in cluster development may not truly help the creative industry.

Whereas the conversion of old factory spaces into new landscapes for the arts is by now common in many cities around the world, and certainly in all the other cities that are the focus of this book, the situation in Singapore lends itself to a different analysis, and thus brings up the rear in the order of chapters (Chapter 11). The flight of industry to China as evident in Hong Kong did not feature as strongly in Singapore. Nor was the closure of state-owned factories, as in China, experienced in Singapore. Old factory spaces are thus not in the same abundance in Singapore as some of the other cities examined in this book. On the other hand, the global cultural city that Singapore aspires to be has benefited from change in another dimension of the urban landscape – the relocation of schools and the resultant availability of old school buildings for alternative use. There are numerous examples: the former St Joseph's Institution now houses the Singapore Art Museum; the former Tao Nan School boasts the Peranakan Museum; the former Convent of the Holy Infant Jesus is a high-end retail complex; the former Stamford Primary School is Stamford Arts Centre; the former Methodist Girls' School was for a time a creative cluster called 'Old School'; and the former Telok Kurau South Primary School is part of the Arts Housing Scheme run by the National Arts Council (NAC) offering space to artists, known since 1997 as 'Telok Kurau Studios'. We focus in this chapter on the last two cases, where old urban spaces have become creative cultural clusters whether by organic evolution or design; we examine the ways in which these new uses have contributed (or not) to creative cultural activity, and ultimately to the ambition and ideal of a global cultural city. The case of Singapore's Telok Kurau Studios demonstrates how, contrary to the claims of cluster proponents, creative aesthetic work is accomplished in spite of the creative cluster, not because of it. It is not the synergistic relationships envisaged of clusters that has supported the creative aesthetic work of the artists. Instead, the relationships within the cluster are marked by hostility and rivalry. There is a lack of dense and mutually supportive intra-cluster relationships and a glaring absence of cooperation. Even though some occupants believe that the cluster can have value, with joint exhibitions and sharing of ideas, in reality, this does not happen. In short, there is no causal relationship between geographical propinquity and the development of positive social relations. Indeed, the close proximity puts strains on relationships, which might not be as immediate or as apparent if it were not for co-location. Nevertheless, the cluster continues to exist and to enjoy its status as an important site for the practice of visual arts in Singapore. This is because of the reputational effect that occupants of the cluster enjoy, drawn from the concentrated location of a significant number of award-winning artists, offering all occupants some much-valued cultural capital. The environment being quiet and one of isolation also allows artists to give expression to their 'individual genius'. Importantly, the subsidized rents of this NAC arts housing facility make co-location a prudent decision. By comparison, the much newer Old School found its new lease of life in 2007 as a complex of heritage buildings housing art galleries, artist studios, an art film theatre, design firms, photographers, musicians and others. A group of three entrepreneurs with an interest in the arts got together and successfully secured the lease from the Singapore Land Authority, with a plan to turn the former school site into a creative hub and to promote 'made-in-Singapore creativity' to the world. With over 30 tenants, the intention was to showcase interesting art forms and provide a place for exchange and stimulation, curation and interaction. The initiative thrived, but the lease ran out as the government turned the land over to private developers for residential development.

The preceding academic 'travel' through the cultural landscapes of the five Asian cities culminates in the final chapter, where we step back from the rich and detailed ethnographic and textual material for each city and the grounded analysis of individual contexts to draw broader conclusions about culture, urban landscapes and global cities. It is our hope that this book addresses the shortage of micro-level analyses of creative or cultural worlds at ground level, and uses this empirical analysis to draw on larger theoretical canvases.

NOTES

1. Friedmann (1995, p. 31) uses the terms 'global cities' and 'world cities' interchangeably.
2. Core countries were identified using World Bank criteria, and included 19 industrial market economies. Semi-peripheral countries mostly included upper-middle income countries with a significant degree of industrialization and an economic system based on market exchange.
3. The word billion is used throughout this book in its US sense, meaning 'one thousand million'.
4. We use the terms cultural industries, creative industries and cultural creative industries (and their derivatives, for example, cultural/creative clusters) interchangeably here; they are related, yet not the same. Studies stemming from Europe (with the exception of the United Kingdom) commonly use the term cultural clusters while those from the United States and Australia appear to favour the term creative clusters. Often, this proliferation of terms reflects the lack of conceptual clarity around the ideas of 'cultural industries' and 'creative industries' themselves. It is not our intention in this book to work through the differences, though we recognize that they are not inconsequential. We recognize that, at a fairly broad level of generalization, the phenomenon that we are interested in does not suffer from the interchangeable use of the terms.

PART I

2. The National Grand Theatre in a city of monuments: discourse and reality in the construction of Beijing's new cultural space

INTRODUCTION

In the wake of the Reform and Opening Up of China, under the guidance of the central government, Beijing has been active in the construction of new cultural space. At the same time, following its successful bid for and subsequent hosting of the 2008 Olympic Games, China has also undertaken to build Beijing into a world-class metropolis. The construction of the highly controversial National Grand Theatre is a good example of this effort. The National Grand Theatre, built on the empty plot of land to the west of the Tiananmen Square and Great Hall of the People, took the Beijing municipal government eight years and three billion renminbi to complete.[1] Designed as a national cultural establishment, it was completed in 2007. Given its relatively short history, any assessment and evaluation of its impact on Beijing's cultural sector and on its development as a global city will be premature. Nevertheless, it is clear that, already, the Grand Theatre has become the pride of the Chinese people, and a must-see for international tourists. Using the National Grand Theatre as a case study, this chapter examines the reconstruction of the cultural landscape in Beijing, underpinned by its aspirations to be a global city. It offers a review of the controversy surrounding the construction of the National Grand Theatre, highlights the contributions of new cultural space in the global city-building enterprise and foregrounds the differences in various social groups' responses to the construction of the Grand Theatre.

The chapter is organized as follows. The next two sections examine the ideological and policy shifts that have marked the history of cultural space construction in Beijing, from the early period of nation-building by the Communist Party to the cosmopolitanization drive of the 1990s. Based on fieldwork findings, the subsequent two sections focus on the case of the National Grand Theatre, discussing debates sparked by its construction as well as its implications for political, cultural and social reconfiguration. This is followed by a final concluding section.

CULTURE, SPACE AND NATION-BUILDING: PRE-REFORM DEVELOPMENTS

Historically, culture has exerted a powerful influence on social and political thought and institutions. The foundation upon which the Chinese communist regime was founded stresses that culture and arts are components of the superstructure of social relations, and that they shape the ideology and the value system of the masses. Accordingly, culture and its expression became major instruments of social control. Consequently, in the period when the Communist Party was establishing a proletarian government, especially during the Mao period, the production and consumption of culture were political and ideological affairs aimed at consolidating the regime. In the 1942 'Yan'an Forum on Arts and Culture', Mao Zedong pointed out that 'Arts and culture belong to the politics of class, and they must fulfil the revolutionary task set by the Party within a certain revolutionary period' (quoted from Wang, Z., 1993, p. 292). As a result, before the period of Reform and Opening Up, the content of cultural activity was not the natural expression of a civic aesthetic but merely an instrument in the nation-building effort, tasked, on the one hand, with reflecting the political will of the leaders and, on the other, with rallying the proletariat class.

This expropriation of culture for nation-building by the Chinese Communist Party was most pronounced during the Mao period. After the founding of the People's Republic of China (PRC) in 1949, with the support of the state, large national exhibition and performance facilities were erected to showcase and rally the masses around political projects and achievements. These facilities were located in a cluster of prominent architectural monuments in the heart of political power, namely, the area neighbouring Tiananmen along the Chang'an Avenue. Prime examples of power-symbolic spaces are the Beijing municipal government building, Tiananmen Square, the Great Hall of the People (1959),[2] Chairman Mao Mausoleum and the Revolution Museum of China (1961).[3] These new spaces, together with the Forbidden City, which represents traditional cultural space, and the nearby political nerve centre Zhongnanhai,[4] turned the area surrounding Tiananmen into a grand spatial representation of the communist regime's political power. When people walk in the spacious Tiananmen Square, the landscape constituted by the concentration of imposing monuments around Tiananmen is powerful enough to make them feel the insignificance of the self and the greatness of the state. As much as the extravagances of this space stand as markers of Chinese nationalism and secure identification of the masses with the national (and party) agenda, they are also intended to publicize the party's achievements to visitors and tourists. Further, while the creation of ostentatious cultural space in the midst of avenues of political power firmly entrenched the political role of culture, it also laid the foundations for Beijing to be irreplaceably installed as the cultural and political capital of the country. Subsequent construction of cultural space in Beijing has followed the early pattern, by expanding along the axis of Chang'an Avenue as a sort of cultural corridor, with Tiananmen Square as the nucleus. Today, the number of national cultural facilities situated on the axis of Chang'an Avenue is testimony to its status as the cultural heartland of the cultural capital (Zhang, J., 2004).

However, although the performing arts were an important component of cultural consciousness-shaping in the Chinese Communist Party's nation-building tactics, monumental performance spaces of the national theatre type were notably absent around Tiananmen Square in the early period of the regime. In contrast, quite a number of theatres and cinemas were constructed in Beijing's Xicheng District in the 1950s and 1960s, making it the most dynamic cultural zone of the time. One good example of early cultural space construction is the Capital Theatre, a dedicated performing arts venue completed in 1956, which served as the venue for the Beijing Opera Gala Performance in 1964.

Most of the cultural-political space construction of that time was concentrated in the part of Xicheng District lying within the Second Ring Road and the inner city. The development of these cultural spaces resulted primarily from a need to promote party-sponsored plays and operas, in order to consolidate the party's power and reinforce its ideology. During this period, with Zhou Enlai as premier, the idea of building a National Grand Theatre on the empty plot to the west of Tiananmen Square was first hatched. The project, designed to showcase the Communist Party's achievements in the first ten years after the founding of the PRC, was later shelved because of a lack of funds and political struggles ensuing from the Cultural Revolution. At that time, official policy required that cultural and artistic activities be linked with the daily life of the people (workers, peasants, soldiers) (see Wang, Z., 1993). As such, the spatial distribution of cinemas and theatres needed to take the distribution of the population into consideration. As a result, these cultural establishments were mainly scattered in the densely populated area within the Second Ring Road, especially in the Xicheng and Xuanwu Districts within the inner city (Zhang, J., 2004). Thus, every aspect of the cultural facilities constructed in the early period, including layout, location and form, reflected the intention of the political leadership to deploy culture in the cementing of national consciousness and in the reinforcement of ideological hegemonies.

CULTURE AND SPACE IN THE MAKING OF A GLOBAL CITY: POST-REFORM DEVELOPMENTS

Beijing and the Making of a Global City: Discourse and Strategy

Although culture retained its political function post-reform, a readjustment of political priorities saw the mandate for culture shift, from forging national identity to helping Beijing realize its aspirations to be a global city. As a result, Beijing's politically inflected cultural space underwent a profound change at the end of the 1990s. The driving force for this change did not originate from a reshuffling of political personnel at the top but from revisions to government policies arising from a rethinking of the state's economic development strategy and political structure. The ideological reorientation had two significant implications: first, developing a socialist market economy became the government's primary task; second, the country opened up to the outside world, actively attracting foreign direct investment and eventually joining the World Trade Organization in 2001, thereby becoming a player in international affairs. This marked a radical departure from the party's previous emphasis under Mao on class struggle and self-reliance, which had a far-reaching impact on the development of cultural space in Beijing. In particular, from the second half of the 1990s, through the 9th and 10th Five-Year Plans under Jiang Zemin and the 11th Five-Year Plan under Hu Jintao, the Chinese government took active steps to integrate cultural development with the development of the urban economy. Establishments were transformed into industries (Kong et al., 2006) through reforms of the cultural system, and cities were encouraged to build massive cultural facilities. In response to these political and economic changes, the Beijing municipal government also invested in the industrialization of culture and the construction of monumental cultural facilities under related Five-Year Plans. Compared with the period before 1990, the development of cultural facilities in Beijing after 1990 was clearly based on the state's characterization of the capital as a cultural city and, indeed, as the nation's cultural capital.

The 'Urban Development Plan of the Beijing Municipality: 2004–2020', revised and approved by the Central Committee of the Chinese Communist Party, describes Beijing as the capital of the nation, international, renowned for its culture and highly liveable. Premier Wen Jiabao pointed out that setting the direction of Beijing's development was by no means an easy matter. Rather, it was the result of several decades of experiment and learning (Wu, L., 2006, p. 4). The discourse on developing Beijing's cultural credentials, emanating from the top echelons of the political leadership, was suitably picked up and repeated at lower levels of government. The Beijing Party Secretary Jia Qinglin, for example, a member of the Politburo of the Chinese Communist Party, stressed that Beijing needed not only to build on its advantage as a political centre but also to function as a cultural hub. Beijing Mayor Liu Qi similarly observed that, as a world-renowned historical and cultural city, Beijing must attach high importance to and vigorously engage in the construction of large-scale cultural facilities. Reflecting the spirit of these remarks, Beijing has entered a new era of development that emphasizes the industrialization of culture as well as the construction of cultural space; this emphasis is central to the strategy of building Beijing into a global city (Tan and Li, 2001).

The discourse underlying Beijing's new cultural space construction is an adaptation of world city development discourses that have gained currency in academic, media and policy literature. This influence can be traced to globalizing forces, which since the Reform and Opening Up have had a most critical impact on the development of the Chinese economy and Chinese cities. The theories of global economy and city development introduced by academics have been influential on decision-makers (Kong et al., 2006). Among economic development strategies, the most influential idea has been the agglomeration of science and technology enterprises, which now constitutes the municipal government's blueprint for Beijing's development (Wang and Wang, 1998; Zhou, Y., 2005; Zhou and Tong, 2003). On the other hand, urban development policy has drawn heavily on the theme of global city competition as articulated in, among others, global city studies by Friedmann (1986) and Sassen (1991). This influence is reflected in the large-scale public investment in infrastructure, such as the building of the international financial centre and related facilities, the international airport and an efficient road network, infrastructure for the manufacturing and service sector in the special economic zone and so forth (Tan and Li, 2001). However, while the infrastructural focus may be traced to the influence of the global city studies mentioned above, the formulation of the cultural strategy has a somewhat different genesis.

In particular, the construction of cultural space in Beijing has been shaped by ideas about urban regeneration at the local level. Early efforts at urban regeneration (as laid out in the 'Urban Development Plan of the Beijing Municipality: 2004–2020', but also preceding 2004) focused on relocating the city's resident population and redeveloping large tranches of the inner city (Chang, 1998; Leaf, 1995). However, this 'bulldozer policy' of inner city redevelopment came under severe criticism for lacking strategic vision and direction. In addition to the debates on land compensation and resident relocation (Leaf, 1995), critics also highlighted the lack of protection of cultural heritage and the lack of consideration for the inner city's regenerative potential (Lu, J., 2007; Wu, L., 2006; Zhou, Y., 1996). Indeed, as Chen (1999) pointed out, this superficial 'cosmeticization' of Beijing resulted in sprawling suburbs and satellite towns, populated by relocated inner city residents, which compromised the principle of urban regeneration and impeded its practice. In response, the municipal government changed its simple land reuse policy and began to pursue a more 'culturally conscious' strategy (Tan and Li, 2001). The cultural focus in this urban regeneration strategy translated, on the ground, into policies for constructing new cultural space, adapting existing spaces for cultural use and promoting cultural activities such as performances and exhibitions. As such, the strategy and related policies are concordant with the state's philosophy on culture, as articulated in the 10th Five-Year Plan, which views culture as capital in the building of a global city. Thus, they are both politically justified and exceedingly popular.

It was under the 9th Five-Year Plan (1995–2000) that extensive, organized cultural space construction took off in Beijing. During this period, the municipal government invested more than two billion renminbi in the construction of cultural facilities that spanned an area exceeding 250 000 square metres. The construction plan and process were guided by a municipal government and Party committee rule stipulating that efforts must be made to preserve as many existing cultural facilities as possible and, where preservation is technically infeasible, the facilities must be rebuilt in the vicinity. A good example is the relocation of the Chang'an Theatre from West Chang'an Avenue to East Chang'an Avenue. Other cultural facilities constructed or relocated in Beijing during the 9th Five-Year Plan include the Music Hall of the Zhongshan Park, the Ping Opera House of China, the Beijing Traditional Opera Theatre, the Seven-Colour Light Children's Theatre, the Capital Theatre, the Beijing Broadcasting Building, the Capital Library and the China Millennium Monument. These cultural facilities have all become icons in Beijing's cityscape (*People's Daily*, 9 October 2000, p. 1). Beijing's pursuit of cultural excellence and visibility is an ongoing project. While the 9th Five-Year Plan pioneered the construction of cultural space, subsequent Five-Year Plans developed the theme by envisaging and executing even grander cultural projects. Under the 10th Five-Year Plan, construction for the National Grand Theatre, the biggest cultural project of the time, got under way. Under the 11th Five-Year Plan, Beijing turned its attention to construction of the Beijing

Art Museum (envisaged to be on a scale rivalling that of the grand Capital Museum) and expansion of the National Museum.

What lent further impetus to the 'culturalization' drive was that the plans for and the construction of these cultural facilities were not isolated items on the agenda of the Five-Year Plans but incorporated into Beijing's overall urban redevelopment strategy, designed with an eye on the Olympics. In fact, the Beijing municipal government declared that the 2008 Olympic Games would be held in a new Beijing that boasted abundant cultural facilities, active cultural performances and a flourishing cultural industry. Furthermore, pursuant to the listing in 2006, by the Beijing municipal government and the central government, of the development of cultural space and cultural industry as a global city development strategy, Beijing set itself the task of building six major cultural centres, each dedicated to developing a particular cultural sector,[5] and increasing the percentage of the cultural industry's share of gross domestic product (GDP) to 9 per cent, thereby making it the backbone of the capital's economy. In this vision, the following large-scale cultural facilities were planned (for construction or expansion), namely, the National Grand Theatre, Beijing Planetarium, Capital Museum, China Film Museum, Fortune Centre, China Central Television Station, Beijing Television Centre and Beijing International Media and Cultural Centre.

Obviously, Beijing's re-engineered urban cultural landscape is an expression of a new political and economic vision that acknowledged the indispensability of cultural development in achieving the goal of reinventing Beijing as a global city. Thus, compared to the cultural spaces built during the Mao period, these new spaces differed in scale, scope and function: the later cultural facilities were significantly grander, more diverse in the activities they housed (the ambit of culture expanded to include media, science and technology) and operated primarily to project Beijing's cultural credentials onto the global consciousness (rather than, primarily, as a mouthpiece of political propaganda). Further, from a theoretical perspective, the new spaces reflected globalization-induced trends and pressures, whereas pre-Reform construction had been driven largely, if not wholly, by an internal, introverted political ethic and expediency. The National Grand Theatre aptly captures these differences.

THE NATIONAL GRAND THEATRE

The construction of the National Grand Theatre has been the focal point of Beijing's new cultural space in the last decade. The amount of investment, its location and design have a far-reaching impact on Beijing's urban development and its global reputation. This chapter examines the following questions. First, what were the political, economic and strategic contexts of its construction? Second, how did the debates on, and interpretations of, the related transformation of urban landscape play out in public forums? Third, what sort of impact did the National Grand Theatre actually have on Beijing's urban development?

Building the National Grand Theatre

Since Reform and Opening Up, every year, during the famed 'Two Meetings', representatives from the culture and arts sector would submit proposals calling for the building of a national theatre. The project, however, did not get off the ground until the 9th Five-Year Plan, which, as stated before, initiated an emphasis on cultural development. In 1996, the 6th plenary session of the Party's 14th National Congress passed 'The Resolution on A Number of Important Issues concerning the Strengthening of Socialist Cultural and Ideological Development', which contained proposals to build a number of high-profile cultural facilities including the National Grand Theatre and the National Museum. In 1997, an empty plot of land west of the Great Hall of the People was chosen as the site for the National Grand Theatre. By this time, the project had gained enough momentum to have become a national image project for the central government. In January 1998, to execute the project, the central government set up the National Grand Theatre Construction Taskforce and the Owners' Committee of the National Grand Theatre Construction Project, comprising officials from the Beijing municipal government, the Ministry of Culture and the Ministry of Construction.

Given that the construction of new cultural space in Beijing is motivated by the city's aspiration to have world-class cultural facilities, there was a desire to adopt highly creative designs and employ the best supervision and construction teams. This entailed drawing on creative talents around the world. As such, the National Grand Theatre became a product of the international division of labour that characterizes globalization.

In the two rounds of tender for the Grand Theatre's design, 40 design agencies from ten countries competed. Out of the 69 proposals submitted, 32 were local (including those from the Hong Kong Special Administrative Region) and 37 were from abroad. At the end of the process, the 'giant egg' design by Paul Andreu of Aeroports de Paris (ADP) eventually won. Andreu, chief architect of Aeroports de Paris, is also the architect of Pudong International Airport in Shanghai and the Guangzhou Stadium. The main reason for his success was his experience with the Guangzhou and Shanghai projects, which enabled him to gain a better understanding of how public projects are managed as well as the specific needs of China's urban redevelopment projects. Another reason for his success may be his cooperation with Tsinghua University's Institute of Architecture, which not only provided him with local credentials but also the requisite insight into the minds and decision-making processes of the top Chinese leadership.

Reflecting practices in a globalized world, the construction of the National Grand Theatre involved the cooperation of several countries. While Andreu from France was in charge of the design, the Opera House and the Traditional Chinese Opera House in the Theatre adopted technologies from Japan. The state-of-the-art pipe organ in the Music Hall employed German technology. Construction of the project was jointly carried out by Beijing Urban Construction Co. Ltd, Hong Kong Construction (Holding) Corporation and Shanghai Construction and Engineering (Group) Corporation. Touted as the symbol of China's Reform and Opening Up, the National Grand Theatre received total funding of about CN¥2.55 billion from the state coffers. Construction work started in 2000 and was completed in 2007. During this period, the Beijing municipal government invested some CN¥966 million (about US$154.6 million) in making improvements to and beautifying the surrounding area. Designated as 'a massive modern cultural facility built by the Chinese government to usher in the 21st century' (Gao, L., 2003), the theatre consists of a 2398-seat opera house, a 2019-seat music hall, a 1035-seat traditional opera house, a small theatre housing 300 to 500 seats and other auxiliary facilities like an art gallery and a communication centre for the performing arts. In terms of size, equipment and technology, the National Grand Theatre can rival national theatres in key global cities.

In its design, the theatre ranks among the most avant-garde in the world. Nestled by a 35000-square-metre artificial lake, the egg-shaped National Grand Theatre is 46.68 metres high and 32.5 metres deep below the ground. Exiting from the West Tiananmen metro station, visitors can immediately catch sight of this 'shiny pearl' surrounded by the lake to the west of the Great Hall of the People on Chang'an Avenue. Designed to stand out and built on a scale that both awes and intimidates, the National Grand Theatre unequivocally asserts China's economic emergence as well as its cultural resurgence.

Cultural Monuments and Global Cities: Accord and Discord

The National Grand Theatre and the Three Gorges project were two of China's largest and most controversial turn-of-the-century public projects. Debates on the Theatre raged almost as fiercely as those on the

Three Gorges and were primarily centred around various aspects of the global city development strategy.

The design and construction of a cultural monument is closely related to the symbolic representation of the city and the state. However, differences over the interpretation of the proposed cultural monument were not seen to constitute a direct challenge to the Chinese Communist Party's control over ideology. As such, the Grand Theatre could be discussed and contested publicly in China. Immediately after Andreu's design had been selected, criticisms of it surfaced and circulated in the design and construction industry. These mainly focused on two issues: first, it was contended that the theatre exhibited no Chinese characteristic at all; second, and relatedly, it was argued that the design was out of harmony with the buildings clustered around Tiananmen Square. Through extensive media coverage, the design issue became a hot topic of debate in local, national and international architectural circles. These debates, conducted on multiple scales, produced a powerful discourse that, by contesting the chosen design, put the government under tremendous pressure.

On 12 June 2000, during a meeting convened by the Chinese Academy of Sciences and the Chinese Academy of Engineering in Beijing, 49 members of the two academies wrote a joint letter to President Jiang Zemin and Premier Zhu Rongji, urging the government to reconsider Andreu's design. In this letter, the scientists enumerated the flaws of Andreu's proposal, suggesting, in addition to the charges levelled above, that the exorbitant cost of the project was not merited by its inadequate functionality (Peng, 2000). Lashing out at the design, they also accused it of being completely out of touch with China's reality and in total disregard of traditional Chinese culture. Shortly afterwards, on 19 June, some 100 architecture experts from across the country also wrote to central government leaders, raising similar objections. If constructed, they observed, the Grand Theatre designed by Andreu would become the butt of jokes for the international community. While the original budget for the National Grand Theatre was about CH¥2 billion, the final cost, according to Andreu's design, would top CH¥5 billion. Averaged out over the Grand Theatre's 6000 seats, each seat would cost CH¥800 000 (*Yangtze Daily*, 14 July 2000). It was alleged that this extravagance diverted public funds from expenditures on education and poverty relief. As one interviewee put it, 'There are so many people who can't even make their ends meet, yet the government is spending so much for the sake of image.'

Concerns about the extravagance, safety (it was suggested that the underground and underwater opera halls would be hard to evacuate in the event of an emergency) and dysfunctionality (detractors suggested that the heavy pollution in Beijing would turn the proposed white exterior of the monument black) of the design aside, the issue around which most critics rallied was the insensitivity of the design to the traditional Chinese architectural aesthetic. In response to the suggestion of the Chinese Ambassador to France that the design conform to Chinese cultural history, Andreu was reported to have retorted, 'My intention is precisely to cut off historical links.' The implied arrogance of the designer's response was highlighted as the clearest indicator of cultural colonialism, constituting an offence to the Chinese people (Peng, 2000). Thus, it was alleged that the Grand Theatre embodied a new type of colonialism practised by developed countries, achieved through capital monopolization and cultural penetration. The attempt to spread the Western way of life, its cultural norms, artistic forms and associated value systems in the developing world revealed a presumption about the cultural superiority of West over East.

As calls from experts for a re-examination of the design grew intense, the project had to be put on hold. In July 2000, construction work on the Grand Theatre was suspended until the criticisms had been adequately addressed. In the face of mounting scepticism about the construction of this new cultural space, the state took a series of crisis management measures. First, in a conciliatory gesture, the State Council and the Ministry of Construction dispatched a special team to Guangzhou, Shanghai and Beijing to explain the design to local architecture experts and also invite their suggestions for improvement. Subsequently, the state-run media was mobilized to reorganize the discourse on the design by getting Andreu to provide clarifications in defence of his design. This constituted a placatory attempt by the government to reduce popular opposition to the project as well as an attempt to give the appearance that, ultimately, the endorsement of the design was the outcome of a consultative process. However, supplementing this tactic, the state media also aggressively reinforced the logic behind the government's cultural space construction strategy and defended its choice of design.

The state media conducted an exclusive interview with Andreu, during which the architect provided clarifications and responses to the criticisms of his design. The interview was published in *Guangming Daily* (19 May 2000) and then republished in some influential newspapers like the *Southern Weekend* in an effort to reshape the public discourse. In fact, most specialists did not understand Andreu's design concept and its underlying urban landscape philosophy. In the interview, besides addressing the issue of the egg shape and the use of water, Andreu responded to concerns about the huge cost and public safety. He also emphasized

My understanding about the National Grand Theatre of China mainly consists of the following four points. First, its location determines its symbolic meaning:

the Great Hall of the People next to it stands for the state's highest political power, so the Grand Theatre should become a cultural symbol; second, it is a new, massive, important building of the new century, a building charged with Chinese people's strong aspirations; third, it should possess comprehensive social functions, that is, it must serve the public well and gain popularity with the public; fourth, its external appearance must be attractive and convey a sense of history and culture. (*Guangming Daily*, 19 May 2000)

In summarizing his views, he remarked

I believe my design will definitely prompt people to think seriously about archi-tecture design in Beijing. In a word, it will not make Beijing ugly, in fact, the opposite is true . . . I'll bet that when people look around in the National Grand Theatre of China once it is completed, the majority of them will like my design. The Grand Theatre is a cultural facility that serves educational purposes. It's a cultural space where people can relax and enjoy themselves. That's the purpose of my design. (*Guangming Daily*, 20 October 2000)

It is apparent that through this act of justification the state, via Andreu, sought to tailor the discourse in a way that would allow the design to proceed intact. Pragmatic issues about cost and safety, among others, were also addressed; once that was done, the original design could proceed with only minor amendments.

After a process of debate, feedback, consultation and clarification, construction work on the Grand Theatre was eventually resumed, dem-onstrating the strength of the political commitment to the project. The government stressed that the idea of building the National Grand Theatre around Tiananmen Square had initially been put forward by Premier Zhou Enlai. The third-generation leaders, with Jiang Zemin at the helm, saw the nation's modernization effort as a logical articulation of that vision. It was argued in the state media that the collective decision to build the National Grand Theatre next to Tiananmen Square, instead of office buildings or hotels, spoke volumes about how much the party and the government cared about the development of culture and arts and the improvement of the cultural life of the people (*Sina News*, 31 March 2000).

The above illustrates that, at the state level, the construction of the National Grand Theatre has been projected as necessary for enabling China's evolution into a 'cultural power', in addition to its growing role as an 'economic superpower'. The strongest argument in favour of build-ing striking, new cultural spaces was their contribution to the city's (and the state's) image in the eyes of the world. Citing the examples of the sail-shaped Opera House in Sydney and the glass pyramid that serves as the entrance to the Louvre Museum in Paris, these arguments pointed out that avant-garde architecture, by definition, often passes through a stage of criticism before being gradually accepted by the public and becoming well-loved landmarks of world cities. Such reasoning was later vindicated by Beijing's successful bid for the Olympics, which was heralded as the world's acknowledgement of the city's cosmopolitan credentials. Following the successful bid, the theatre was classified by the state as a major cultural facility serving the Olympics; accordingly, any remaining obstacles to its construction were easily circumvented. The government's aggressive marketing of the theatre was complemented by efforts undertaken by the media, various cultural organizations and the real estate and construction sector to mobilize popular support for the construction of the Grand Theatre in particular, and new cultural spaces in general. As a result, construction of the theatre, which had been put on hold in July 2000, was officially resumed on 13 December 2001 and completed in mid-2007.

THE CHALLENGES AND DILEMMAS FACING THE GRAND THEATRE

Although the Grand Theatre is unequivocally iconic and its contribution to the city's international imageability is not in doubt, question marks remain over its contribution to the city's cultural development, for two reasons. First, it is holistic, broad-based cultural development and not merely the construction of eye-catching cultural space that promotes a city's claims to being global. Second, as highlighted earlier, the government had clearly identified social functionality as a non-negotiable benchmark by which the theatre's success could be measured. Although the limited time for which the facility has been operational entails that any attempt at evaluation must necessarily be taken as only preliminary, the following discussion suggests that gaps between discourse and reality remain, rendering as compromised the theatre's advocacy of Beijing's global city claims.

The Functional Conflict: Balancing Profit and Public Function

As mentioned earlier, the huge cost of the theatre was one of the focal points of the controversy surrounding its construction. The large investment indicated a need for commensurately high rates of return, prompting the question 'Who will the Grand Theatre serve after completion?' The dilemma was clear: if the theatre operated as a private commercial enterprise, that would call into question the judiciousness of allocating public funds for its construction; on the other hand, if the facility operated for public benefit, the prudence of the scale of investment would be open to challenge. Ultimately, under enormous political pressure, the central government chose to designate the Grand Theatre as a public enterprise. In doing so, it stressed that the Grand Theatre should cater to the general public by staging as many quality performances as possible, by widening its audience base and by serving the public, cultivating the people's appreciation of the arts and boosting interaction and cultural exchange between national and international artistic organizations.

However, though managed as a public enterprise, the Grand Theatre must operate as a commercial entity. While this is critical to ensuring the theatre's long-term economic sustainability, it is also mandated by the government's strategic vision for the cultural sector. The industrialization of cultural activity has been the explicit state policy since the 10th Five-Year Plan. The designation of the Grand Theatre as a public enterprise contravenes this national policy. Although there is no necessary contradiction in supposing public enterprise to be potentially independently profitable, the constraint on ticket pricing implies that recouping the initial investment costs and covering the substantial operational expenditures will be impossible without continual state funding. A functionary of the theatre puts this predicament in perspective: 'Of course, the ticket price of each show also has to do with market supply and demand, as well as the production cost. So low ticket prices cannot be understood as absolutely low. It's just that we'll try to use marketing tactics so that the price would be relatively lower under given circumstances' (*Southern Weekend*, 4 June 2007). It is hard to imagine the price-control mechanism as a viable long-term tactic.

The Grand Theatre: Symbol or Resource?

From the outset, the official literature had made clear that the Grand Theatre was designed as a public cultural facility. Consequently, during construction, the government stressed the provision of auxiliary facilities to enhance the theatre's functions. Officials pointed out that through public tours and lectures, 'we must try to make the public feel that they are spiritually connected with the National Grand Theatre' (*Southern Weekend*, 4 June 2007). The National Grand Theatre is envisaged as China's top stage for the performing arts, a platform for interaction between domestic and overseas artist networks and a medium of arts and cultural education for the public. The Grand Theatre was also conceived as a space where arts-related commercial ventures like specialist bookstores could be set up.

Nonetheless, it is unlikely that the theatre can maintain its status as a public resource, since the low ticket pricing is not so much a realistic tactic as sop to the critics of the project. Moreover, the level of public utilization of the auxiliary facilities will be restricted by operational costs. On this basis, it appears that, ultimately, the theatre's value as a symbol will outstrip its functional value; as such, its contribution to residents' wellbeing will be marginal.

Conflict over Control

The conflicts over the theatre's identity, function and finances result in and are reinforced by ambiguities in its administration and control structure. In the project's planning stage, the central government set up the National Grand Theatre Owners' Committee,[6] a preparation committee comprising officials from the Ministry of Culture and the Artistic Committee of the National Grand Theatre, both bodies being considered possible administrators of the theatre, either individually or jointly. However, during its launch by the Jiang Zemin administration, it appeared increasingly likely, based on government pronouncements, that the Ministry of Culture would take charge after completion. However, as the Jiang administration completed its term before authority could be delegated, the administration of the theatre quickly became a political problem. During the National Political Consultative Conferences of 2003 and 2004, Hu Zuqiang, director of the former National Artistic Committee, made it clear in his proposals that the Ministry of Culture should be the administrator of the Grand Theatre. He argued that its status as a national cultural establishment (not just a local theatre) determined that the Ministry of Culture was better suited than the local government to manage the facility in the state's interest.

Although the Two Meetings, which were held in March 2006, deliberated on Hu Zuqiang's proposal, no clear mandate for the ministry emerged (*Southern Weekend*, 4 June 2007). The sticking point was the operational cost of the theatre. While there is no official estimate of these costs, according to the interviewees, the figure was expected to be in the vicinity of CH¥300 million every year. Both the Beijing municipal government and the central government were unwilling to pay for this. Protesting against the central government, which was increasingly keen on delegating administrative responsibility to the municipal government, the latter echoed Hu's argument and augmented it with concerns that it was not equipped to make critical operational decisions concerning the theatre (including how to choose between performances, how to organize appearances by overseas artistes and how to prioritize between local and national performance groups). In the face of these arguments, and with the dates for trial performances approaching, a compromise was eventually reached in 2007. The Grand Theatre would be administered by a joint owners' committee made up of officials from the municipal government and the central government.

The shared administrative responsibility translated, naturally, into shared financial responsibility. Over the first three years of the theatre's operation, about 80 per cent of the operational costs were financed by subsidies shared by the central and municipal governments. The remainder was contributed by the theatre's own revenues (income earned from commercial shows, exhibitions and conferences, sightseeing tours and food and beverage services) and by funding raised from the public (sponsorship received from companies, foundations and individuals). The high proportion of subsidies in the theatre's funding mix keeps the owners' committee sceptical about its ability to keep the Grand Theatre independently financially sound. As a result, it was very ardent in advocating maintenance of the theatre's status as a national, public enterprise in order to ensure its continued access to huge government subsidies. This, however, contradicts the central government's stated policy of cultural industrialization.

The Representational Conflict: Exclusive Performance Space or Platform for Local Cultural Development?

The Grand Theatre was completed in 2007 and started operations in September of the same year. In a short period, the institution has established itself as one of Beijing's cultural icons, as well as a landmark of the city's reinvented urban landscape. It has also been a site of hectic cultural activity. Between December 2007 and March 2008, 183 shows, with overseas productions and domestic productions accounting for 30 per cent and 70 per cent, respectively, were staged in the various facilities of the theatre (*China Times*, 22 September 2007). While the National Grand Theatre's first complete performance season kicked off only in September 2008, programming was already scheduled into late 2009 even before the first season. It was expected that, annually, the theatre would host some 500 shows, spanning genres as diverse as opera, drama, folk music and chamber and orchestral music.

The National Theatre was designed as the premier display space for China's performing arts. As such, a 'first-rate only' principle governs the selection of shows; only first-rate international and domestic groups are considered for performances at the venue. However, critics argue that the Grand Theatre's 'first-rate' criterion, implemented by the National Artistic Committee, is structurally discriminatory. Under this regime, it is hardly possible for local performance groups that have yet to establish a reputation or those that enjoy no support from the state to use the theatre for performances. This systematic exclusion implies that the majority of Beijing's performing arts bodies cannot benefit from this project. As the Grand Theatre essentially becomes an exclusive performing space for top artistes and groups, the elitism becomes increasingly hard to justify in light of its mandate to promote local cultural development. Further, given the importance of such local cultural development in installing China as a cultural superpower and Beijing as a global city, the continued failure of the theatre on this count is likely to be hotly contested in the future.

CONCLUSION

That the construction of cultural space in Beijing is politically motivated is not new. Under Mao, culture was conscripted to serve in the Communist Party's nation-building discourse, not valuable in itself but only as the means to a greater political end. In the post-Reform period, especially in the 1990s, the nation's cultural strategy underwent a significant transformation. As promoted by the central government, culture began to be interpreted as a form of capital in urban redevelopment and, accordingly, an asset in the building of a global city. This, in turn, prompted the Beijing municipal government to vigorously engage in the construction of new cultural spaces. What is noteworthy, however, is that, under the reinterpretation, culture did not cease being a political metaphor; what changed was the use to which culture and cultural spaces were politically mandated.

The reconfiguration in political priorities in conjunction with the 'New Beijing, New Olympics' slogan that came to characterize Beijing's successful bid further spurred a wave of construction of cultural spaces and facilities. It was during this process that the National Grand Theatre for performing arts was conceived, to showcase to the world Beijing's cultural credentials as well as its formidable economic and social achievements since the Reform. Further, as a monument in Beijing's revamped urban landscape, it was designed to evoke civic pride and foster civic consciousness. Its avant-garde design, notwithstanding the contestations, symbolized the nation's readiness to embrace modernity and display its cosmopolitan colours. After a protracted process of debate, discussion and clarification, the discourse underpinning the construction of this formidable and world-rivalling space went beyond the venue's symbolic goals in emphasizing its functionality, including particularly local cultural development and the enrichment of the cultural life of Beijing residents.

In the relatively short period that it has been operational, the theatre appears to have satisfied its mandate to internationalize Beijing's cultural visibility. However, question marks over its functional effectiveness remain. Conflicts between the discourse supporting its construction and the realities of its operation surface in several forms: the designation of the theatre as a public enterprise runs contrary to the government's strategic vision in favour of a cultural industrial sector; the use of the theatre as a symbol compromises its functional capacity as a resource; the early lack of consensus on where the locus of its administrative control should be and its use as an exclusive performance space marginalizes local artistes' access to the theatre and impedes cultural development. In order to meet the functional mandate attributed to the Grand Theatre, a delicate balancing act that reconciles these tensions is necessary. Many of these tensions surface in the mega-cultural spaces in the other cities that this book examines – a turn to Shanghai in the next chapter demonstrates the shared dilemmas and challenges confronting global cultural city aspirations.

NOTES

1. The exchange rate was about US$0.16 for a renminbi in 2014. The final accurate cost is CH¥2.69 billion, equivalent to US$430.4 million.
2. Initially constructed for the occasion of the tenth anniversary of the founding of the PRC, it was intended to showcase the nation's achievements over the past decade. It is the venue for the National People's Congress, the Chinese People's Political Consultative Conference (together with the National People's Congress, often known as 'Two Meetings' for short) and the five-yearly National Congress of the Communist Party of China.
3. It features China's modern history from the Opium War in 1840 through to the founding of the PRC. The exhibitions are threaded by the theme of Western powers' invasion and collision with Chinese feudal forces, thereby turning China into a semi-colonial, semi-feudal society; the Chinese people's struggle against imperialism and feudalism; and finally the glorious achievements under the leadership of the Chinese Communist Party.
4. Zhongnanhai is the seat of the State Council and the Central Committee of the Chinese Communist Party. It is also home to several political leaders. Zhongnanhai is therefore a synonym for top political power in China, akin to the White House.
5. These are the National Performance Centre of Culture and Arts, the National Publishing and Property Rights Trading Centre, the National Movie and TV Programme-making and Trading Centre, the National Animation and Internet Game Research and Manufacturing Centre, the National Exhibition and Conference Centre of Culture and the National Antique and Arts Trading Centre.
6. This committee was made up of officials from the Ministry of Construction and the Beijing municipal government.

3. Rivalling Beijing and the world: realizing Shanghai's ambitions through cultural infrastructure

INTRODUCTION

Shanghai has long felt a sense of rivalry with the national capital, Beijing, desirous as it is to gain a primary position in the national imaginary. In recent times, Shanghai has also sought visibility on the world stage as a global city. In some ways, it may be said that the latter ambition is really about reclaiming its past character and reputation as 'the Paris of the East'. In 1842, with the signing of the Treaty of Nanjing, Shanghai and four other Chinese ports were opened to Western trade, leading, by the 1930s, to Shanghai's position as one of the world's five most important commercial centres and the second busiest port. But while Shanghai has always been seen as China's leading commercial, trade, shipping and financial centre, it is not known to be China's cultural capital.

In its present-day quests for national and international standing, Shanghai has invested significantly in culture, in the belief that cultural life and achievements stand a city apart from its rivals. Whether it is to aid the attraction of global elites, tourists or investments, or to enrich the cultural life of residents, solidify civic identity, contribute to local cultural development or promote the development of cultural/creative industries, municipal authorities have paid more attention to culture than would otherwise be expected, given the way the city has represented China's embrace of the market economy rather than its cultural pride.

In this chapter, we examine two of the most significant (official) cultural projects of recent years in Shanghai, namely, the Shanghai Grand Theatre (SGT) and the Oriental Art Centre (OAC). In particular, we examine the ways in which cultural infrastructural projects have been used to articulate the city's aspiration for global status, their influence on the city's cultural landscape and their impact on various cultural groups in Shanghai. The chapter begins with an account of the evolution of Shanghai's cultural infrastructure, including the political and economic contexts of policy transitions that have guided these developments. The chapter then considers the functions of cultural infrastructure in the city and the changed role of government in constructing and operating such infrastructure as a response to the desire to attain global city status, using SGT and OAC as case studies. Subsections analyse how such infrastructural developments reconfigure the city's cultural landscape and assess their impact on populations, including global and local artists, tourists and residents. The chapter concludes by identifying the contradictions inherent in the pursuit of global city status by these reshapings of the city's cultural spaces.

REINVENTING CULTURAL SPACE AND FUNCTION IN CHINA

As in Beijing, Shanghai's cultural affairs prior to reform were a platform for ideological activity and expression. Accordingly, they remained under the state's supervision (Mitter, 2004). Large performance spaces or cultural infrastructure were part of a political project to showcase the country's development to the populace. The construction of large cultural infrastructure was expected to imbue the local population with a sense of glory about the nation and establish a coherent national identity. Cultural infrastructure, as political apparatus, functioned to assemble people for ideological education and as the site of national identity building projects. This situation changed in the late 1990s, corresponding to changes in China's political and economic context. As the state acknowledged the importance of establishing global connections in its drive for higher economic growth, the development of a culture-based industry and the construction of cultural facilities began to appear on the development agenda. This transition to a more economically driven motivation was shaped by an ambition to successfully compete for global city status (Kong, 2007).

Under the open-door policy, Shanghai became a focal point for high-level international cultural activities and attracted renowned performance groups from around the globe. The surge in demand for cultural infrastructure, combined with its lack of high-quality cultural facilities, convinced decision-makers of the pivotal role that investment in such infrastructure could play in the city's economic development. In the 1990s, the city devoted significant resources to redress the short supply of cultural infrastructure. Despite these interventions, Shanghai's push to be the pre-eminent cultural destination in China has faced stiff competition from Beijing for state attention and resources. State ambivalence to the idea of Shanghai as a cultural capital is exemplified in the state-authorized

Shanghai Master Plan 1999–2020, which articulates ambitions to reposition the city as a global economic, financial, trading and shipping centre (Shanghai City Government, 2004), while remaining silent about its cultural aspirations. The silence is deafening, suggesting that at the highest level the city's cultural ambitions were not deemed significant. However, in the more detailed near-future action plan for achieving the Shanghai Master Plan, it was indicated that the city would make efforts to become an international cultural exchange centre, to enhance the city's cultural life and lift the quality of its cultural contents. This inconsistency of the state seems to imply a certain ambivalence about the significance and role of culture in Shanghai's development plans.

Notwithstanding these apparent contradictions, the development of Shanghai as an international cultural exchange centre has been pursued on many fronts. The first is in the spatial arrangement of cultural infrastructure, to form a coherent and complementary cultural space. Second, there has been a concerted effort to expand and support traditional cultural activities, while simultaneously organizing high-quality and high-profile international cultural events. Third, the focus has been on the construction of cultural infrastructure, such as libraries, museums, cultural centres, art galleries and so forth.

The strategy, outlined above, to refurbish and revamp Shanghai's cultural identity highlights how such infrastructure has reverted to performing an essentially cultural function from its erstwhile political one, in conjunction with the shift in state attitudes towards openness. Cultural infrastructure is expected to execute this function through the performance of multiple roles that include supporting cultural development by offering high-quality space for artists; enhancing local artists' ability to perform and local people's capacity for cultural appreciation; promoting the development of creative or cultural industries; and enhancing the city's image and assisting the development of tourism. It is worth noting that the unifying theme of Shanghai's efforts to become an international cultural centre is an expansion and liberalization of cultural space. While infrastructure construction creates and modifies such spaces, the city's welcoming stance towards artists and creative talents from other cities and countries by promoting artistic collaboration and competition constitutes a deregulation of the artistic playing field. This development approach has been named the Shanghai Development Pattern.

The construction of cultural mega-infrastructure has been a significant part of Shanghai's reinvigoration of the cultural landscape since the 1990s. In the next section, two of the most significant cultural projects in Shanghai post Reform, namely, the SGT and the OAC, are examined. The focus is on the ways in which cultural infrastructure projects have been used to promote the city's claims to global status and the impacts on various groups in Shanghai.

SHANGHAI'S CULTURAL MEGA-STRUCTURES

For the performing arts, SGT and OAC are without doubt the most significant cultural projects of recent years in Shanghai. Constructed by the municipal government, these facilities reiterate the city's intent to acquire and maintain global city status, as well as its attempt to deepen its global linkages and expand its sphere of cultural influence. SGT and OAC are thus instructive case studies for discussing the influence of new cultural monuments on the urban cultural landscape and on various groups.

The Shanghai Grand Theatre

SGT sits at the intersection of Central Boulevard and Huangpi South Road in the northern part of People's Square, neighbouring the premises of the city government, the Shanghai Urban Planning Exhibition Centre, and the Shanghai Museum (another major cultural infrastructure that speaks of the changing attitudes towards culture in the 1990s). The construction of SGT cost the city more than CH¥1.2 billion without central government subsidies (Beech, 2000). Designed by French architect Jean-Marie Charpentier, the 40-metre-tall, 70 000-square-metre building is equipped with top-quality acoustics and lighting equipment. It also has world-class stage facilities, designed and fabricated by Mitsubishi. It has three theatres: the largest one, with 1800 seats, is designed for ballet and opera; the medium theatre, with 550 seats, is a drama and chamber music venue; and the smallest theatre, with 250 seats, is used for modern drama and dance performances.

The strong mandate for the city government's plan in 1993–94 to build SGT rode the wave of liberalization. Shanghai was perfectly poised to be China's gateway to the world. One of SGT's artistic directors mentioned that, since the implementation of the open-door policy, Shanghai has had many opportunities for high-grade cultural interactions; however, in the early days of open doors, Shanghai did not have an infrastructure commensurate with the scale, scope and quality of these events (Ma, 2007). Nonetheless, much as the construction of SGT was owed to the practical need for a venue to accommodate large-scale, high-profile cultural events, it has also been interpreted as a bold statement of intent by Shanghai to stake its claim to global city status (Kong, 2007). By choosing to site the facility in a central location where land values are the highest, right next to the municipal administration centre, city planners demonstrated their acknowledgement that honing the cultural element to noteworthy standards is essential to competing substantively in the race for global city status. Inviting a well-known architect to design this top-quality cultural palace was another acknowledgement of the importance placed on this facility. The same intent may be discerned in SGT's mission, as publicly articulated: to display first-class artistic works; to provide first-class artistic experiences and art education; to become the model for all Chinese theatres; and to develop the prestige and cultural creativity of the city (Shanghai Grand Theatre, 2014).

Since opening in August 1998, SGT has successfully staged various kinds of cultural performances, including operas, musicals, ballets, chamber music concerts and Chinese operas. It has hosted solo concerts by Pavarotti, Domingo and Carreras; several European operas (*Aida, Faust, The Flying Dutchman, Eugene Onegin*); the world's top philharmonic orchestras (Philadelphia, Washington National, San Francisco, Russian, Japan NHK, Vienna, Berlin and others); and famous ballets (such as *Romeo and Juliet* performed by the British Royal Ballet, *Cinderella* performed by the Belgian Royal Ballet of Flanders, and so forth). In addition to these successful stagings, SGT has received favourable reviews from both domestic and international artists and visitors. It has been widely acknowledged as an important platform for cultural exchange between China and the world, a bridge for artistic communication between genres and a platform for Chinese artists to develop and display their creativity.

On the evidence outlined above, it seems uncontroversial that SGT has established itself as an excellent artistic centre and as a stage for international cultural exchange. Consequently, it has been used as a symbol of Shanghai's cultural image and prestige. The theatre has also performed its envisaged role in expanding cultural linkages. It has been instrumental in forming performance networks in Asia, cooperating with other cities by sharing costs and fees and inviting top performance groups from around the world. Besides, in order to support local artists, to enrich local cultural life and to augment residents' aesthetic sensibilities, SGT abides by a government-imposed operational guideline of balancing the minimum of 250 shows among overseas, national and the city's local performance groups (Xie, 2005). Based on an examination of the 2007 and 2008 programmes, performances by international arts groups comprised approximately a third of all performances. Further, SGT also provides a venue for public art education via a series of art classes, such as 'appreciating the classics', 'conversing with masters' and 'working with children'.

SGT's financial management has been carefully arranged, while its operational management is expertly undertaken. The financial arrangements are uniquely designed to spare the city administration from the potential financial burden that might arise from the operation of the theatre. Under the arrangement, the theatre assumes ownership of profits and losses in exchange for a waiver of the construction loan and a promise for help in replacing infrastructural capital. The organizational arrangement is called *wenhua shiye danwei qiyehua guanli*, which means a public institution operating like a commercial enterprise (Kong et al., 2006; Xie, 2005; J. Wang, 2003, p. 7). In terms of operations, the management of SGT has passed ISO9002 certification. In 2006 and 2013, it even won the 'Best Theatre Management Gold Award in China'.

Despite the carefully thought-out financial arrangements and an acclaimed management structure, balancing the operational budget by relying only on income from the sale of tickets has posed a challenge. Accordingly, several strategies have been adopted to increase revenue. One of these income-supplementing measures takes the form of organizing art popularization and training classes conducted by renowned artists. SGT also provides agency services for talented Chinese individuals and groups, presenting them in the theatre and promoting them aggressively on the overseas performance circuit. According to an interviewee, these projects not only increase SGT's income but also contribute to fulfilling its express aim of introducing Chinese cultural/performance groups to the world. Thus, SGT serves as the display window for Chinese show business. Similarly, popularization activities increase audiences and boost ticket revenues.

SGT has also enlisted the support of commercial enterprises. Under the terms of support, the latter defray the theatre's performance expenses or purchase a certain number of tickets in exchange for publicity on SGT's marketing materials. While sponsorship for public relations is common practice, SGT in some instances allows supporting enterprises space within the theatre or in the lobby for displaying their products.

The Shanghai Oriental Art Centre

The Shanghai OAC is located in the central zone of Pudong New District. Funded by a joint investment of over CH¥1 billion by the Shanghai city government and Pudong District government, OAC covers 40 000 square metres. It is designed by the famous French architect Paul Andreu (who also designed Beijing's National Grand Theatre, discussed in Chapter 1). The construction started at the end of March 2002; the centre was inaugurated three years later on 1 July 2005. From a vantage point, the centre gives the impression of a butterfly orchid in full bloom. The five petals of the orchid represent the entrance, the exhibition gallery and the performance, concert and opera halls. OAC is equipped with advanced acoustic and lighting technologies that are adaptable to various performance needs.

The concert hall has 1953 seats and boasts the largest pipe organ in China, the Austrian Rieger pipe organ. The opera hall has a seating capacity of 1015 while the performance hall has 333 seats. The performance hall is distinguished by its amphitheatre-like design (which facilitates performer-audience interaction) and a rotating stage for enhanced visual effects. Designed as a highly specialized venue for musical performances, OAC fills a gap in the supply of space for chamber music performances in Shanghai. Thus, as a technological achievement and a design marvel, OAC qualifies as a world-class cultural facility.

OAC's goals include providing new cultural space for 'enjoying arts and enjoying service', achieving the status of domestic leader and receiving regional and global acclaim (Shanghai Oriental Art Centre, 2014). To meet these objectives, its management team has directed efforts at establishing four platforms: (1) for both the world premieres of Chinese artworks and of foreign artworks in China; (2) for carrying out various kinds of artistic activities (such as art training, art education and art competitions); (3) for recording and producing music; and (4) for fostering talent managers. Since its inauguration in July 2005, OAC has presented many high-quality performances; the Berliner Philharmoniker Shanghai Premiere Concert is just one such example.

To select its operational team, the city government invited tenders from around the country in September 2003. The Poly Culture & Arts Co. (later reorganized and renamed to Beijing Poly Theatre Management Co. in June 2009) became the successful tenderer. As a joint venture between Poly Culture & Arts Co. and Wenhui Xinmin United Press Group, the Shanghai Oriental Art Centre Management Co. was set up with responsibility for the management and operation of OAC and its subsidiary facilities. An artistic committee was also established, comprising invited local and renowned foreign artists and outstanding arts managers. This committee provided suggestions for the operation of OAC, especially with regard to performance design and long-term vision. For incorporating unique elements into its design, providing high-quality performance space and professional management, OAC has been awarded regular accolades. It has been listed as one of 'Shanghai's Ten Fashionable Landmarks' and praised as 'The Latest High Art Location in Shanghai'. In November 2006, it became the first theatre in China to acquire the ISO9001 quality management certification and the ISO14001 environmental management certification.

The use of invited tenders to select its management team places OAC in the same league as SGT in terms of market-oriented operational practices. Nevertheless, OAC has had to face competition from other cultural venues, especially SGT and the Shanghai Music Hall. From a location standpoint, SGT and the Shanghai Music Hall (located in the city centre) have a competitive edge over OAC, which is in relatively remote Pudong. To offset this disadvantage, it is imperative that OAC develops a specialized capability to provide niche services. An example is OAC's commitment to developing expertise in music recording and production. It has been suggested, to this end, that the rehearsal hall be redesigned and redesignated as a recording room. Since Shanghai has traditionally lacked high-quality recording infrastructure, such a step would position OAC as the base for the recording industry in Shanghai.

The sustainability of 'mega' cultural centres like SGT and OAC, where governments have absolved themselves of responsibility for their balance sheets, crucially depends on a large audience base. The premium placed on audience numbers has led SGT and OAC to make efforts to popularize art activities, such as free admission days, art appreciation lectures, music lectures and student tickets. While these efforts have increased the demand for tickets to various performances, management at both venues acknowledge the challenges that lie in both broadening – by inducing more people to attend performances – and deepening – by encouraging the casual performance-goer to attend performances habitually – the demand base. One manager puts the current situation into perspective:

> The number of annual performances in Shanghai has surpassed 10,000, and the size of the audience has increased to six to seven million. We did not dare to imagine such an achievement even a few years ago. However, Shanghai has 18 million residents. If we calculate the proportion, it indicates that one in every two to three persons has only attended one performance each year. There is a very large scope for the growth of the performance market. (Liang, 2007)

SGT's and OAC's pre-construction context, the high-profile nature of the design and construction process and the scale of financial investment lend credence to the thesis that Shanghai's investment in cultural infrastructure is largely motivated by its aspiration to be a global city. While these icons in Puxi and Pudong are conceived as integral to building 'brand Shanghai', they are also intended to develop local cultural assets. In this light, the cultural element of establishing and sustaining the status of a global city may be considered to consist of these separate but connected dimensions: first, the emphasis on visibility, by distinguishing the cityscape with identifiable cultural monuments; second, the attempt to build a stock of differentiated, marketable, local cultural goods for domestic and international consumption; and finally, the attempt to build a critical mass of local culture patrons to sustain the operations of the facilities.

With respect to the last two dimensions, the financial arrangements for the operation of 'mega' cultural facilities assume a critical importance. The operational design of the SGT and OAC envisions them as financially autonomous entities to ensure that international cultural activities do not compete for government resources with local cultural development and educational objectives. Further, the roles of these facilities have been conceptualized so as to harness the complementarities of cultural exchange. Accordingly, in addition to being responsible for showcasing global 'high' culture in Shanghai, the facilities are mandated to promote local cultural talent in global markets. SGT and OAC execute this role through their agency function.

SGT and OAC: The Cultural Balance Sheets

The cultural landmarks in Puxi and Pudong mark for cultural institutions a shift away from a predominantly political role towards a primarily cultural and economic role. In this sense, the contrast between the SGT and the OAC and monuments (like the People's Assembly Hall) from the pre-liberalization period is fundamental, yet subtle: while the latter represent a political space where cultural events were staged, the former demarcate a cultural space where politically inflected events (like the New Year Celebration Assembly) are held. This realignment of political and economic domains is re-emphasized by the insistence on a market-oriented approach to the operations of the SGT and OAC, which highlights a supplanting of political motives by cultural and commercial considerations.

The discussion in the previous section indicates the facilities' success in installing Shanghai, if not yet as a global culture hub, then at least as the cultural centre of the Yangzi Delta region and as a primary cultural gateway to mainland China. The involvements of acclaimed architects in their design, their technological capabilities and their résumé of successful performances by internationally renowned groups have given the venues a high cultural profile that the city enjoys, vicariously. As further evidence of this rapidly evolving visibility, the SGT and OAC cater not only to a local audience, but also to audiences from neighbouring provinces (Jiangsu and Zhejiang) as well as international tourists. Commensurate with this increasing regional and global recognition, a strong civic bond has crystallized around these monuments. Many of the residents interviewed in the course of this research reported a sense of pride in the construction of the SGT and the OAC.

While visibility is crucial to establishing cultural credentials, participating in cultural networks is equally important for building cultural capital and acquiring cultural leverage. A key success of the SGT and OAC has been in integrating these diverse functions as centres for cultural exchange. Responding to economic constraints as well as in leveraging opportunities, SGT and OAC have embarked on a strategy of cooperation with institutions in other regional cities (such as Hong Kong, Singapore, Tokyo and Taipei). While this reduces operational costs by spreading the substantial burden of performance fees, it has helped Shanghai integrate into the international performing arts system and to connect to global cultural networks. Thus, the city acquires the potential to help its local artists or cultural groups penetrate into other cultural destinations. SGT has used these networks to introduce the Shanghai Broadcast Symphony Orchestra and the Shanghai Ballet Troupe to other cities around the world.

However, such achievements do not imply that there is no contestation over the value of the projects. For projects based on significant investment of public funds, their accessibility to ordinary citizens and their role in the enrichment of citizens' cultural lives are important benchmarks for evaluation. Despite its central location, SGT's proximity to the seat of the city's government causes it to seem politically intimidating. The theatre's design has also reduced its accessibility to the general population, with very high steps at the entrance. The presence of a security enclosure continually manned by security guards makes approach and access even more forbidding. Further, buying a ticket is the only way to enter the SGT. To make matters worse, high ticket prices – due, in part, to high operational costs – put entrance beyond the reach of a large section of the general population. Denouncing the high premium on cultural appreciation and enjoyment, a local newspaper reported:

> SGT's high ticket prices have been widely denounced in society. However, the question of how ticket prices can be lowered is a difficult issue. (Lianhe Shibao, n.d.; Zhongguo Jingjiwang, 2013)

Clearly, cultural performances in Shanghai (and, especially, at the SGT and OAC) face the issue of there being only a small number who are able and willing to pay for a performance ticket (Xie, 2005). Despite their efforts to expand their audience base – for example, by offering half-price tickets to students – overall, ticket prices still remain so high as to deter ordinary people and students from attending performances. On this basis, it may be said that SGT and OAC remain spaces that are the preserve of international tourists and of the upper classes of society. The theme of the physical and economic inaccessibility of these facilities resonated through the responses in several interviews conducted in this study. In a survey of more than 100 students in Shanghai's universities (Tongji, Fudan and East China Normal University), very few acknowledged having bought a ticket to a performance at the SGT or OAC. The inability to afford the ticket was cited as the primary reason. Conversations with many ordinary residents in Shanghai, from taxi-drivers to salespersons and even office workers, revealed that the cost of tickets was prohibitive. This corroborates the comment by an OAC manager that, on average, each Shanghai resident attends less than one performance every two years (Liang, 2007).

The preceding discussion highlights a problem of cultural trickle-down inherent in grandiose cultural infrastructural projects like the SGT and OAC. It demonstrates how operational constraints and socioeconomic realities can combine to prevent the vision of universal cultural participation from being realized. In the case of SGT and OAC, despite their express commitment to enriching the cultural life of Shanghai residents, a substantial section (if not proportion) of the population continues to remain excluded from these performance spaces. Thus, while as landmarks and symbols of cultural aspiration they inspire civic pride and a sense of association, as purely functional performance spaces, they restrict participation, accentuate social distinctions and, hence, antithetically to their objectives, promote cultural elitism.

Given their range of responsibilities, the operational sustainability of cultural venues like SGT and OAC is a particular area of concern. This worry becomes especially germane when the size and constitution of Shanghai's culture-consuming population is taken into account. The proportion of the art-appreciating population in Shanghai is relatively low compared to other cities in more advanced countries. The consideration of volumes and costs, combined with a responsibility for the balance sheet, puts a high premium on tickets for performances, which serves to further truncate the audience base. The ensuing vicious cycle is hard to interrupt without state support or subsidies. In the absence of the same, SGT and OAC have had to rely on support from enterprises to strike a balance between ticket prices and audience numbers. As mentioned earlier, the current model requires a guarantee from supporting enterprises to buy a certain number of high-priced tickets. The enterprise assigns these tickets to its staff or to its consumers. The ticket-holders may go to the performance themselves or give the tickets to their relatives or friends. This so-called consumption by public money distorts the make-up of the audience for performances. The people who attend the performance are not necessarily arts lovers or have the capacity for artistic appreciation; indeed, they may not be familiar with the etiquette required of an audience at a performance. There was an incident at OAC where a member of the audience was so disruptive that the performer had to stop the performance and ask the person to leave (*China Daily*, 21 June 2006). SGT's and OAC's capacity to plan perform-ances well in advance is also impeded by Shanghai cultural consumers' habit of not ordering tickets ahead of time. This burdens cultural venues with an enormous risk in inviting internationally reputed performance groups. While arrangements for groups to come and perform have to be made at least a year in advance, the audience invariably buys tickets two to three days before the performance. The resulting uncertainty in projected revenue serves to increase ticket prices further by including a premium for the risk. Thus, with a host of structural and behavioural factors that threaten the operational stability of SGT and OAC, it is clear that the two bodies face a significant challenge in expanding their audience base and in changing audience behaviour.

Another criterion in evaluating the performance of SGT and OAC is their impact on local artists and groups. There is no immediate evidence to suggest that their construction has directly facilitated the development of Shanghai's cultural industry, particularly with regard to original artworks with local cultural content. However, by attracting famous international groups to Shanghai, SGT and OAC have provided local art groups the opportunity to learn by observing and emulating their creative and man-agement skills. While the tangible benefits from such interaction can be substantial, local performances by established international performers can be even more important in providing creative stimuli and suggesting directions for future artistic development.

In addition, SGT and OAC have attempted to be the face and voice of local cultural accomplishments in China, the region and globally. SGT currently schedules and manages the performances of cultural heavy-weights like the Shanghai Broadcast Symphony Orchestra, the Shanghai Ballet Troupe and the Shanghai International Performance Corporation. Furthermore, it provides agency services to outstanding local performance groups and artists. Although the main aim of this is to increase SGT's operational income, it also helps the contracted artists to build up both performance skills and visibility, by giving them the chance to perform in SGT as well as abroad.

Nevertheless, to local performing artists, particularly small cultural groups and young artists, SGT and OAC remain remote. Many local artists use other, more affordable spaces for their performances and, accordingly, are better positioned to attract a local audience. SGT's and OAC's market orientation inevitably leads them to focus almost exclu-sively on those local cultural assets that they consider to be marketable. By implication, a relatively small section of local artists and groups are contracted to be represented and managed. This selective provision of agency services runs the risk of marginalizing groups whose cultural aesthetic is not mainstream (and, hence, not marketable) or those groups whose artistic expression is so distinctly local as to lack regional or international appeal. This bias towards marketable cultural expression has the potential to erode diversity and, in the worst case, accelerate the extinction of endangered forms of local culture. In this context, institutions like SGT and OAC face the challenge of reconciling the needs of the market with that for sustainable cultural development. In the longer term, it is imperative that these facilities spread access to their services over a much larger group of local artists and groups, especially those whose artistic vision incorporates uniquely Chinese cultural characteristics. SGT and OAC need to be able to manage a shift in focus of the merchandising of culture to the culturing of culture.

In this regard, the content of these institutions' programming has also been challenged. Here, the contention revolves around the quality of local and international performances at the venues. One of the interviewees, a professor in a local university, mentioned:

> International performance groups present their cultural content. The contributions or achievements of these foreign performance groups in cultural exchange have never been evaluated. But I am sure that these performances have nothing to do with the local cultural identity. I also doubt that the SGT's operation can help local artists or contribute to the development of local cultural identity. Although one-third of annual programmes are contributed by local artists, most of them are in the nature of charity performances. Most of these programmes do not sell tickets in public, but mobilize students to attend the performance. Foreign performance programmes are also biased towards Eastern European and Russian performing groups. I am not saying they are not good. But they are cheaper than performances from Western Europe and North America. The aim of international cultural exchange would not achieve its goals due to the problem of lack of diversification. (Personal interview, 15 October 2007)

It is reasonable to assert that, in ensuring a lasting validation of Shanghai's cultural credentials, the quality of the performances is as crucial as the quality of the infrastructure. Further, to sustain Shanghai's appeal as a cultural destination for performers, it is essential to initiate a bandwagon effect by establishing the venues' reputation as high-quality performance spaces. To that end, SGT and OAC, as previously mentioned, have played host to numerous high-profile cultural events; however, it is alleged that a large proportion of the performances were mediocre. At a basic level, the explanation for this is economic. While these facilities are treated as self-managing economic units, the choice of performances must answer to cost-benefit calculations. Therefore, in certain circumstances, the choice of 'cheaper' performance groups may be economically justified. This throws up interesting philosophical questions about the judiciousness of burdening such flagship cultural institutions, which have a mandate to generate positive externalities for society, with the responsibility to be commercially viable as well (Ma, 2007). Implied in such considerations is the thesis that the purely cultural and educational functions of an institution that is entirely commercially run might be unsustainable in Shanghai's cultural environment.

A final concern about sustainability addresses the (de)merits of locating two premier cultural destinations (SGT and OAC) in close proximity to each other. The small local market for cultural/artistic consumption lends weight to the view that cultural infrastructure projects (like investments in other physical infrastructure) are deprived from enjoying economies of scale by being forced to compete against each other. Not only do SGT and OAC have to compete against each other, they also have to fend off facilities in several southern Chinese cities, such as Guangzhou, Shenzhen and Ningbo, which have also built their own grand theatres. Besides concerns about the inefficacy of a competitive structure in this context, the projects have also been criticized as being redundant investments and a waste of public funds (Xie, 2005). A proposed solution to this problem involves product differentiation. Competing cultural facilities can distinguish themselves operationally by creating niches that they may then monopolize. As mentioned by the manager of OAC, 'we should shift our focus from theatre construction to theatre operation. Only by developing our own characteristics can we make the theatre a cultural symbol for the city and thus to maintain competitiveness' (personal interview, 5 January 2008).

CONCLUSION

The construction of cultural facilities has been regarded as one of the main means for Shanghai to contest the status of global cultural hub. In the pursuit of such recognition, these mega-projects have also been expected to play multiple roles, including supporting the development of cultural industry; promoting the city's image and attractiveness; developing abilities for arts appreciation; enriching citizens' cultural lives; strengthening global linkages; and facilitating cultural exchange. The case studies of SGT and OAC presented here reveal that the monuments are potent emblems of Shanghai's aspirations for cultural greatness. Compared in terms of design, technological capabilities and versatility, these performance spaces rank alongside those in other global cities. As a result of efforts spanning the past two decades, Shanghai has achieved visibility as a cultural destination by attracting artists and groups of international repute and by integrating into regional and global cultural networks.

Despite this, there are concerns about the sustainability of this model of cultural development. The inadequate cultural trickle-down implies that the facilities cater to foreign tourists and local elites. Thus, the envisioned enrichment of residents' cultural lives remains a remote objective. The capacity for artistic appreciation among residents in Shanghai remains inchoate – in contrast to the culturally established cities in Europe and North America – which requires the institutions to step up efforts for popularization. However, a market-oriented operating structure restricts SGT's and OAC's ability to expand art popularization and education programmes. This research also highlights how commercial concerns might foster a tendency for selective support to those assets of local culture that are considered marketable. Such selective patronage might contribute to the demise of more esoteric forms of artistic and cultural expression along with those forms that are deemed too local to have any demand in other markets. A final challenge for sustainability of these cultural infrastructure projects is constituted by their mutual competition for a small local market. As such, the economic logic of situating both SGT and OAC in relative proximity to each other must by questioned.

The success and failure of these projects is perhaps best captured in Kong's (2007) assessment of SGT: 'The Shanghai Grand Theatre is symbolic: it represents what the communist authorities do best and worst. The infrastructure is state-of-the art, but artistic expression has not been commensurately supported.'

The construction of cultural buildings might be great attention-grabbers, but to keep global attention over the medium and long run and to secure global recognition of its cultural sophistication and quality, Shanghai will need to support hype with substance. This includes stable economic development; the gradual opening up of society to provide an ambient climate for art appreciation; the promotion of local cultural development by assisting the growth of local artists; support for works of art with local cultural content; and the provision of space and opportunities to local artists to showcase their work. For now, spaces such as SGT and OAC have not yet been able to fulfil these roles.

4. Hong Kong's dilemmas and the changing fates of West Kowloon Cultural District

INTRODUCTION

Hong Kong is not a place usually associated with rich culture and thriving arts. Instead, it is better known as a centre of commerce, finance and telecommunications. Its recent branding efforts have focused on establishing itself as 'Asia's world city', a positioning 'designed to highlight Hong Kong's existing strengths in areas such as financial services, trade, tourism, transport, communications, and as a regional hub for international business and a major city in China' (Hong Kong Government Information Centre, n.d.). Its 2001 Brand Hong Kong programme, intended as the platform for promoting itself internationally as Asia's world city, was focused primarily on economic opportunity and entrepreneurship. As a corollary, the programme acknowledged the significance of culture. The focus, however, was on hardware – the plan was to develop 'world-class cultural infrastructure' in the form of a new 40-hectare arts district (the West Kowloon Cultural District (WKCD), facing the central business district on Hong Kong Island). The plan proclaimed that the district would be a 'cultural oasis', designed to 'enrich the lives of Hong Kong residents, attract visitors from neighbouring cities and enhance even further one of the most beautiful skylines in the world with a new, distinguished landmark' (Hong Kong Government Information Centre, n.d.). The reference to a 'cultural oasis' amounts to a self-acknowledgement of the relative lack of a thriving arts scene in this Special Administrative Region of China. Indeed, no new public performance venue has been built since 2000 and no new territory-wide, purpose-built performing arts venue has been built since the completion of the Hong Kong Cultural Centre in 1989 (Subcommittee on West Kowloon Cultural District Development, 2007a). Unlike in Taipei, the private sector is not active in providing arts facilities, and the Hong Kong government owns most of the performance venues in the territory, under the Leisure and Cultural Services Department (LCSD).

LCSD operates 13 performance venues and one indoor stadium, a visual arts centre, a film archive, 12 museums and 72 libraries (Subcommittee on West Kowloon Cultural District Development, 2005b). Given the paucity of new public facilities for the arts, the development of WKCD might have been a welcome addition. On the contrary, it has drawn abundant criticism, not least from the arts community. Academic assessment has also been harsh. In the midst of public criticism and what seemed like project abortion, Tai-lok Lui (2008, p. 215) delivered a scathing verdict, calling it a 'typical package of urban entrepreneurialism, with an emphasis on chasing after mega-projects, iconic buildings and media visibility', while avoiding 'questions concerning the substance of the entire project, consensus from below and the vision of cultural development'. Consequently, Lui concluded that 'city competition by means of developing global architecture, mega-projects and fabricated urban culture is inevitably futile'.

GENESIS OF THE IDEA

The idea of a cultural district in West Kowloon first came about in 1996 when the Hong Kong Tourist Association shared the results of a survey highlighting how tourists to Hong Kong showed a strong interest in arts-, culture- and entertainment-related events. The association thus proposed that more large-scale performance venues be developed in Hong Kong (Subcommittee on West Kowloon Cultural District Development, 2005b). A report published by the association in 1999 pushed for a new performance venue in Hong Kong for several reasons. First, existing performance venues were already utilized to the maximum. Second, it believed the availability of new performance facilities would support the development of arts and culture locally and enable Hong Kong to become Asia's arts and cultural centre. Third, it felt additional large-scale performance venues would boost tourism to Hong Kong, and develop Hong Kong into the 'event capital' of Asia (Taoho Design Architects and Hong Kong Tourist Association, 1999). The report also recommended the development be modelled as an 'arts district', with the inclusion of commercial areas, in order to be commercially viable. In addition, it identified a site on West Kowloon as a potential location.

Plans for development in West Kowloon were officially announced by the government in 1999. Then-Chief Executive Tung Chee Hwa ordered a 40-hectare site in West Kowloon to be developed into an integrated arts, cultural and entertainment district. An international competition held in 2001 for the district's design concept was won by the British firm Foster + Partners, whose design included a distinctive 25-hectare canopy (Legislative Council, 2005). However, subsequent feedback from the community forced changes to the design concept. In 2003, a call for proposals was launched to select a developer for WKCD. The winner would be expected to develop a theatre complex, a large-scale perform- ance venue, a museum cluster, art exhibition centre, water amphitheatre, piazza areas and the canopy (Subcommittee on West Kowloon Cultural District Development, 2005c). Significantly, in the call for proposals, global ambition was clearly articulated: WKCD would be a 'cultural icon' that is part of Hong Kong's 'positioning as a world city' (D. Tsang, 2003). One of the selection criteria was the ability to create a unique architectural landmark that would draw visitors (D. Tsang, 2004). Added to this is a litany of ambitious objectives: WKCD is to 'enrich cultural life by attracting internationally acclaimed performances and exhibi- tions; nurture local arts talent and create more opportunities for arts groups; enhance international cultural exchange; put Hong Kong on the world arts and culture map; provide state-of-the-art performance venues and museums; offer more choices to arts patrons; encourage creativity; enhance the harbour front; attract overseas visitors; and create jobs' (D. Tsang, 2003).

A PROTRACTED CONTROVERSIAL PROJECT

The project has been characterized by controversies and dilemmas. Its chequered history is summarized in Table 4.1.

Soon after the project was announced, an international competition for the district's concept was launched on 6 April 2001. It attracted 161 entries, 71 of which were from Hong Kong. The results were announced on 28 February 2002, with British firm Foster + Partners emerging the winner. The significant feature of the winning design was its 25-hectare canopy, of which the jury said, 'the sinuously flowing form of the site contours and the canopy produce a memorable effect' (Legislative Council, 2005, p. 6). Foster explained his design: 'It is a canopy, not a roof because it never goes down to the ground. It is not enclosed and encourages the flow of air' (Chau, 2002). In September the same year, a Steering Committee for the Development of WKCD was established, the first governance structure to be put in place. At the same time, with Hong Kong facing an economic downturn due to the Asian financial crisis and the severe acute respiratory syndrome (SARS) outbreak, it was decided that private investment was needed for the project. The private sector, with its commercial knowledge, was felt to be in a better position to develop WKCD to meet the pressing

Table 4.1   A summary of WKCD's chequered history

Years	Event
1996–99	Genesis of the idea
2001–02	First design competition
2002	First governance structure
2003	First signs of public unhappiness mixed with government unilateralism
2004–05	*First round of public consultation (x 2)*
2006	Government rethink: consultative committee formed
	Second round of public consultation
2007	*Third round of public consultation*
2008	Formation of West Kowloon Cultural District Aauthority; consultation panel formed
2009–11	*Fourth round of public consultation (x 4)*
2013	Development plan approved; West Kowloon Waterfront Promenade (a temporary site at the tip of West Kowloon Reclamation) opened to public with arts and community activities initiated to positive public response; commencement of construction
2020	Targeted completion of WKCD Phase 1
2031?	Targeted completion of WKCD Phase 2

demand for arts and cultural facilities (Subcommittee on West Kowloon Cultural District Development, 2005a). This would soon lead to an open tender for a developer to undertake the work, which would in turn open the floodgates for the expression of a multiplicity of divergent views as to how the project should proceed.

The first stirrings came from the Culture and Heritage Commission, a high-level advisory body established in 2000, responsible for advising the government on cultural policies as well as funding priorities in culture and the arts. The commission's members, appointed by the chief executive, have as their key responsibility the formulation of a set of principles and strategies to promote the long-term development of culture in Hong Kong. In March 2003, the commission put forward its report, with some 100 recommendations on overall policies and specific implementations. It focused on a 'community driven', 'people-oriented' approach (Culture and Heritage Commission, 2003, p. 1) and recommended that the government pay attention to integrating the facilities in WKCD to create a 'lively and vigorous environment'; ensure that the district complemented other cultural facilities in Hong Kong; and, importantly, that the government consider the 'software' before planning the 'hardware'.

The commission's views notwithstanding, on 5 September 2003, the invitation for proposals (IFP) for the development of WKCD was launched. A number of mandatory requirements were stipulated: a complex comprising three theatres, with seating capacities of at least 2000, 800 and 400 seats; a performance venue with seating capacity of at least 10 000; a cluster of four museums of different themes; an art exhibition centre; a water amphitheatre; four piazza areas; and a canopy covering at least 55 per cent of the development area (Subcommittee on West Kowloon Cultural District Development, 2005c). As part of Foster's design, 39 per cent of West Kowloon would be set aside for arts and culture, 17 per cent for office developments, 16 per cent residences, 21 per cent retail and the rest for community use (Hui, 2004b). In announcing the IFP, then-Chief Secretary for Administration Donald Tsang said control would be given to one developer, to 'ensure its concept would be consistent' (*The Standard*, 2003). It would be granted 30 years' sole rights to the development. Then-acting Chief Secretary Michael Suen Ming-yeung warned that the canopy was a 'must' and that tenders that did not provide for the canopy would not be considered (M. Wong, 2004).

The predetermination of cultural facilities, the assessment criteria and the single-developer approach came under fire. Stephen Tsang et al. (2009, p. 105) pointed to this as evidence of the deficiencies in the strategies of public participation adopted by the government, revealing public dissatisfaction with the manner in which the government had purportedly invited only 130 (pro-government) practitioners to provide inputs to the development plan. Regardless, in June 2004, five proposals were received; in November, after the first round, three developers who had complied with the mandatory requirements were shortlisted. These were Dynamic Star International (a joint venture between Cheung Kong and Sun Hung Kai), World City Cultural Park (Henderson Land) and Sunny Development (a consortium formed by Sino Land, Wharf (Holdings), Chinese Estates Holdings and K. Wah International). One proposal, by Swire Group, was rejected, partly because its concept did not include the canopy and 'would not create a unique architectural landmark for WKCD to attract visitors. It would not group together the facilities in the district. It would not allow the public to enjoy the facilities in an open setting. The merits expected of the canopy design are lost' (D. Tsang, 2004). The three shortlisted proposals were exhibited as part of a public consultation exercise.

However, the public had begun to express its disapproval of the project from the time the IFP was launched. There were diverse views on several issues, such as the single-developer approach, the mandatory huge canopy and the lack of consultation with the arts and cultural sector. The 1.5 kilometre-long canopy, which was to have a 120 metre-high roof, stirred much discussion, with many highlighting its potential problems, including maintenance and the requirement of special ventilation. Builders and construction contractors questioned its feasibility, especially with regards to how the canopy was to be supported (Fenton, 2004). More importantly, many began asking, as one reporter did, 'Is the canopy, which creates the intended icon, the best way to showcase Hong Kong culture?' (Loh, 2004).

Representatives at a public forum from the cultural and architectural sectors called WKCD a 'property project' (Hui, 2004c). The government was attacked for its decision to hand over the management of WKCD to a single consortium for 30 years, especially to developers who had no experience in arts and cultural projects. It was felt that the single-developer approach restricted the participation of small- and medium-sized developers. In a newspaper article, Professor Bernard Lim, chairman of the Board of Local Affairs of the Hong Kong Institute of Architects, argued that the government and developers had no experience in partnering with each other in large-scale cultural projects (Hui, 2004a). Also, as the project was to be run on a self-financing basis and would not involve public funding, it was not necessary to seek funding approval from the Legislative Council. This raised questions as to whether the government was circumventing the normal approach to seeking funds for public works (Subcommittee on West Kowloon Cultural District Development, 2005c).

In acknowledgement of the significant public unease, a public consultation exercise ran from December 2004 to June 2005. It was conducted by the Public Policy Research Institute of Hong Kong Polytechnic University. At a Legislative Council meeting in early January 2005, Chief Executive Donald Tsang continued to reject calls to scrap the single-developer approach and the canopy, saying that the canopy was integral to the hub and that scrapping either feature would mean starting over again, with a further delay (Yeung, 2005). However, the first indication that the community's views were having an influence on the government emerged when Rita Lau Ng Wai-lan, Permanent Secretary for Housing, Planning and Lands, told the Legislative Council Subcommittee that the government might consider setting up a statutory body to manage WKCD (Lai, 2005b), comprising not just legislators but also those from the arts and cultural community. Telephone polls and other submitted public opinions showed that the majority was against the single-developer approach, but views were mixed on the issue of the canopy. Another point put across in the public consultation was a preference for less residential and commercial development, and more open and green areas. The public also favoured a lower plot ratio (Home Affairs Bureau, 2005). Various organizations also raised their voices. The Legislative Council's

Subcommittee on West Kowloon Cultural District Development, set up on 21 January 2005, continued to push for a master plan for the West Kowloon site (Legislative Council, 2007).

The single-developer model was dropped in October 2005, 'to satisfy public demands' (A. Lam, 2006). The Executive Council approved a revised plan that gave one developer the arts district, a minimum of 30 per cent of the total project area, and half of the land for residential and commercial development; the rest would be put to open tender. The winning developer would have to pay HK$30 billion to set up a trust fund to support WKCD and a statutory body would be established to oversee the district. The government kept its plot ratio of 1.81. However, the canopy continued to be a main feature of WKCD, despite reservations expressed by Sino Land and Henderson Land, two of the property giants in the bidding. As Henderson Project Director Lau Chi-keung said in July 2005: 'If the government really is cutting the project into a number of pieces, can the canopy be built? The canopy is a one-piece design that sleekly stretches along the site' (Lai, 2005a).

With the new financial requirements, there was speculation that bidders might drop out, but the project was saved at the last minute when two shortlisted bidders expressed their continued interest, just hours before the 27 January 2006 deadline. The other bidder had done so on the 26 January. However, the developers did not state explicitly if they had accepted the revised terms. A *South China Morning Post* article noted that the bidders had raised questions about the project's specific conditions, such as the HK$30 billion fund, but would not say if they would negotiate with the government on possible compromises (Wong and Hung, 2007). This information concerned the legislators and the public. Subcommittee on West Kowloon Cultural District Chairman Alan Leong Kah-kit said 'The three bidders have not confirmed their compliance with the new terms set out [by the administration] in October. This is not something they can meet to discuss and handle behind closed doors with the three bidders' (Chan and Crawford, 2006). Lobby groups and pro-democracy groups also urged the government to confirm the bidders' compliance with the terms. Thus, the project was sent back to the drawing board, with the government announcing a rethink of the arts hub in February 2006. It decided to set up three consultative committees to assess the arts hub plans before proceeding any further.

The Consultative Committee on the Core Arts and Cultural Facilities of the West Kowloon Cultural District and its three advisory groups (Performing Arts and Tourism Advisory Group, Museums Advisory Group and Financial Matters Advisory Group) were set up in April 2006 to 're-examine and reconfirm if appropriate the need of the CACF (core arts and cultural facilities) and to assess the financial implications' (Subcommittee on West Kowloon Cultural District Development, 2007a, p. 1). The Performing Arts and Museum Advisory Groups conducted a public consultation exercise from May to June 2006 to gain views from the public as well as from the arts and cultural sectors. Many more views continued to be received by the administration (see later discussion). In a paper published in June 2007, the committee laid out its recommendations. The Museums Advisory Group put forward its idea of a mega-museum, M+ (Museum Plus), to focus on twentieth- and twenty-first-century visual culture from a Hong Kong perspective. The recommendations from the Performing Arts and Tourism Advisory Group included a total of 15 performing arts venues of various types and sizes, such as a chamber music hall, four black boxes and a performance mega-venue with a 15 000-seat capacity. Further, the committee recommended that the government set up a West Kowloon Cultural District Authority.

The consultative committee's public consultation exercise notwithstanding, another public engagement exercise was held almost immediately after the recommendations of the consultative committee in June 2007. This third round of public consultation lasted some six months, after which a new start for the arts hub was unveiled. Control was to be handed over to a new authority, and the government would inject HK$19 billion from the sale of more than 40 per cent of the area's gross floor area for residential and commercial development; 15 arts performance areas, a mega-museum and a convention centre would be built in two phases, with the first phase to be completed by 2015 and the second in 2026. The project was expected to create more than 40 000 jobs in the first 30 years (Wong and Hung, 2007). The government said it had struck a balance between development and public open space, with some 23 hectares of the latter (Hung and Wong, 2007). It was later revealed that only two of the 17 arts and cultural facilities – the 15 000-seat venue and the 10 000-square-metre exhibition centre – were likely to be financially self-sufficient. The government estimated that the arts and cultural facilities would generate a deficit of HK$6.7 billion over the course of 50 years, but that revenue from rents and land sales would be able to cover it (H. Wu, 2007). When the details of the new proposal were released, it seemed as if the canopy had been dropped, but in effect it was in limbo, as Chief Secretary Henry Tang Ying-yen indicated on 20 September 2007: 'Whether there should be a canopy, how it should be built, or whether there should be a canopy on a smaller scale – we should leave this to the future authority' (Ng, K., 2007).

Critics expressed their views in multiple ways, through media commentaries, public statements and symposia, workshops and talks.

Additionally, some 3800 public views were received as part of the public engagement exercise, which closed on 12 December 2007. The result was largely in support of WKCD, according to the Legislative Council Subcommittee report (Subcommittee on West Kowloon Cultural District Development, 2008). However, the official online discussion forums showed that respondents were divided on whether WKCD should proceed immediately or undergo another round of planning and consultation, as many felt that it was a high-risk investment. Like the critics from the arts and culture sector, many respondents were concerned about the lack of 'software'; others worried that WKCD would end up a white elephant and a waste of public funds (Home Affairs Bureau, 2007).

The Subcommittee on West Kowloon Cultural District recommended in January 2008 that the bill for establishing the West Kowloon Cultural District Authority be passed before the current session ended, and that Legislative Council approval be sought for an upfront endowment of HK$21.6 billion (Subcommittee on West Kowloon Cultural District Development, 2008). The West Kowloon Cultural District Authority Bill was tabled in February 2008. The role of the authority would be to develop and operate the arts hub, set up committees to facilitate its operation, decide land use, invest funds, borrow money or raise funds to perform its functions and determine and collect fees and charges for the arts hub (Home Affairs Bureau, 2008). The bill was passed in July 2008, but observers worried that the authority might be too powerful if it received a one-off grant of funds (O. Wong, 2008).

In a bid to prove to sceptics that it would be inclusive, the newly formed authority established a consultation panel made up of members from a wide spectrum of backgrounds and fields. The authority spent the next three years in public engagement: Phase 1 in 2009, Phase 2 in 2010 and Phase 3 in 2011. To illustrate just how protracted and (over-) involved the process was, Phase 1 comprised three public forums, including one special forum for students and youth; 61 focus group meetings with over 20 stakeholder groups; 66 public engagement events; and the administration of 7000 questionnaires. Phase 2 involved another three public forums, including one special forum for students and youth; roving exhibitions of the conceptual plans; and another 7300 questionnaires. Finally, Phase 3 comprised an exhibition of the modified conceptual plan and information on the proposed development plan with guided tours and presentation sessions. There were also conferences held with professionals, stakeholders, arts and cultural groups and students and youth.

In the face of so many divergent views and public engagement efforts, progress on WKCD has been slow. Since the plan to build WKCD was announced in 1999, the master plan has undergone several re-evaluations. In terms of construction, the first phase is scheduled for completion only in 2015; the entire project is estimated to take up to 32 years, if 1999 is taken as the starting point and 2031 the completion date, as currently estimated. By the time the development plan was approved in February 2013 and construction was scheduled to begin, the equivalent of approximately seven years had been dedicated to multiple rounds of public consultation. At the time of writing in 2014, this constituted nearly 50 per cent of the total time dedicated to the project to date.

IN SEARCH OF A SUSTAINABLE MODEL

By far, Hong Kong's WKCD represents the most protracted and controversial of the cultural projects discussed in this book. WKCD has met with widespread opposition within Hong Kong and, in response, the city government has rolled out exercise after exercise of public consultation and engagement. The myriad views about the project from the public and interest groups may be characterized as follows. The first set of concerns focus on WKCD's long-term sustainability as a cultural project serving the arts and cultural life of Hong Kong. Critics believe that attention should be paid to 'software' development (social institutions that support cultural industries) rather than 'hardware'. The second set of anxieties relate to WKCD as a social project – how the views of the community that the district is to support and serve have not been consulted. These objections foreground especially the social role of the arts and culture, and the need to take into account the community's needs and aspirations. The third set of concerns centre on WKCD as part of Hong Kong's urban landscape, and express the desire to see the urban project speak to the needs of the population and the identity of a people. The final set of issues relate to whether the project will be economically viable for the long term. In the earlier rounds of consultation, the views revolved around more abstract issues, such as the need to encourage organic growth of arts and cultural activities and facilities, particularly at the community level; the need to involve the community in its planning; the importance of providing the public with open and green spaces; providing support for the development of local talent; maintaining the aesthetics and relevant symbolism of the proposed district; and ensuring its environmental sustainability. As some of these concerns came to be addressed, later concerns addressed more practical, specific details of organization and management.

Cultural Sustainability

A concern for cultural sustainability underlies many of the objections raised against WKCD. Observers and interested parties expressed the view that WKCD would be truly sustainable only if a clear philosophy and strategy underpinned its development as an arts hub (personal interviews with Chow Chun-fai, 12 January 2008, and Kong Kee, 17 January 2008). The advisory committees were perceived to have failed to take 'a macro-view in the formulation of a holistic and integrative public policy for the development of art and culture' (Museum of Site, 2006). Critics called for the government to outline its cultural development strategy for Hong Kong. In an opinion piece in the *South China Morning Post*, Paul Zimmerman, convenor of Designing Hong Kong Harbour District, called for a comprehensive plan for Hong Kong's arts and cultural development (Zimmerman, 2007).

In addition, concerns were expressed over how the government lacked clear plans for the development of arts and cultural software to accompany the physical development of WKCD. The Hong Kong Academy for Performing Arts, for example, pointed out that the future viability of WKCD depends on the 'training of new artistic talent', as well as an 'improvement in curricular arts content' that would stimulate audience development (Hong Kong Academy for Performing Arts, 2006). The People's Panel on West Kowloon (2005) also highlighted that for WKCD to be sustainable and continue as a 'cultural project', it must have 'cultural substance'. It urged that attention be paid to 'cultural depth' in the development of WKCD, cautioning that neglecting this critical aspect would result in a failed cultural project, and ultimately reduce WKCD to a mere property development project (People's Panel on West Kowloon, 2005). Sharing similar concerns, one prominent civic group calling itself 'Project Hong Kong', and led by internationally renowned film director Tsui Hark, protested against the development of the cultural district, calling for a focus on talent development (for example, establishing a film school) instead. Similarly, a prominent arts director, critic and academic, Oscar Ho Hing-Kay, stressed the importance of accelerating 'the training of local professionals to meet the future cultural needs' of Hong Kong (Ho, 2007). Likewise, Margaret Yang, Chief Executive Officer of the Hong Kong Sinfonietta, a mid-sized orchestra, felt that without efforts to develop local talent and software, the 'iconic structures will be, at best, mere shells' (Yang, 2007). Others, such as the organization Zonta Club, stressed that priority should be placed on building up cultural software first, and that cultural development plans for WKCD ought to be suspended until issues involving support for the arts and the current quality of arts education were ironed out (Zonta Club, 2005c).

Attention was also drawn to the specific programming and management policies of WKCD. These were thought to be as vital as the physical infrastructure development. 'As important as the bricks and mortar, will be the programming and management policies which will govern WKCD's operations and its role in Hong Kong', the Hong Kong Arts Administrators' Association stated. It felt the arts community should have control over determining such policies, while the government should act only as a facilitator (Hong Kong Arts Administrators' Association, 2007). In this regard, there was concern over whether adequate local expertise would be used in the management of WKCD to engender and embed a local sense of identity. The local chapter of the International Association of Art Critics voiced its concern, calling for local expertise to be involved and empowered, alongside international experts. This, it stated, 'is a key prerequisite to making WKCD or any other new cultural institutions truly reflective of Hong Kong's unique cultural perspective on an international scale' (International Association of Art Critics – Hong Kong, 2007).

Social Sustainability

Along with concerns expressed about the cultural character and sustainability of WKCD were anxieties about social sustainability. In the early years of the project, many expressed unhappiness that the authorities had failed to engage the participation of diverse parts of the community, and believed this lack of inclusiveness undermined WKCD's potential role as an instrument of social cohesion.

Various organizations and individuals vociferously expressed their views about the lack of public consultation. The local chapter of the International Association of Art Critics called for more discussion and debate as to how the cultural district would serve as a cultural hub and who the target audience would be (*South China Morning Post*, 2 June 2004). The 'Citizen Envisioning a Harbour' lobby group also expressed concern that community needs were neither solicited nor considered. As a senior member of the group argued: 'This is supposed to be a cultural centre for the community – what do private developers know about the cultural needs of a community?' Further, 'huge sectors of the community were not included in the planning of this site – people who it is supposed to be there for' (*Agence France Presse*, 29 April 2004). There was widespread sentiment among Hong Kongers that their opinions were being ignored. Based on a public opinion survey conducted in 2006, Hong Kong Alternatives, an advocacy group representing Hong Kong residents, declared that 'there is a clear discrepancy in what the people wants and what the government is providing or planning to provide'. Evidence of this lay in data showing that only one-fifth of the respondents in the survey 'considered the government to have respected public opinion in its planning for the WKCD' (Hong Kong Alternatives, 2006). In recognition of the importance 'for the general public to develop their sense of ownership' in the WKCD project, Robert Chung, Director of the Public Opinion Programme at Hong Kong University, advocated a consultation process based on democratic means (Chung, 2007). Even the Zonta Club, a service organization of executives and professionals working to advance the status of women, added its voice, recommending that the government delegate the supervision and implementation of WKCD to a statutory body comprising 'experts in arts and development and administration, artists, financial advisors, architectural planners, and able civic leaders' (Zonta Club, 2005a). This has eventually come to pass.

Artists and professionals who expressed concern at the lack of consultation feared that the district would be less a cultural hub than a 'developers' colony' (*South China Morning Post*, 17 June 2004). In particular, there was strong worry that this was really a real estate enterprise that would benefit developers who knew and cared little about culture, rather than an important part of the city's cultural infrastructure that would help develop creativity and the arts. Some went so far as to reject a government-driven initiative, calling instead for organic evolution. For example, Jaffa Lim, artist and founder of Artist-in-Residence, was highly critical of WKCD's commercial and residential portions, and called instead for the entire district to be left to organic development by artists (personal interview, 10 January 2008).

Even as the project has moved beyond the multiple public consultation phases towards construction, doubts still linger over whether it will successfully encourage public involvement and participation. Arts critic Oscar Ho Hing-Kay pointed out the need for the government to nurture an 'understanding of and participation in arts and culture at a *broader, community level*'. For instance, he believed M+, the mega-museum planned for WKCD, should 'dismantle the esoteric image of museum' and instead 'make arts approachable to the public' (Ho, 2007). Others called for the facilities and programming of museums in WKCD to cater to children as well (International Association of Art Critics – Hong Kong, 2007). In addition, the Action Group on Protection of the WKCD stressed that the plan for WKCD needs to consider the cultural needs of different social strata (Subcommittee on West Kowloon Cultural District Development, 2005b). Indeed, many groups emphasized the need for WKCD to engage diverse parts of the community, as they realize a healthy arts and culture ecology is a prerequisite for social sustainability (Subcommittee on West Kowloon Cultural Development, 2007b).

Urban Sustainability

Perhaps the most fundamental objection to WKCD is the one that questions the need for it. As one critic argued forcefully, is such a planned cultural district really necessary since Hong Kong already has a natural cluster? (Zimmerman, 2007). The Harbour District, an area between the Eastern Harbour Crossing and Western Harbour Tunnel, has 90 per cent of all arts, cultural, entertainment, financial and commercial facilities (*South China Morning Post*, 29 April 2004). This is corroborated by many first-hand accounts from film industry interviewees who argue that in a small place like Hong Kong, the effort to cluster activities in one place made no sense since most places were within easy reach (see Kong, 2005). In fact, the Hong Kong Institute of Planners stated that developing a 'high concentration of arts and cultural venues in WKCD is unhealthy', and proposed the alternative of developing existing local cultural venues in other districts instead (Subcommittee on West Kowloon Cultural District Development, 2005a; see also Zimmerman, 2007). Others, like the Zonta Club, felt WKCD would not be a suitable site for a community of artists, as it would be 'artificial and removed from artists' natural neighbourhoods' (Zonta Club, 2005b). Supporting these views were calls for the land to be used for other purposes that could preserve or enhance the landscape. For example, Hong Kong Alternatives proposed that instead of allowing development, the West Kowloon area should be made into an integrated green park (Hong Kong Alternatives, 2007). The funding that would have gone into developing WKCD could be put to other uses. For example, Jeffrey Au of the local think tank Professional Commons believed WKCD funds should be used to advance cultural sectors and talent development, as well as to provide for arts and cultural facilities in other parts of Hong Kong, such as Wanchai or the New Territories (personal interview, 12 January 2008).

For those who accepted that a cultural district would be a good addition to the urbanscape, there were nevertheless views about how the area should be developed aesthetically. Some simply wanted to ensure that WKCD would not become too densely built up. As one of the public consultation exercises revealed, the public had a preference for more open and green areas, and less residential and commercial development within the district, as well as a lower plot ratio (Home Affairs Bureau, 2005). The integration of residential and commercial buildings with arts facilities within WKCD also warranted concern. For example, the Hong Kong Institute of Architects strongly believed that residential and commercial developments intended for WKCD should 'contribute meaningfully to the promotion of arts and culture', and must be compatible with the overall

WKCD goals before being accepted (Hong Kong Institute of Architects, 2007).

Others focused on the physical design of WKCD, especially the canopy feature. As highlighted earlier, the canopy stirred up much discussion over its appropriateness in representing Hong Kong culture, its ability to integrate with surrounding urban forms and its purported lack of character (Subcommittee on West Kowloon Cultural District Development, 2005c). Furthermore, Zonta Club believed the canopy would obstruct views across the harbour, arguing that 'in the current context, the canopy is an irrelevant and almost undesirable feature' (Zonta Club, 2005b). It also felt 'the existence of a gigantic canopy over a group of nondescript buildings' would lack appeal.

Beyond the aesthetics and internal planning parameters, many were also concerned about integration with the neighbourhood. The People's Panel on West Kowloon, for example, was of the view that West Kowloon planning 'must interface with nearby districts' and should 'complement that of harbour development' (People's Panel on West Kowloon, 2005). This rightly contextualizes WKCD as part of a larger urban landscape that should not exist in dissonance with its neighbourhood.

Financial Sustainability

A fourth broad area of consideration that exercised critics and observers was the financial sustainability of the project. After the rounds of public consultation, the government settled in 2007 on a method of financing. It would request an upfront endowment of HK$19 billion (subsequently increased to HK$21.6 billion in 2008) from the Legislative Council to establish a statutory authority, called West Kowloon Cultural District Authority, to operate the project (So, 2007; Subcommittee on West Kowloon Cultural District Development, 2008). The authority would then use recurrent income from retail and restaurant space rents in WKCD to offset operational deficits of the arts and cultural facilities (So, 2007). In other words, under this financing model, income from retail and dining business would pay for the arts and cultural programming expenses. Paul Zimmerman, the principal of a policy and strategy consultancy and Chief Coordinator of Designing Hong Kong Harbour District, whose views have already been cited above, expressed concern that this was a less secure source of programme funding. He also expressed doubt that such a financial model would 'fulfill the government's policy objective of creating an environment that is conducive to free artistic expression' (Zimmerman, 2007).

With the hefty bill, attendant risks and the many misgivings expressed on numerous fronts as outlined, some critics urged the funding be used to develop cultural software instead (personal interview with Jeffrey Au, 17 January 2008). Others took a less diametrically opposed position. The Hong Kong Society for Education in Art and Hong Kong Arts Development Council, for example, called for part of WKCD funding to be allocated to education and training (Subcommittee on West Kowloon Cultural District Development, 2005c).

CONCLUSION

The story of Hong Kong's WKCD presents us with two points of note. The first has to do with Hong Kong's motivations in developing WKCD. The second relates to the protracted process, with myriad views from multiple quarters shared, whether solicited or unsolicited, reflective perhaps of the democratic spirit in search of a voice in a post-handover Hong Kong of the twenty-first century.

Hong Kong's motivation in developing WKCD is clearly and largely economic in nature. The project is part of an aggressive cultural economic policy (see Kong et al., 2006) that aims to stimulate the Hong Kong economy, which has somewhat lost its lustre in the twenty-first century, and to assure Hong Kong's position as a global city. This is part of the global neoliberal agenda and logic that other cities examined in this book also manifest. On the other hand, unlike the cases of Beijing and Singapore (and to an extent Shanghai), for Hong Kong, the issue of national identity does not emerge in the discursive space surrounding WKCD except insofar as the district is seen as 'an integral part of what will make a postcolonial Hong Kong "different" from other rapidly expanding centres in China' (Raco and Gilliam, 2012, p. 1432). Whereas the other cities in China are keen to establish themselves in the national imaginary and whereas securing prideful positions in the global city hierarchy is driven at least in part by a desire to emplace China globally, the frame of reference for Hong Kong is not the nation but the city and its global interconnections. This is consistent with the larger ongoing negotiation of Hong Kong identity, which Anthony Fung (2001) argues is an insistently local identity rather than a national one intertwined with the mainland. Thus, Hong Kong's cultural infrastructural projects as represented by WKCD speak little to the project of national identity. In fact, economic imperatives and global aspirations underlie Hong Kong's motivations as a city. In this case, both the nature of public response (protest) to WKCD and the frame of reference for the debate underscore a political culture and identity where the 'nation' and 'national' are the constitutive outside in the city's cultural-global strategy. This is consistent with Degolyer's (2001, p. 170) observations of Hong Kong people as being 'exceptionally outward looking' with an '"unpatriotic" internationalistic orientation', considering themselves 'citizens of the world, first; secondarily, citizens of the SAR [Special Administrative Region]; and finally, and for many, reluctantly, citizens of the PRC'.

The global neoliberal agenda notwithstanding, local political conditions, institutional powers, relationships between civil society and authority, cultural legacies and changing social identities have played a huge role in shaping the project's chequered history. In other words, local political and social conditions were far from 'residualised' (Clive Barnett, 2011, quoted in Raco and Gilliam, 2012, p. 1425). WKCD as it is today is not 'merely' the outcome of an abstract neoliberal policy that privileges urban entrepreneurialism, but a project deeply implicated in the social and political relations in Hong Kong in a particular historical moment (Raco and Gilliam, 2012, p. 1426). The nature of the public response to WKCD and the protracted processes of public consultation that have lasted, to date, a cumulative total of seven years, demonstrate the far-from-residual relevance (indeed, the centrality) of local history, politics and culture.

The seven years of public consultation are, by any standard, extensive – some might even say excessive. Extensive public involvement is not unique in Hong Kong, even though the example set by the WKCD project is singular. Other projects in Hong Kong nevertheless also demonstrate the political culture that is developing around urban planning and development, such as in the development of the former Kai Tak airport site (Delang and Ng, 2009) and the harbour reclamations (Ng, M., 2010, 2011; Ng et al., 2010). As Ng Mee Kam (2008) characterizes it, the shift is one from government to governance, in which political activism has grown since the 1980s, both formally and informally (Lam, W., 2004). Formally, voting records show that support for pro-democracy parties has increased (Lam, W., 2004, p. 235). Informally, there has been a rise in citizens' movements, political commentary groups and political parties (Lam, W., 2004, p. 234). A number of external and internal factors account for this. As the time approached for the handover from Britain to China in 1997, British encouragement of citizen participation and China's Reform and Opening Up created a set of conditions conducive to growing activism. Internally, as Hong Kongers lived an increasingly more comfortable life made possible by economic growth, a desire grew for greater involvement and to have a voice in matters affecting them. At the same time, with government leaders politically appointed rather than democratically elected,[1] issues of representational legitimacy provided the context for community engagement as a way to derive legitimacy from projects. One might say that *de facto* democratic participation has resulted from *de jure* democratic underachievement. This is a kind of 'contingent engagement' or 'contingent democracy', engagement that occurs because it is dependent on or conditioned by some other factor. The outcomes in the WKCD project, insofar as they are stable for now, represent a furtherance of civil society participation, a movement beyond tokenistic participation evident even in the mid-2000s (Ng, M., 2008), and a continued search for the institutionalization of a more participatory mode of planning governance. Such furtherance has not always been linear, but there is no mistaking a new type of politics that includes participation and democratic involvement. In many ways, debates over projects such as WKCD, Kai Tak and the harbour reclamations are as much about the merits of individual projects as they are about the ways in which locals can have a voice in the city's future at a particular moment in post-handover Hong Kong and post-handover politics, with its ongoing search for democratization.

NOTE

1. Secretaries of departments and directors of bureaus, under-secretaries and political assistants are all appointed. The chief executive is elected by an election committee, not through universal suffrage.

5. The making of a 'Renaissance City': building cultural monuments in Singapore

SINGAPORE AS A 'LINCHPIN OF THE NEW GLOBAL CAPITALISM'

Without a doubt, Singapore has global aspirations to be in the superleague of cities. Indeed, some argue that it can already claim global city status (Baum, 1999, p. 1098), as a 'linchpin of the new global capitalism' (Chua, 1993, p. 105). Sally (2014) goes even further, asserting that there are only four truly global cities – London, New York, Hong Kong and Singapore. There are numerous reasons for this confidence. Baum (1999, p. 1098) attributes it in part to Singapore's physical infrastructure – its 'efficient transport system and telecommunications network, modern and efficient airport and sea terminals, efficient business districts and a highly developed public housing system, all of which act to strengthen the city-state's global competitiveness'. It is also a function of Singapore's 'international presence as a major commercial and financial centre as well as a significant location for the regional headquarters of major multi-national corporations' (Lim and Malone-Lee, 1995, p. 90). Baum (1999, p. 1098) further points to the increasingly 'global reach of both the economy and society', evidenced by the 'numbers of foreign-controlled companies, the amount of foreign capital invested in Singapore and the extent of international transport flows, both cargo and passenger'. These passenger flows, in turn, are of multiple hues, ranging from the business and professional class to unskilled immigrant workers and tourists.

This global orientation has major implications for the ways in which Singaporeans understand the meaning of the 'nation', and how the government is engaged in the project of nation-building. Rather than submit to what some researchers warn to be the demise of the nation with globalization (Gereffi, 1996; Guehenno, 1995; Ohmae, 1995), the government of Singapore has since independence in 1965 engaged in a series of projects to build a 'nation' (Hill and Lian, 1995; Kong and Yeoh, 2003), including social and spatial strategies pertaining to housing, education, language, race, religion and community development. Cultural policy and cultural infrastructure have similarly been pressed to service. At the same time, the global orientation of the city-state presents a challenge in this nation-building endeavour – the global city in all its openness and associated mobilities renders the making of the nation a particular challenge, and cultural policy and infrastructure have to serve the minimally dual purposes of addressing a global and local audience, and manifesting a global and local character.

In this chapter, we examine how the global city and city-state of Singapore negotiates its cultural identity via its cultural mega-structures (recognizing that this is but one of many platforms through which cultural identity is negotiated and forged). Unlike the other cities discussed in this book, for Singapore the city *is* the country, the local *is* the national. Thus, while global city aspirations have contributed to the rationale for building cultural mega-infrastructure, the desire and need to develop a national and cultural identity that unites the city-state has contributed to numerous strategies to 'nationalize' and 'localize' the facilities and programmes to ensure social and cultural sustainability.

The chapter is divided into three sections hereafter. First, we outline the larger state discourses and policies pertaining to arts and culture in Singapore over time, highlighting the ways in which culture's economic potential is (to be) harnessed. This sets the stage for the second section, in which we document the evolving cultural infrastructure landscape in Singapore, concomitant with the changing ideologies about culture's place in Singapore's economy, society and landscape. Third, we turn to a close examination of one major cultural 'monument', the Esplanade – Theatres on the Bay, addressing the promises and perils confronted in negotiating the economic and social-cultural agendas of cultural policy, as well as the global aspirations and local demands for cultural and social sustainability.

CULTURAL POLICY

The larger state discourses and policies on arts and culture in Singapore may be framed in terms of the intersection between economic and socio-cultural agendas behind cultural development policies. In this section, we briefly introduce cultural policy in the 1960s and 1970s as a backdrop to the main discussion, which focuses on the rise of cultural economic policy in the 1980s and 1990s.

Singapore's cultural policy in the 1960s and 1970s was focused primarily on how artistic and cultural activities could be used for nation-building purposes and how the negative influences associated with the 'yellow culture' of the 'decadent West' were to be avoided. A statement by the Minister for Culture, Mr Jek Yuen Thong, in 1974 made this point distinctly:

> Literature, music and the fine arts have a significant role to play from within the framework of nation building. A truly Singaporean art must reflect values that will serve Singapore in the long run. Faced with threats from the aggressive culture of the West, our own arts must reflect countervailing values that will be helpful to Singapore. (Press release, 28 June 1974)

This view was variously repeated by other members of government, for example, when government MP Tay Boon Too argued that 'the various orchestras, dance troupes and choirs in the National Theatre should be regarded as a cultural army representative of Singapore' (*Parliamentary Debates*, 22 March 1971, col. 998) and when the Parliamentary Secretary to the Minister for Culture, Inche Sha'ari Tadin, asserted that 'the arts can play a vital role in nation-building through the inculcation of correct values', especially since, 'more than ever', Singapore was faced with 'the threats from the aggressive culture of the West' (press release, 30 November 1974). Popular cultural products from the West were deemed 'unhealthy' 'yellow' culture that 'destroy [young people's] sense of value, and corrode their willingness to pay attention to serious thought' (K.C. Lee, 1967). By the mid- to late-1970s, the government encouraged the composition of songs by Singaporeans to help 'develop a sense of national identity and instil a sense of patriotism in our young people' (*Parliamentary Debates*, 16 March 1977, col. 1078). Engagement in the arts, it was hoped, would also 'redeem us from the ill-effects of a materialistic, money-oriented exist-ence' (Inche Sha'ari Tadin, press release, 30 November 1974), especially important given the emphasis on economic development in the newly inde-pendent state. Artistic pursuits, defined by the state, were to be purveyed to the person in the street, with the introduction of, for example, a series of monthly 'Art for everyone' exhibitions that toured the community centres, organized by the Ministry of Culture.

In short, the sociopolitical agendas of cultural policies were pre-eminent in the 1960s and 1970s. Conversely, the conception of a cultural economy was somewhat circumscribed. The only significant cultural economic policy was a tourism strategy that sought to promote Singapore as a desti-nation where tourists could enjoy, *inter alia*, the arts and cultures of Asia in one destination, using the banner of 'Instant Asia' as a promotional tool. This was the tack that the then-Singapore Tourism Promotion Board took from about 1969 to the late 1970s. However, apart from the active pursuit of a tourist cultural policy, recognition of and efforts to tap the economic potential of the arts and culture in other ways were, at best, feeble, including, for example, turning arts and crafts products into souvenirs for the tourist industry (press release, 19 July 1973).

At the start of the 1980s, the official view of the relationship between culture and economy was still one in which culture was thought of as the superstructural icing on the Marxist cake. The state was clear that the economy had to be taken care of first, while artistic pursuits could follow later. Suppiah Dhanabalan (1983, p. 16), then Minister for Culture, expressed this unequivocally when he said

> We often talk of improving the quality of life in Singapore as distinct from improving the standard of living. We have concentrated, and rightly so, on improving the standard of living of Singaporeans . . . Without better standards of living – more jobs, more housing, more education, better health – one cannot hope to improve the quality of life.

The quality of life, in his estimation, referred to more 'peripheral' issues such as artistic and cultural pursuits. The view was taken further with the position that economic prosperity was a necessary precondition for artistic creativity (Sabapathy, 1995, p. 16), a view that was not borne out in reality.[1]

By 1985, however, when Singapore was in the midst of an economic recession, the Economic Committee tasked with charting future directions for growth proposed diversification strategies, and some attention began to be paid to the arts as a potential growth area. It was deemed part of the 'service sector', albeit a relatively minor part. Specifically, 'cultural and entertainment services' were given brief attention as one of 17 service categories that could be further developed.[2] Several recommendations were made as to the role of the cultural and entertainment services, defined to include the performing arts (popular music, symphony, drama), film production (for theatres and television), museums and art galleries, and entertainment centres and theme parks. These recommendations were made in recognition of the fact that such services were economic activities in their own right; that they enhanced Singapore as a tourism destination; improved the quality of life and helped people to be more productive; and contributed to a vibrant cultural and entertainment scene that would make Singapore more interesting for foreign professionals and skilled workers, and could help attract them to work and develop their careers there (Economic Committee, 1986, p. 211). They represented the first explicit, albeit somewhat *ad hoc*, acknowledgement of the economic potential of artistic and cultural activities, and although there were few clear signs that the recommendations were systematically taken up in the three to five years following the report, many have since then been given serious attention and carefully developed.

Growing cognizance at the highest level of the economic potential of culture and the arts emerged in the 1990s. A new Minister for Information and the Arts, George Yeo,[3] appointed in 1991, gave renewed attention to the arts and culture. Yeo was most active among ministers in publicly suggesting that 'to be competitive in the next phase of our national development, we need to promote the arts' (Yeo, 1991, p. 56) and that while Singapore had been 'an international market for rubber, for spices, for oil, for Asian Currency Units, for gold futures, and for many other things', it also hoped to be 'an international market for the arts' (Yeo, 1993, p. 66). This was because

> We should see the arts not as luxury or mere consumption but as investment in people and the environment. We need a strong development of the arts to help make Singapore one of the major hub cities of the world . . . We also need the arts to help us produce goods and services which are competitive in the world market. We need an artistic culture . . . we also need taste. With taste, we will be able to produce goods and services of far greater value. (Yeo, 1991, p. 54)

Some of these views were echoed by government MP Heng Chiang Meng, who used economic arguments to ask for better financial support of cultural activities. He suggested that

> . . . such funding can be viewed as supporting an infant industry. Looking at the arts industry in London and New York, I see no reason why Singapore cannot be a major arts centre if we put our minds to it . . . all the necessary ingredients for the promotion of arts as an exportable industry are here . . . (*Parliamentary Debates*, 21 March 1991, col. 944–46)

He cited for support the view that a wide range of industrial products not only needed to be functional and durable but that, increasingly, there was demand that they also be well designed and aesthetically pleasing. Hence, an artistic base was crucial to industrial progress.

The chairman of the National Arts Council, Liu Thai Ker, also articulated the view that there was nothing wrong in the arts being 'aligned with economic impetuses'. He argued that while the arts was traditionally associated with the need for subsidization, the government now recognized that the economic gains were potentially far greater than the expenditure, which made government spending on the arts justifiable. His view was that investment in the arts was the act of a 'responsible government' (personal interview, 12 May 1997).

Given official acknowledgement of the economic value of arts and culture, the government began in the 1990s to pursue more rigorously policies and strategies to harness the economic potential of the arts.

Singapore's cultural economic policies may be conceptualized into three categories, following Frith (1991): an industrial cultural policy; a tourist cultural policy; and an urban cosmetics policy. The first entails the local production of cultural goods to be consumed nationally or exported. Through state agencies such as the Economic Development Board (EDB) and Trade Development Board (TDB), cultural goods such as electronic goods (radios, data discman and so on), the mass media (film, television programmes and so on), artistic productions (theatre, dance and so on) and fashion have been produced and promoted (see Kong, 2000a, 2012a). Specific efforts to export cultural goods are also apparent. For example, the National Arts Council (NAC) established an International Relations Unit in 1998, which selected cultural acts by groups/individuals to perform overseas in order to enhance their reputation, to sell the image that Singapore is not only a city of business but also a city of arts, and to earn revenue. Pioneer efforts include NAC's selection of 17 art groups/ individuals for marketing at the Australian Arts Market in Adelaide and Montreal in 1998. More recent efforts include 'Singapore Day' in cities such as London, New York and Shanghai, which though targeted at overseas Singaporeans, and involving food and other festivities besides performances by local artistes, also function as a showcase of Singapore culture to non-Singaporeans.

While aggressively pursuing an industrial cultural policy, the state has also adopted a tourist cultural policy and an urban cosmetics policy that reinforce each other. This is reflected most unequivocally in a statement by government MP Yu-Foo Yee Shoon (*Parliamentary Debates*, 23 March 1990, col. 764) that Singapore was well placed to 'absorb the best of Eastern and Western arts and culture for the smooth development of tourism and economic development', so that both tourists and international investors could enjoy 'a certain degree of cultural life'. The value of culture and the arts to tourism is acknowledged by Tong Min Way, director of corporate affairs at the Ministry of Information and the Arts (MITA), who announced in 1995 that the state intended to develop 'cultural tourism' as a 'distinct industry' (Brady, 1995). At the same time, Yeo (1993, p. 65) also made explicit the fact that the multitudinous actions to generate artistic activity in Singapore also belied an urban cosmetic policy:

> We want to make Singapore a centre for the arts partly for its own sake and partly because we need the arts to help make us a centre for brain services. We want talent from all over the world to meet here, to work here and to live here. They must enjoy being here – the people, the food, the music, the cosmopolitan air. We cannot work the magic without the arts. This is why we will be spending quite a lot of money – about a billion dollars – over the next five to 10 years building new cultural facilities and expanding existing ones.

Tamney (1996, p. 154) has expressed this pointedly as the government's belief that 'educated, affluent people will be more content if there are various artistic and literary works for their amusement and enlightenment'. Bringing in the major international art and antiques fair in Singapore, Tresors d'Arts, was one example of a strategy to bring major art galleries and antique dealers from Asia and Europe to Singapore and attract collectors, buyers, sellers, dealers and art professionals from all over the world. The Singapore Tourism Board has also worked closely with the NAC and EDB to bring in more and more major pop and rock acts, from the late Michael Jackson, Paul Simon and Natalie Cole to Jacky Cheung and the late Anita Mui, which has brought in their regional audiences, particularly rich Filipino and Indonesian young-sters (Substation, 1995, p. 147). London West End and Broadway musicals have also been brought in, such as *Cats* and *Les Misérables*, not only to 'keep Singaporeans entertained' but to 'draw art lovers from other parts of the region' (Brady, 1995). This is done in full recognition that 'for every dollar spent on a theater ticket, six or seven more are spent on related services' such as meals, lodging and souvenirs (Brady, 1995). For this reason, the EDB has 'opened doors' for companies such as Cameron Mackintosh Pte Ltd, encouraging it to set up a Southeast Asian base in Singapore, as has Andrew Lloyd Webber's Really Useful Group (Brady, 1995, p. 40). The outcome of the synergies generated is that big companies have bought blocks of seats for performances, catering to touring groups – 'just as they do in Sydney, New York and London' (Brady, 1995, p. 40). Indeed, Yeo (1993, p. 65) has used *Cats* and *Les Misérables* as a measure of success, indicating that if they are able to attract not only Singaporeans but also bring in audiences from the region, then 'Singapore will be on its way to being a theatre hub in Southeast Asia' (see Kong, 2000a, 2012a).

This vision of being a cultural hub for the region is indicative of Singapore's larger ambitions in general to be a global city, the hub of multiple flows of talent, capital and ideas. It is a city that is creative and vibrant, best captured perhaps in the aspiration to become 'Renaissance City Singapore', as expressed in the *Renaissance City Report* of 2000 'amidst an uneasy mix of millennial celebration and pessimism from a prolonged economic downturn' (K. Tan, 2007, p. 2):

> Renaissance Singapore will be creative, vibrant and imbued with a keen sense of aesthetics. Our industries are supported with a creative culture that keeps them competitive in the global economy. The Renaissance Singaporean has an adventurous spirit, an inquiring and creative mind and a strong passion for life. Culture and the arts animate our city and our society consists of active citizens who build on our Asian heritage to strengthen the Singapore Heartbeat through expressing their Singapore stories in culture and the arts. (Ministry of Information and the Arts, 2000)

CULTURAL INFRASTRUCTURE IN THE CITY-STATE

The various policies and strategies introduced to harness the economic potential of arts and culture in Singapore have been supported by a large injection of state funds to develop new and upgrade old cultural facilities. It was a necessary development, given the state of cultural infrastructure right up to the 1990s.

At independence in 1965, the desperate lack of venues for the performing arts was stark. There were only three: the National Theatre, Victoria Concert Hall and Victoria Theatre. By the 1970s, the situation had not improved very much. The most popular concert hall in the 1970s was the Singapore Conference Hall, which, while ideal for orchestral and choral performances as well as instrumental recitals, had difficulty in attracting foreign orchestras, as a capacity of at least 2000 seats was required before it could be commercially viable (the Conference Hall had only 1024 seats). Despite good acoustics, it was also built more for conferences and seminars, and was a poor choice for dance and drama performances because of the small stage, absence of curtains and inadequate lighting (*The Straits Times*, 16 October 1979). Other venues posed different problems: the Victoria Theatre had mediocre acoustics while the National Theatre, a semi-open structure, had poor acoustics, carried noise from passing traffic and insects, had no air-conditioning and was open to rain, insects, bats, birds, lightning and clinking bottles (from canteen boys stacking drink crates after the interval) (*The Straits Times*, 16 October 1979, 4 December 1982, 9 January 1984).

By the 1980s, the facilities had deteriorated further. In 1989, a major landmark report was produced, titled *Report of the Advisory Council on Culture and the Arts* (Singapore Advisory Council on Culture and the Arts, 1989) (more popularly labelled the *Ong Teng Cheong Report* because the then Second Deputy Prime Minister chaired the council). The report was to form the blueprint for cultural policy in Singapore. It gave due acknowledgement to the importance of the arts for 'personal enrichment', that is, 'broaden[ing] our minds and deepen[ing] our sensitivities'; to 'improve the general quality of life', 'strengthen our social bond' and 'contribute to our tourist and entertainment sectors' (Advisory Council on Culture and the Arts, 1989, p. 3). It outlined as key strategies the need to

> ... encourage more people to develop an interest in culture and the arts, to take part in art activities as amateurs or as professionals, to build up a pool of good artistes, arts administrators, arts entrepreneurs and other related

professionals, to develop more modern purpose-built performing, working and exhibition facilities for the arts, libraries and specialized museums/galleries, to step up the level and tempo of cultural activities and have more works of art in public places, and to encourage and promote more original Singapore works. (Advisory Council on Culture and the Arts, 1989, p. 3)

The substantive outcome of the report was the establishment of the NAC and the National Heritage Board (NHB) to spearhead the development of various aspects of the arts in Singapore. The decision to establish the Esplanade was also a direct outcome of the council's recommendation, although it took 12 years before this major performing arts infrastructure was eventually built and open for operation (in 2001).

The specific recommendation to build the Esplanade came from a Committee on Performing Arts, appointed by the Advisory Council on Culture and the Arts in 1988 'to examine the present status of performing arts in Singapore and to recommend strategies which could lead to the integration of the performing arts as a permanent and visible manifestation of Singapore's cultural lifestyle' (MITA, 1988, p. 2). The committee's recommendation was based on its assessment of the dire lack of performing arts venues. Victoria Theatre and the Drama Centre were suitable only for small to medium-sized performances, leaving no possibility for large professional companies; moreover, their stage equipment was out of date and the environment 'decidedly aged'. The Victoria Concert Hall suffered the same problem of a lack of audience and stage capacity while the Kallang Theatre inherited limitations arising from the fact that it was built for some other purpose (MITA, 1988, p. 26). Given these inadequacies, it was difficult for creative works that called for differences in ambience to achieve their optimal effect (MITA, 1988, p. 50). The same committee also highlighted the fact that total performances had increased in the 1980s from 789 in 1982 to 1539 in 1987. Hence, apart from the inadequacies of venues, there was also a general insufficiency: 'with an average utilization rate of 70 per cent in 1987, performing arts groups found increasing difficulty in booking venues on preferred dates and during certain periods of the year' (MITA, 1988, p. 36). During the Festival of Arts, non-performance designed venues such as conference auditoria had to be used (MITA, 1988, p. 50).

Given all these constraints, the committee strongly recommended the construction of a performing arts centre. It led in 1992 to the formation of the Singapore Arts Centre (now the Esplanade Company Limited), which was to build the Esplanade – Theatres on the Bay. It is to this cultural mega-infrastructure that we now turn.

ESPLANADE AND THE MAKING OF A RENAISSANCE CITY

An Ambitious State-of-the-art Facility

Esplanade – Theatres on the Bay was officially opened on 12 October 2002. Its iconic structure covers six hectares of prime waterfront land, and is made up of the two distinctive domes with spiked sunshades, which has earned it the colloquial name of 'Durian', for its likeness to this well-loved (or much-disliked, but rarely eliciting indifference) tropical fruit. Whereas it had also been likened to the eyes of a fly, this comparison has not worked its way into the popular imagination. It is sited within Singapore's civic district, just by Marina Bay at the mouth of the Singapore River, displacing a popular (especially in the 1970s) food haunt for Singaporeans, known as the 'Satay Club', an open-air collection of stalls selling the favoured aromatic meat skewers.

The Esplanade was designed by two architectural firms, well-known Singapore firm DP Architects and London-based Michael Wilford and Partners. They had won the project in a design competition. Although they started work on the project together, the latter left the project in May 1995 once the general set-up of the major elements was complete. Indian-born Singapore resident Vikas Gore of DP Architects remained as the main architect.

The original design was presented to the public in 1994, to much criticism. It comprised two unadorned glass cases over the theatres, subjecting the facilities to a greenhouse effect in Singapore's equatorial climate. Critics labelled them 'two copulating aardvarks'! According to Gore, the intention was always to have some form of shading: the final design revealed a cladding of aluminium sunshades that offered the 'durian' effect. The project has won multiple national and international awards, including the BCA Energy Efficient Award (1st Prize, 2004), the President's Design Award (2005), the FIABCI Prix d'Excellence Award (2004) and the Royal Institute of British Architects Worldwide Award (2006).

The Esplanade's two main venues are the 1600-seat Concert Hall, with acoustics by Russell Johnson of ARTEC Consultants, and the 2000-seat theatre, which is an adaptation of traditional European opera houses in horseshoe form. It also has smaller spaces, such as a 245-seat recital studio (ideal for chamber music and solo recitals, cabarets and jazz concerts), and a 220-seat theatre studio (ideal for experimental theatre and dance presentations). The Esplanade's outdoor spaces are also available for use. The roof terrace, for example, may be hired for private performances or functions, and offers spectacular views of the bay and city skyline. Finally, the Esplanade has a dedicated visual arts space, Jendela (which means 'window' in Malay), for exhibitions and a public library (the only one with a dedicated performing arts collection in Singapore).

The Esplanade, costing S$600 million, probably represents the state's most ambitious and expensive venture into the production of new space for the arts. It represents what Singapore hopes to realize: the vision of a global city, acting as a hub not only for banking, finance, manufacturing and commerce but also for the arts, thus helping to 'create new ideas, opportunities and wealth' (Yeo, quoted in Singapore Tourist Promotion Board, 1995, p. 5). Its first executive director, Robert Iau, articulated the vision pointedly: the facilities would cater to the needs of the '240 million people in the region' rather than the three million in Singapore (personal interview, 20 May 1997). In this way, the Esplanade would help Singapore become at least a regional hub for the arts, rendering possible the vision of the city-state as a Renaissance city.

An Elite, International Space?

In its early stages of development, cultural practitioners in Singapore – playwrights, actors, directors, dancers and other artists – expressed serious reservations about the Esplanade (Kong, 2000a). They were persuaded by the need for 'community self-development and self-expression' (Bassett, 1993, p. 1785), privileging a cultural paradigm that celebrates indigeneity. In seeking to develop a Singapore idiom and an original voice in their cultural products, they endeavour to draw from local cultural resources as well as contribute to community life, so much so that artistic and cultural activities may become part of the warp and woof of daily life, generating a pulse and rhythm in the city. The cultural spaces that they seek are those in which '[a]rt, artists and art-lovers mingle, muse and meditate', and where there is as much room 'for eloquent failures as for resounding successes' (T. Sasitharan, on an older version of the Substation website that is no longer live). The Esplanade was not this kind of space, in their view.

In particular, the Esplanade did not sufficiently encourage Singapore art and local expression, as one playwright put it, because, with such heavy financial investment in the infrastructure, there would be a need to 'go for surefire successes' that would cover the cost of renting the space and eventually recovering the investment. He, along with other practitioners, all recognized that few local groups could afford to use the spaces because 'profit-making theatre' will be favoured above 'exploratory, indigenous forms', with the result that:

people who are still exploring new forms feel the pressure to have to abandon more of those projects and go for more audience-determined plays so that they can economically justify [their work], so that they can feel that there is an audience to their theatre. (quoted in Kong, 2000a, p. 419)

Many in the arts community expressed the view that the Esplanade unfortunately pushed back the schedule for developing small performing spaces in favour of bringing forward the large facilities. In that sense, the Esplanade in effect delayed opportunities for experimentation to find a distinctively Singapore idiom. Such pessimism may not have been unfounded in the 1990s. The anxiety amounted to a fear that urban cultural entrepreneurialism would create a city in which cultural substance was lacking while 'aesthetics replace[d] ethics' (Harvey, 1989, p. 102). What the artist community was seeking was support for local expression and implicitly an assurance of long-term cultural sustainability. While acknowledging that global cities have world-class cultural infrastructure, the arts community in Singapore argued that providing the 'hardware' (infrastructure and facilities) without concomitant attention to the 'software' (creative development) would be regressive for the development of local/indigenous arts. Members of the arts community further argued that the development of large cultural infrastructure attracted large exhibitions and shows (such as the Guggenheim, Tresors, *Cats* and *Les Misérables*), but left little room for local communities to develop their own art forms (Kong, 2000a). While a global flavour is apparent, so too is the absence of well-developed indigenous arts. Such a reality, in which Singapore is 'a kind of emporium for the arts', offering yet another retail space (quoted in Kong, 2000a, p. 419), they argue, will stymie the blossoming of local styles and the maturing of national identities. In as much as a global city is not only about hardware, it is also not only about showcasing the works of international artists. No global city is worth its salt if it does not have a strong base of indigenous works that express local flavours and national identities.

The Esplanade has worked hard, after initial criticism, to be inclusive. If 'cultural entities – as places where people meet, talk, share ideas and desires, and where identities and lifestyles are formed' (Bianchini, 1993b, p. 12) should afford social inclusion of different communities, then the Esplanade has sought to create occasions for social participation and integration. In an explicit statement of intent, the Esplanade aims to be a performing arts centre for everyone and for its programmes to cater to diverse audiences.

The theatre's official website today explicitly points to three objectives in its programming: to provide access to the arts for the community; to provide opportunities for local arts groups; and to provide a platform for major international productions to feature in Singapore. Through various programmes in different festivals and series, a broad range of audiences are therefore targeted. As evidence of the diversity, the in-house programming team presents over 14 festivals and 20 ongoing series throughout the year.

To widen access to the community and thus be a socially inclusive space, the programmes include PLAYtime! for toddlers, Bitesize (a monthly talk and workshop taster series for a range of arts topics), At The Concourse (a free music series that runs every day of the year), MoonFest (performances including Chinese opera, Chinese orchestra and lantern-making in celebration of the Mid-Autumn Festival), Coffee Morning Afternoon Tea (concerts every first Monday of the month featuring nostalgic English and Chinese golden hits by veteran local artists) and Lunchbox (lunchtime concerts). It should be noted that, on occasion, the Esplanade organizes activities for community groups in and around its premises, which may incorporate elements of the performing and visual arts, though only as a part of larger events and activities. In other words, in turning itself into a site of social activity and interaction, the strategies do not always foreground the artistic and cultural. Two examples will illustrate. Every year, the Mid-Autumn Festival is celebrated at the Esplanade with an annual Lantern Walkabout. About 1500 members from community clubs and voluntary welfare organizations are invited, and families and friends stroll with lanterns along the Esplanade's waterfront under the bright, full moon. An artistic element is provided in the form of music by two *dizi* and *sheng* musicians, while volunteers add to the festive mood by dressing in traditional Chinese costumes and mingling with the crowds. The event is one of several successful efforts to turn the Esplanade into a site of active participation, even if the performing arts are not the primary reason for such participation. Another example, which draws more firmly on artistic contributions, is the invitation of various communities to performances. For example, the performance of *Calonarang* in early 2007 was a collaboration between master of Javanese Bedaya dance Retno Maruti and internationally renowned Balinese Legong dancer Bulantrisna Dielantik. With the support of a philanthropic foundation, over 400 children, seniors and nursing staff from homes run by Jamiyah Singapore, a Muslim missionary society, were invited to enjoy the performance. In this sense, there is more commonality with the work groups in Shanghai whose attendance at the Shanghai Grand Theatre are sponsored.

In terms of championing local acts, the Esplanade hosts various series such as Beautiful Sunday (free concerts by home-grown music groups held once a month on a Sunday at the Esplanade Concert Hall), Chinese chamber music by the Singapore Chinese Orchestra every quarter, Late Nite (a series of intimate concerts every last Friday of the month featuring established and upcoming Singapore talents) and Limelight (showcasing the best of school choirs and concert bands). Like the community programmes introduced above, the efforts to showcase local talents typically pay attention to performances from Singapore's different ethnic groups; in that sense, they reinforce the racial categorization so prevalent in official Singapore policy and discourse.

In terms of international acts and performances, Esplanade has played host to a wealth of big names, including the Queen musical *We Will Rock You, Avenue Q*, the Bolshoi Ballet, *Les Misérables* and many more. Different genres are featured, appealing to different tastes and preferences, and indeed drawing audiences from the region (personal interview, programming officer, 20 October 2010), as its inaugural executive director intended.

Apart from direct efforts by the Esplanade to bring people to its spaces and activities, it is observable that many among the general population visit the venue for events and activities that are not related to the performing or visual arts. Instead, many are engaged in social activities, spending time with friends and family, which very often involve patronage of the food and beverage (F&B) outlets there. Many in the local population also go there to enjoy the waterfront atmosphere and the scenery and sunset. Even for audiences of the different shows, the shops and restaurants entice them to stay, as a member of the audience shared: 'At the Esplanade, you'd definitely wanna stick around and explore the place and shops within, whereas at the other places I mentioned, there's nothing much to stay around for after your concert' (personal interview, 23 November 2010). Others enjoy the rooftop garden, describing it as 'simply marvellous', for, with the 'unblocked view of the entire bay area', it affords enthusiastic shutterbugs a treasure trove of photo opportunities: 'this place is one of my favourites to snap pictures of sunsets' (personal interview, 11 December 2010). Still others wax lyrical about the environment: 'For the not so artsy people, the night lights along the river, the soothing music played by outdoor bands, and the cool breeze, make for a really relaxing walk. One does not have to be interested in the arts to come to the Esplanade to enjoy a lovely evening' (personal interview, 13 August 2010). To that extent, the success of the venue in integrating the larger community and stimulating social interaction and activity augurs well for social sustainability.

CONCLUSION

Today, the Esplanade has become a distinctive icon for Singaporeans, fondly referred to as the 'Durian'. The vociferous criticisms levelled at its architecture in the early planning stages by members of the public and architectural critics seem to have given way to tacit approval. The expressions of disapproval about the lack of a distinctive Singaporean identity have become muted, perhaps when the sunshade features were added and the distinctive local idiom became apparent. Among many ordinary Singaporeans we interviewed, many knew it as an iconic presence by the waterfront. Others are familiar with the food outlets associated with its mall. Some attend performances there. While the arts community has been disappointed by the Esplanade's lack of appropriate space for the nurturing of local (and 'national') expressions, thus frustrating what they believe to be the genuine way to truly achieve global status, public reactions to the icon have become more positive over time. There is not always great depth in the public's engagement with the space; often, it is more a part of the national imagination than a space frequently experienced. Yet, its place in the national imagination cannot be belittled for its symbolic significance as a place to be proud of, and a place that represents global competitiveness.

Concomitant with Singapore's interest in the 'creative economy' and the identification of arts and culture as one key sector in that economy (Kong, forthcoming), many more spaces have become available since the Esplanade was established. Some have come about through the conversion of existing buildings such as the Old Parliament House and the former Supreme Court and City Hall to cultural use; others have been established via the non-governmental sector (such as the Star Performing Arts Centre, a 5000-seat performing arts theatre – interestingly, constructed by New Creation Church for its services but used extensively for performances); still other existing facilities have been refurbished to grandeur such as the Victoria Theatre and Victoria Concert Hall. They complement the large, state-vaunted cultural spaces – in this case, the Esplanade – that are in size and scale deliberately iconic, and which might best be constituted and theorized as a distinct category that specifically supports the ambition of the city to be global.

Providing space for the performing arts clearly does not involve merely providing performance venues. Each production entails months of preparatory work, which may include rehearsals, sectional practices, building of props and sets as well as administrative activities such as fund-raising and repertory planning. Appropriate rehearsal spaces are needed, as are workshops, storerooms and office space. As important, if not more so, 'performing arts groups also have a psychological need for a place they can call "home" to give members a sense of permanency and security and to build group loyalty and support' (MITA, 1988, p. 27). Despite the acknowledgement, even today, many groups do not have fixed locations for rehearsals and work. Most rent space on a sessional basis at theatres, schools and community centres. Some operate from the private homes of members, a highly unsatisfactory situation given that the high-density housing situation in Singapore generally means constrained spaces and noise disturbances. A few have been fortunate to have purchased sub-urban premises in the past, but these were few and far between (MITA, 1988, p. 28). It is in this context that the relatively rare organically evolved spaces in Singapore must be understood, prompting the state to step in with an Arts Housing Scheme, a subsidized housing scheme for arts groups, introduced in 1985 under the purview of the then Ministry of Community Development. In the second part of this book, we return to a discussion of this dimension of arts spaces in urban Singapore.

NOTES

1. In the 1950s and 1960s, when Singapore was economically not very well developed, some exciting work was produced in the visual arts by artists such as Cheong Soo Pieng, Liu Kang, Chen Chong Swee, Chen Wen Hsi and Georgette Chen. They 'examined conventions in the light of the realities in this part of the world, consolidated fresh imagery and subjects, created distinct visual languages and produced innovative work that crystallized formative, historical phases of art in Singapore' (Sabapathy, 1995, pp. 16–17).
2. The others were classified under six divisions: transport and communications; business services; financial services; commerce; personal and social services; and others.
3. George Yeo was Minister for Information and the Arts until mid-1999.

6. In search of new homes: the absent new cultural monument in Taipei

INTRODUCTION

As the capital of Taiwan, Taipei has always been the flagship in Taiwan's development. It is also the main site of Taiwanese cultural infrastructure investments. During the era of 'anti-communism and revival of the country' from the 1950s to the 1990s, and even to the present day, these cultural facilities have important ideological and political functions. The government has used them for political ends to indicate that Taiwan is still the legitimate heir to Chinese culture. In addition, these facilities have been used for ideological education internally, to support anti-communism efforts.

Since the early 1990s, Taiwan's political-economic landscape has undergone significant changes. The government rescinded martial law in 1987 and turned towards democratization. In the course of these changes, many assembly halls previously used for political functions have been released for cultural use. This has quickly transformed Taipei's cultural landscape and contributed to more diversity in cultural life for citizens.

In the late 1990s, with increasing globalization and its related rapid flows of people, goods, capital, information, ideas and technology, many cities had to compete to attract international investments and global elites, a process that continues today. In the midst of this competition, Taiwan recognized the value of its cultural assets and the need for supporting facilities to stay competitive. Decision-makers therefore began to consider constructing new cultural infrastructure aimed at celebrating Taipei's cultural assets and energies, as well as to promote civic cultural life.

Over the years, the main function of cultural facilities has shifted from political propaganda and ideological education to offering spaces for the development of the arts, as well as providing its citizens more diversity in the arts. This transition has changed the pattern and content of and ideology behind cultural construction. Taipei's cultural landscape has thus been restructured significantly. Furthermore, it has encouraged transcultural interactions, deepened local cultural content and stimulated local cultural workers.

This chapter explains political and economic contexts in Taipei and the ways in which they have influenced the evolution of cultural infrastructure development in the city. It describes interactions between the state, cultural workers and other actors in the course of the construction and changing use of cultural infrastructure. It then analyses the impact of such infrastructural developments on Taipei's cultural development, particularly on artists and the cultural life of its citizens. It also explores the dynamics of global-local cultural interaction and the influence of such dynamics on Taipei's urban landscape.

The chapter is structured as follows. It begins with an overview of the evolution of cultural infrastructure in the city. This is followed by a discussion of the transforming functions of the pre-existing, essentially political and administrative spaces, using Zhongshan Hall and Chiang Kai-shek Memorial Park as examples, to illustrate the new cultural uses to which they are put. This is followed by a discussion of another type of cultural space, that established and run by the private sector. The chapter then ends with Taipei's comparatively belated efforts to construct a new cultural mega-structure and monument to support its competition with other cities. The challenges encountered in developing Taipei's new infra-structure are discussed within the context of its political and economic environment.

THE EVOLUTION OF CULTURAL INFRASTRUCTURE DEVELOPMENTS

With the end of martial law in 1987, and since the 1990s, many assembly halls previously used for political functions have been released for cultural use. This has provided more space for the development of the arts, as well as more opportunities for citizens to enjoy a diverse variety of arts. These cultural monuments have also functioned as places for global cultural exchange and transmission. These changes have collectively and significantly restructured Taipei's cultural landscape. This section examines this evolution of Taipei's cultural infrastructure, drawing attention to the transforming functions of infrastructure and the changing role of the state in building and operating cultural infrastructure.

As the main site of Taiwanese cultural infrastructure investments, Taipei houses major assets such as the National Palace Museum, the Sun Yat-sen Memorial Hall, National Theatre Hall and National Concert Hall. All these structures served political functions from the 1950s to the 1990s. On the one hand, these facilities supported the Republic of China (ROC) government in signalling to the world that Taipei still had legitimacy in Chinese cultural production. At the same time, they were used to implement ideological education in order to unite the people in support of anti-communism. During those decades of martial law, the state exercised complete control of these facilities to host various kinds of political activities. Cultural groups could use these spaces only when they were not being employed for political use. Permission to use these spaces for cultural activities would have to be granted by a government agency. Artists did not have a say in the decision process.

After martial law was lifted in 1987, the situation changed in the early 1990s. Many assembly halls previously used for political functions were released for cultural use, for example, Zhongshan Hall and Chiang Kai-shek Memorial Park. Even the mayor's official residence was converted into the Mayor's Residence Arts Salon (an auditorium with 100 seats). The cultural community also got involved in deciding what kind of arts/performances would be hosted in these facilities.

In the late 1990s, as many more cities competed to attract the influx of investments and global elites, recognizing the value of cultural assets in that competition, the construction of world-class cultural monuments (such as museums, grand theatres, concert halls and cultural centres) became an important strategy. Taipei similarly became alert to the value of unique cultural assets in strengthening its competitive advantage and securing its status as a global city. Decision-makers began to plan the construction of new, key cultural facilities to celebrate Taipei's cultural assets and promote civic cultural life in order to establish global link-ages, nurture cultural development and disseminate local culture. In this way, the city authorities hoped to attract global elites and tourists, and to develop related high value-added industries.

The acknowledgement of culture's potential led to an announcement from the central government in 2003 that cultural infrastructure would be among the 'new ten big development projects'. The central government's commitment would be to fund the construction of world-class cultural monuments in several Taiwanese cities. The policy document was explicit: cultural infrastructure would serve not only local artists and the citizenry but be a platform for establishing global cultural linkages, strengthen-ing the city's position in the midst of global competition by enhancing the city's image and supporting the development of tourism and creative industries. This shift also influenced city planning. In laying out a city's future development, planners and policy-makers were expected to pay attention to the provision of cultural facilities.

Another way to understand the evolution of cultural infrastructure in Taipei is to consider the shifting role of the state in the provision and operation of such infrastructure. While only the state provided and controlled the utilization of cultural facilities during martial law, today there are many types of cultural facilities that are either provided or operated by government, cultural foundations (non-govermental organizations (NGOs) or non-profit organizations) or the private sector. According to a survey conducted by the Department of Cultural Affairs of Taipei City Government (2007), Taipei has six halls and theatres capable of hosting professional musicals and performances, each with a seating capacity of about a thousand or more. These include the National Concert Hall (with 2070 seats), the National Theatre Hall (1526 seats), Sun Yat-sen Memorial Hall (2514 seats), Zhongshan Hall (1122 seats), City Stage (1002 seats) and Novel Hall (935 seats). In addition, Taipei has many small and medium-sized facilities at universities, schools, government agencies, community centres or even at temples or churches, totalling nearly 600 sites that may be used as performance venues. These reflect a range of ownership and operational patterns, divided into three categories.

The first category is made up of those facilities built and operated by the government (either the central or city government). The larger facilities belong to this category, and include the National Theatre and Concert Hall (built in 1987), Sun Yat-sen Memorial Hall (1972), Zhongshan Hall (1936) and City Stage (1964). These halls were built as cultural infrastructure by the state for supporting cultural development, or for government use (for example, to commemorate Sun Yat-sen or to function as Taipei City Hall) and turned later to cultural use. They contributed to the government's political agenda of signalling that the ROC bore the legitimate legacy of Chinese culture and in creating the perception that Taipei was the cultural capital of China.

The second category of cultural facilities involves those built by government but contracted out to and operated by NGOs, such as the Museum of Contemporary Art (MOCA Taipei),[1] Red Theatre and the Mayor's Residence Arts Salon. Some of these public cultural facilities have been handed over to professional groups or NGOs to operate in order to more closely meet the needs of cultural groups and the general public.

The third category of cultural facilities are those built and operated by private companies or cultural foundations. The most well known of these is Novel Hall, which was built and supported in its operational costs by a single private company, Chinatrust Commercial Bank. The bank donates more than NT$10 million annually to support operations. Additionally, the city has at least 13 small theatres, with capacity of up to 500 seats each, run by NGOs, such as TaipeiEYE and Guling Street Avant-garde Theatre. These theatres are mainly used by small local arts groups. These privately operated cultural facilities are self-financed and enjoy their autonomy. The development of such cultural facilities is beyond the state's provision and domination.

In the course of Taiwan's democratic development, the first category of cultural facilities shed their political roles. The government not only withdrew its control over the use of space and the content of cultural activities, leaving them to the management of professional arts groups, but also provided space to the local community for conducting cultural activities. The government's reduced involvement in the cultural and arts scene has led to growth in the participation of civic resources in Taipei's cultural development. The result of these managerial changes is not only an increase in Taipei's cultural space that meets the needs of arts groups and local cultural activities but also a boost to the establishment of Taipei's international cultural connections. Diversity in cultural development has also enriched the cultural life of citizens and redrawn the cultural landscape of this city. The next section discusses specific cases of (a) the shift from government-built and -controlled administrative space to arts facility (Zhongshan Hall) and (b) the change from government-built and -controlled political (commemorative) space to performance facility (Chiang Kai-shek Memorial Park).

OLD BUILDINGS, NEW USES

In this section, we examine two buildings in Taipei that have become cultural facilities, transforming from their primarily political roles of an earlier time. They now act as main sites for supporting local cultural development and as venues for consumers of local arts and tourists to enjoy performances. They also assist in promoting the city's status within the global cultural arena with their ability to host high-end performances, cultivate local artists and develop global linkages. The two facilities that underwent this functional transformation are Zhongshan Hall and Chiang Kai-shek Memorial Park.

The Reinvention of Zhongshan Hall

Before Taiwan was ceded to Japan in 1895, the ground where Zhongshan Hall now stands was occupied by the government office of the Qing Dynasty. During the early period of Japanese colonization, that office served as the residence of Taiwan's governor, before a new residence was built in the 1920s. Following that, the colonial governor attempted to show that Taiwan had developed into a modern democratic society and conceived the notion of building an assembly hall to serve as an icon and gathering place for citizen discussions. The colonial governor asked each Taipei citizen to donate at least one dollar to build the Taipei City Hall. The building was completed in 1936.

The Zhongshan Hall building was based on a complex construction pattern. The front part of the building was a performance hall, while the rear of the building housed the assembly hall and dining room. The equipment in its interior was considered quite modern for the time, with elevators, an air-conditioning system and a dumb waiter in the kitchen for delivering food between floors. The building was also quite advanced in other ways: the four-storey steel structure of the building was designed to be fire-resistant and to withstand severe quakes and typhoons. The building featured an arched entrance, sharp window arcs and other design elements evocative of the Spanish architectural style. The hall was designed not only with aesthetics in mind but also in accordance with certain military defence elements for protection. Its outward facade was coloured mainly green. With a footprint of 44 179 square feet, the total floor area of the building was around 113 750 square feet, thus making it the fourth-largest city hall of Japan at the time, smaller only than the city halls of Tokyo, Osaka and Nagoya.

In 1945, Taiwan was returned to China, after 50 years of imperial Japanese rule. In the same year, the Taipei City Hall was renamed Zhongshan Hall and functioned as an official meeting place. It was always one of the formal reception venues for welcoming foreign guests-of-honour, including former US President Richard Nixon and other presidents or sovereigns of many countries. The building also hosted memorial ceremonies such as the signing of the Sino–US Taiwan Mutual Defense Treaty and formal inauguration ceremonies of successive ROC presidents. It clearly played an essential role in Taiwan's political history.

Zhongshan Hall was the first place to be released for cultural use in the course of Taiwan's democratic development (Xue, 2004). From the early 1970s, the Hall was gradually made accessible to the general public. Many civic and cultural activities took place there, such as the hosting of Taipei's mass marriages, the Golden Horse Awards show and the Asia and Pacific Film Festival. The hall soon became Taipei's and Taiwan's top venue for hosting arts performances. For example, the Boston Symphony Orchestra performed there in the 1970s. It was also the venue where the Cloud Gate Dance Theatre and Taiwan Folk Song Company presented their first performances. At that time, it could be said that Zhongshan Hall was a 'mecca' for young people to gather at for music.

In the late 1980s, however, Zhongshan Hall gradually came to be neglected by the arts and cultural community. Two main factors account for this. First, the development of Taipei's new central business district

(CBD) in the eastern part of the city caused a decline of the entire old CBD, the Ximending area, which contributed to the faltering attractiveness of Zhongshan Hall. Second, new cultural infrastructure had been constructed not far from Zhongshan Hall. Specifically, the National Theatre and Concert Hall were constructed and started to operate in 1987. These two halls have more advanced facilities than Zhongshan Hall.

Zhongshan Hall's fate was to change again in the 1990s. Its historical value drew special attention from preservationists; in 1992, it was designated a major national cultural monument. Furthermore, in line with plans for the city's development and regeneration of the Ximending area, the city government decided in 1998 to close Zhongshan Hall for renovation. Soon after, in 1999, the rights for use and management of the hall were reassigned from the Department of Civil Affairs to the Department of Cultural Affairs. This marked the official conversion of the hall into a cultural facility. In 2002, Zhongshan Hall reopened as a professional theatre after four years of renovation, with its main auditorium providing a capacity of 1122 seats and its two smaller halls 400 seats each. Since then, Zhongshan Hall has become one of the most important sites for the cultural activities of Taipei, providing a venue for musical, theatrical and dance performances. To the present day, annual music festivals use Zhongshan Hall as their main performance venue. Zhongshan Hall is now not only a public space for local cultural activities but also a key site for international cultural and performance arts.

Chiang Kai-Shek Memorial Park – the National Theatre and Concert Hall

The National Theatre and Concert Hall are located in Chiang Kai-Shek Memorial Park. The park was built to commemorate Chiang Kai-shek, leader of the Kuomintang and successor to Sun Yat-sen. The whole area covers 25 hectares, with the main building – Chiang Kai-shek Memorial Hall – situated in the centre of the park. The design of this hall in 1976 embodied rich symbolic meaning, especially in terms of representing legitimate rule. It functioned as a key political space. Just before the 2008 presidential election, the Democratic Progressive Party (DPP) renamed it 'Democratic Square', as an election strategy against the Kuomintang's presidential candidate, Ma Ying-jeou.

In 1975, the state began to construct a theatre to the right of the Memorial Hall and a concert hall to its left. The construction of these two halls, costing NT$7 billion (the exchange rate in 2014 was about NT$30 to US$1), was completed in 1987. During the nearly ten years of construction, Taiwan became a highly industrialized society, one of Asia's 'tiger economies'. The completion of the National Theatre and Concert Hall

(NTCH) heralded a new era of art and culture. That year was a special year for the Taiwanese. Politically, the lifting of martial law made possible political reforms onto the path of democracy. Culturally, the opening of NTCH was a symbolic realization of the long-term hopes of the arts and cultural community, and marked the start of Taiwan's Renaissance. NTCH is not only the best performance venue in Taiwan but heralds the internationalization of Taiwan's performing arts (National Theatre and Concert Hall, n.d.).

NTCH features a traditional Chinese palace structure with gold roofs, red Chinese colonnades and colourful arches. The roof of the National Theatre Hall is evocative of the Tai-He Hall of Beijing's Imperial Palace, while that of the Concert Hall imitates Bau-He Hall. The architectural design is intended to showcase Chinese palace-type architecture in all its splendour, and to create a strong cultural aura. The two buildings and the four adjacent plazas form one of the significant landmarks of Taipei.

The auditorium of the National Theatre has four levels, accommodating 1526 audience seats. The third level of this building has a small but well-equipped Experimental Theatre for small dramatic productions and dance groups; it is usually used by local theatrical companies. The auditorium of the National Concert Hall has 2070 audience seats. It also has a small Recital Hall, with 363 seats, located in the basement level, providing a venue for chamber music, recitals and other small-scale performances.

When NTCH was first completed, it played an instrumental role in elevating Taiwan's art scene by introducing world-famous artists and organizations, such as the New York Philharmonic, the Martha Graham Dance Company and the Three Tenors. Gradually, it started to present local arts groups such as the Cloud Gate Dance Theatre, the Legend Lin Dance Theatre, the U-Theatre and the Han Tang Yuefu. These local groups first gained a footing in Taiwan and shared what they accomplished in art production with the local people, following which they connected with the international community to showcase the beauty of Taiwanese art. It helped Taiwanese groups to pursue international careers and promoted inter-cultural communication.

After more than 20 years in operation, NTCH has become a cultural rather than political space. Physically, it has been made more accessible to the public through improvements in its connections to the mass rapid transit (MRT) station and facilities. Some have even suggested that the Chiang Kai-shek Memorial Park's enclosing wall should be demolished in order to eliminate the atmosphere of authority and allow nearby residents easier access. Another suggestion was for the park to be renamed 'Democratic Square' to indicate that it is a public space for cultural or other activities (as mentioned earlier, this came to pass in 2008).

Before 1 March 2004, NTCH was managed by the National CKS Cultural Centre, a subordinate organization to the Ministry of Education. Restructuring in March 2004 changed the centre into an executive juridical organization, making it the first cultural executive juridical body in Taiwan. Thereafter, NTCH possessed both financial and operational autonomy. It became capable of organizing various cultural activities and, in line with globalization, connecting to internationally famous arts groups, all of which helped to build Taiwan's image and showcase its cultural richness. NTCH has developed an online ticketing system to provide audiences with a convenient system of booking and collecting tickets. It adopts a differential pricing strategy. For the same performance, the price of the best seats may reach US$200, while seats that are less optimally located are offered at only US$10–15. This strategy is designed to cater to different income or social groups, enabling people from a range of financial backgrounds to have the opportunity to enjoy arts and cultural activities, with higher-income groups subsidizing lower-income groups. Special discount tickets are offered to the elderly, students and disabled people. Occasionally, there are half-priced tickets available for students. Through this strategy, art and cultural consumption has increased. With its advanced facilities and supportive management practices, NTCH has provided citizens and tourists with rich and diverse performing arts activities. Since its opening more than 20 years ago, NTCH has contributed greatly to the cultivation of local artists and the fostering of inter-cultural relationships. It is currently one of Taiwan's most important cultural places.

PRIVATE SECTOR PROVISIONS

Besides cultural facilities that originated as political spaces, Taipei has many cultural facilities that have been built and run by NGOs or the private sector. To a certain extent, the emergence of private cultural facilities was related to the lifting of martial law, which laid the foundation for an open society. Citizens found new freedom to publicly express what they thought and desired. In addition, the state adopted a policy of privatization, encouraging the private sector to invest in infrastructure intended for public use. The increasing number of small- and medium-sized, privately provided arts facilities has resulted in more dispersed control of cultural facilities in Taipei, as control is no longer held solely by political entities. This development not only symbolizes the evolution of the performing arts in Taipei but also reveals the contribution of the private sector to cultural development. Deeper engagement by the private sector has come to drive

Taipei's development of the arts. The most famous privately managed cultural facility is Novel Hall, which, as mentioned earlier, was built by the China Trust Commercial Bank (CTC). The auditorium of Novel Hall seats 935 people. The hall started to operate in 1997. Since then, it has provided a mid-sized performance venue in eastern Taipei for musical, dance and drama activities. The hall is located in Taipei's new CBD in the Xinyi area,[2] currently the most prosperous area in Taipei, and easily attracts the masses to the performing arts. It supports local cultural groups – both traditional arts groups (such as Peking opera, Taiwanese opera, Crosstalk, Kunju opera and so on) and avante-garde performing arts groups. Novel Hall has been heavily utilized since its opening and acknowledged as a culturally significant performance venue by citizens and artistes alike.

The construction of Novel Hall and the success of its operation demonstrates that the state is not the only provider of cultural infrastructure in Taipei. The commitment, ability and resources of the private sector cannot be underestimated. Many cultural foundations funded by private enterprises play an essential role in Taipei's cultural development. Nevertheless, the effort required to mobilize and coordinate resources from the private sector still requires the assistance of the state.

The combination of public and private initiatives has provided much space for cultural activities in Taipei. Nevertheless, while Beijing, Shanghai and Singapore forged ahead with their major performing arts infrastructure (construction on Beijing's National Grand Theatre began in 2001, with completion in 2007; on the Shanghai Grand Theatre in 1993–94, with completion in 1998; and on Singapore's Esplanade in 1995, completion in 2001), and Hong Kong first announced its West Kowloon Cultural District in 1998, Taipei relies on converted spaces well into the 2010s, alongside reinvented auditoriums; its newest facility for cultural performances (NTCH) dates from the 1980s. Nevertheless, many local arts groups, such as the Cloud Gate Dance Theatre, the U-Theatre and Ju Percussion Group, have built an international presence through performances in these spaces. Local artistes still find opportunities to collaborate with other artistes on an international level, and to learn from their performances and techniques, their stage and costume design, management and operation, promotion and marketing. The cultural life of Taipei citizens has been lively, and the growth of an arts audience in the city is apparent.

IN SEARCH OF A NEW HOME

Even while cultural life in Taipei appears to have thrived despite the lack of new facilities, globalization and competition among cities has grown into an important force compelling it to invest in the construction of new cultural monuments, not unlike the other cities discussed in earlier chapters. These external pressures, coupled with internal needs, appear to have been brought to bear somewhat later in Taipei so that the construction of a new grand theatre started only in 2012, with completion scheduled in 2015.

Since the opening of NTCH in 1987, the state had not invested in any cultural infrastructure in Taipei. From the early 2000s, NTCH had been heavily utilized to the maximum of its capacity. According to a survey conducted by the Council for Cultural Affairs in 2006, the National Theatre Hall had hosted performances every day of the year, and the National Concert Hall, 336 days of the year. Even the Experimental Theatre was used for 362 days, and the Recital Hall for 354 days. Performance groups were required to submit their proposal 18 months in advance in order to be put on the waiting list. Some could not even be accommodated in the schedule due to the lack of available performance slots (personal interview with Cultural Affairs Department Officer, 25 April 2008). To satisfy the growing audience for the performing arts, many local groups and artists called on the state to construct a new concert and theatre hall. They argued that a new facility would support local performing arts as well as bring in international high-end performances. In response, the central government supported the renovation of NTCH and Sun Yat-sen Memorial Hall in 2004 but sought only to upgrade equipment and facilities, not to expand capacity. In 2005, the central government approved the construction of a new theatre in Taipei – the largest in Taiwan – known as the Taipei New Grand Theatre, in the new Banqiao CBD of Taipei County. It was hailed as one of the 'Ten New Major Construction Projects'. The aim of this initiative was to provide all Taiwanese with top-quality infrastructure for cultural activities, support the creative industry's development and attract the best international performance art groups in order to develop Taipei into a performance arts hub in the Asia-Pacific region. The policy document indicates that the construction of the Taipei New Grand Theatre was motivated by the need to gain a competitive edge over other cities by developing cultural assets to attract investment and resources.

It is no coincidence that the 'Ten New Major Construction Projects' of the 2000s makes for a different list from the 'Ten Major Construction Projects' of the 1970s. The earlier list was focused on key utilities such as highways, seaports, airports and power plants, while the later list focused very notably on cultural and educational facilities, in addition to highways, seaports, metro systems and sewers.

Despite the clear motivation, the process of constructing the new theatre has been difficult, due to Taiwan's economic troubles and the contentious political struggles in the 2000s. Economically, Taiwan's growth has been in slowdown for many years. Its economic performance has lagged behind the other 'Asian tigers', Hong Kong, South Korea and Singapore. This has resulted in the reduction of government revenues obtained through taxation and other income streams. At the same time, the government of the day (led by Chen Shui-bian of the DPP) emphasized the policy of balancing development among Taiwan's various regions. In order to build Taichung's and Kaohsiung's global functions, the state invested more resources in the central and southern regions, including the construction of cultural facilities, such as the National Palace Museum Southern Branch (for which construction began in 2005), Taichung Metropolitan Opera House (2005) and Kaohsiung's Wei-Wu-Ying Centre for the Performing Arts (2006). All these investments used up a large amount of the government's financial resources, thus reducing those available for Taipei's cultural infrastructure. Under these circumstances, the state looked to the solution of mobilizing private developers' resources. Having succeeded in getting the private sector to build Novel Hall, the state once again sought to mobilize private developers' resources in the building of the Taipei New Grand Theatre.

The mechanism adopted was to attract a real estate developer to invest in the New Grand Theatre project, and to adopt a BOT (build, operate and transfer) method. In this approach, the developer would propose a development plan to build and operate the cultural infrastructure and, in return, would obtain a permit to build and sell a certain amount of residential and commercial space to balance its financial sheet. The main intention was to use developers' resources and abilities to provide cultural infrastructure for public use while releasing publicly owned land to build real estate products that could be sold in the property market. The land area is 3.3 hectares. The total floor space that can be developed is up to 200000 square metres, while the space to be used for the New Grand Theatre is 30000 square metres, accommodating an auditorium seating at least 3000 people, and two halls each with seating capacity of 500. The rest of the 170000 square metres can potentially be developed into residential and commercial property, such as offices, hotels, retail shops or shopping malls. In 2006, the government opened tender to all companies interested in the project, with intended completion set for the end of 2009. By the closing date, numerous developers had submitted proposals, but their development plans did not receive support from either the state or the cultural community due to their focus on real estate development rather than the grand theatre. New regulations regarding the design and another round of open tendering caused the project to be delayed

(Wikipedia [Chinese], n.d.). Further delays ensued due to contentious political struggles in the late 2000s, resulting in the Premier being replaced and the cabinet (the Executive Yuan) being reorganized several times. When the DPP lost the 2008 presidential election, the tender had still not been completed. Nevertheless, the new KMT government picked up where things had been left by the DPP, and the plan to build the Taipei New Grand Theatre remained bogged down in planning and arguments (Xu and Huang, 2008).

The suitability of the BOT mechanism for developing cultural infrastructure was always in question. Real estate developers are concerned about profits, and naturally aim to realize the maximum possible. Given the primary profit motivation, developing the Grand Theatre was not likely to be the main focus. The cultural facility was treated primarily as a marketing strategy. Private developers also lacked the ambition and vision to build a cultural facility with the most creative design and of the highest construction quality, thereby running contrary to the original intention of developing a cultural icon worthy of representing Taipei's cultural richness, revitalizing Taipei's cultural landscape and helping to strengthen Taiwan's visibility among competing global cities.

By comparison with the central government's stagnant plans for the Taipei New Grand Theatre, the Taipei city government effectively planned for and invested in another infrastructure project, the Taipei Performing Arts Centre (TPAC). In January 2009, the city government selected the design submitted by the Office for Metropolitan Architecture (OMA) (led by Rem Koolhaas) from a number of submissions in an international competition. The city announced its investment of NT$5 billion to build a theatre with 1500 seats and two mid-sized performance halls with 800 seats each. In 2012, ground was broken, and completion is expected in 2015 (Liberty Times Net, 2011). The unique design of the performing arts centre ignited a debate among architects at its unveiling. The main theatre appears as a large sphere on the outside, while the two smaller theatres are peripheric cubes. There is a central cube that houses all stage accommodations, so that the theatres may be used independently or together. Not unlike Beijing's CCTV building (also designed by OMA), there is a 'public loop' for circulation through the building that reveals all the space and equipment that make TPAC work. These are typically hidden spaces: their exposure is the equivalent of rendering visible the engine room. This public loop is open to the public, including those not attending performances in TPAC, thus drawing in a larger public than might ordinarily be the case.

The project is currently under way – the aim is to provide a top-quality hall for hosting international performances and to satisfy the needs of local artists and audiences with respect to their cultural activities and cultural life. The city government's investment reflects its desire to place Taipei among other cities striving for global city status. Such competition provides the city government with both the motivation and justification for constructing large cultural facilities. At the same time, the international design competition attracting world-renowned architects was also intended to promote the city's prestige. Even as construction proceeds apace, efforts to develop Taipei's cultural infrastructure already lag behind those of its neighbouring cities, as earlier chapters clearly demonstrate. For 25 years, Taipei has not been able to build major new space for cultural activities. This has drawn criticism from those in the arts and cultural fields, and even from the tourism industry, which has complained that the lack of cultural facilities does nothing to help attract tourists to Taipei (personal interview with arts agency, 20 August 2008).

Critics have argued that cultural development cannot rely solely on the construction of one or even several cultural monuments or depend on branding and imaging as projected by monuments designed by internationally acclaimed architects. The symbolism of physical cultural monuments cannot override 'true cultural intent' (*Artist Magazine*, 2008). This is not an unfamiliar argument, as preceding chapters demonstrate. Nevertheless, for cultural practitioners in Taipei, the building of a major new facility after a 25-year hiatus – whatever the controversies – is a welcome development.

CONCLUSION

Taipei's cultural infrastructure landscape reflects closely the city's economic and political vagaries. The release of political assembly halls such as Zhongshan Hall and Chiang Kai-shek Memorial Hall for cultural use was a direct outcome of the changing political situation, particularly the lifting of martial law and the democratization that contributed to the formation and development of an open society. The contributions of the private sector have come about because of political decisions to invest in other parts of Taiwan and because of the economic slowdown overall, which placed constraints on the public sector budget. Taipei has been able to develop its cultural life in the past decades, despite the lack of new infrastructure, and has nurtured many performing groups, some of which have made a name for themselves in Taiwan and Asia. In many ways, given that Taipei is home to noted arts and cultural groups committed to developing their art, the city is in a good position to compete with other

Asian cities in terms of being a vibrant site of cultural activity. However, a continuing concern is that the construction of cultural infrastructure has not kept up with the development of cultural and performing arts in Taipei society in the past 25 years. Politics, a slowing economy and administrative instability and inefficiency are to blame. Of all the cities examined in this volume, Taipei has perhaps had the most trouble economically and the most contentious political struggles in recent years. In that sense, it has been distracted; resources have been diverted from its ambition of becoming a global city. Long after Beijing, Shanghai and Singapore have constructed their cultural monuments in the form of iconic performing arts theatres, and long after Hong Kong has identified the need for one, Taipei is finally building its own in the form of the Taipei Performing Arts Centre.

Yet, building cultural infrastructure is but one step in facing down the global urban competition. Several issues need to be addressed if the city still harbours ambitions to catch up with other cities in the race to become a global city. First, the balanced development strategy of the DPP has resulted in insufficient resources for Taipei, thus reducing its ability to become a global or even regional cultural centre. Despite the city's investment in building TPAC, a continual flow of resources will be needed to maintain its operations. Second, there is the difficulty of mobilizing private resources to build new cultural infrastructure, resources that may still be needed post construction in other ways (such as sponsorship), given that the state lacks adequate financial resources of its own. Third, there is a need to establish an understanding between the central government and local authorities about relative responsibilities and contributions in the construction and maintenance of cultural facilities. An issue such as this does not arise in the case of a city-state like Singapore, but clearly already features in Beijing's experience, as shown in Chapter 2. A fourth and final issue is that of how resources will be assigned to support the construction and maintenance of different cultural facilities and activities within Taipei. Balance will need to be struck between support for the large cultural monuments like TPAC and that for the small- and mid-sized venues that have long sustained cultural life while the state looked elsewhere; support must also be allocated among state-built and -operated facilities, state-built and privately operated facilities, and privately built and operated facilities; as between infrastructure and artists. The success of Taipei in sustaining a vibrant cultural life will depend on a judicious balance of all these factors, going far beyond the act of building a new home for cultural activities.

NOTES

1. Formerly the Taipei Government City Hall, the building has been designated a historic site and refurbished for the MOCA Taipei since 2001. Since then, it has become a new landmark on the city's cultural map. It is operated by a cultural foundation. It is an example of the redevelopment of old public buildings to support arts and cultural activities (see http://www.mocataipei.org.tw/index.php/2012–01–12–02–47–11/about-moca, accessed 15 July 2014).
2. The Xinyi area as Taipei's new CBD was a joint project of the city government and the central government, and targeted to enhance Taipei's global city functions.

PART II

7.   Cultural creativity, clustering and the state in Beijing

INTRODUCTION

While the preceding chapters focused on state-vaunted cultural monuments, the next five chapters turn the gaze to 'bottom-up' initiatives that demonstrate the cultural life of each of the cities. The focus is on organically evolved cultural clusters, which, nevertheless, often attract the attention of city governments, resulting in transformations of various kinds and degrees – for better, but often for worse. In this chapter, we begin our analysis with the capital of China, Beijing.

We highlighted in Chapter 2 how the Beijing municipal government, as part of its effort to build Beijing into a global city, has been actively engaged in the creation of cultural space since the latter part of the 1990s. This strategic, government-sponsored development of cultural space comprises the construction of infrastructure, the industrialization of culture and the building of a market system. The state's discourse, which underpins its strategic intervention, highlights its preference for a model of cultural industry development based on spatial agglomeration. Another aspect of this discourse emphasizes how the development of creative culture is key to the success of the state's project. As a result, unlike other Chinese cities that attach importance to the development of cultural industry, Beijing puts a premium on the development of creative culture. It is plausible to think of creative culture as having its origins in, and being sustained by, the social tectonics of dense interactions among members of a city's closely knit creative community. The creative impetus generated within these network-based interactions has a self-perpetuating dynamic that drives the organic development of the creative cluster. Agglomeration of creative industry, in turn, depends on how organically embedded creative/cultural networks are.

Using the idealized model of the organic cultural network as a yardstick, this chapter examines components of Beijing's cultural development strategy – in particular, the development of cultural clusters – and evaluates their effectiveness in producing institutions that fulfil the blueprint. While there are clearly different clusters with their own histories and directions, this chapter is grounded in a case study of the well-known cluster, 798, which has been widely hailed by domestic and international media alike as a poster child of the success of Beijing's initiatives to develop a creative culture and promote cultural industry.

The 798 cluster originated as a bottom-up initiative, but its success quickly attracted official municipal attention. The subsequent state-sponsored recreation of the creative space emphasized the construction of infrastructure and institutions at the expense of artist and creative networks. If 798 is taken to be representative of the articulations of government strategy, then this preference for the construction of physical infrastructure impedes, rather than encourages, the organic development of cultural space. To bear out this argument, the chapter is organized as follows. The next section focuses on state discourse and strategy on cultural industrialization in Beijing, examining how the role of culture has been redefined, the influences on and motivations behind the city's creative culture development and the local application of a global city discourse involving cultural industries. This is followed by an analysis of the 798 Art Zone.

CULTURAL INDUSTRIALIZATION IN BEIJING: STATE DISCOURSE AND STRATEGY

Redefining the Role of Culture

The discourse surrounding the cultural industrialization of Beijing made its first official appearance in the Party's 10th Five-Year Plan, formulated in 2000. The plan proposed to 'promote the development of cultural industry by deepening reform of the cultural system, improving cultural and economic policy, strengthening management and construction of the cultural market, and combining information and cultural industry' (Chinese Communist Party, 2000). The state's acknowledgement of the nexus, both direct and synergistic, between cultural and economic development heralded a departure from traditional modes of thinking about culture. Accordingly, it provided space for revisions and redefinitions of the scope and function of cultural development.

Modelled to meet the indoctrination and socialization needs of a planned economy, China's traditional cultural system emphasized culture's role in moral and civic education, and functioned as an apparatus of the state's ideological control. This highly delimited conception of culture neglected, or even excluded, culture's commercial and economic potential, both as an object of consumption and as a driver of economic development. The operational mode of this 'cultural enterprise system' involved financial guarantees from the state, in accordance with its status as a 'social charity', and is encapsulated in the pithy motto, 'the state sponsors culture' (Chinese Academy of Social Science and Shanghai Jiaotong University, 2002). The state's sponsorship of cultural expression and activity cohered with the narrative of culture as a manifestation of state agency. Through the state's monopoly over its production and distribution, culture had, essentially, been designated as a wing of state bureaucracy; hence, the financing of culture was another form of public expenditure. However, the reappraisal of culture's role, which took place in 2000, translated into a realignment of the state's responsibilities from 'sponsoring culture' to 'managing culture'. In the reconfigured ideological landscape, where culture was recognized as an economic asset, the state ceded to the market control over (and corresponding financial obligations for) cultural production, retaining only its regulatory and consultative functions (Chinese Communist Party, 2001). This privatization of culture, through a market-based allocation (distribution) of cultural resources (products), may be seen as an attempt to attune the production of cultural output to its marketability.

Beijing's Creative Culture Development: Influences and Motivations

In developing its cultural industry, the Beijing municipal government places a premium on creative culture. The argument for Beijing's creative culture industry is rooted, primarily, in the city's strategic advantage as the nation's capital. Other advantages include a cultural pedigree that is the source of creative inspiration; a large pool of talent that guarantees the vitality of the creative culture industry; a capacity for scientific innovation that provides the creative culture industry with solid technological support; and a large market that generates a robust demand for cultural consumption (Zhang, C., 2006).

In the 31st Meeting with Experts of Science and Technology, a platform for communication between the city's political leaders and its social and natural scientists, the Beijing Mayor and the Party Secretary stressed the importance of developing creative culture as a way of diversifying the city's growth base and reinforcing structural change as a model of scientific development (*Beijing ribao*, 2006). The impetus for this surge in the discourse on creative culture development may be traced to the drive to position Beijing as a global city. In particular, after the successful hosting of the Olympics, cultural industries have been identified as an iconic institution for showcasing Beijing's creative potential and reinforcing its claim to the status of a global city.

In this sense, the formulation of Beijing's creative culture policy was not so much a result of careful strategizing by planners and bureaucrats but academic discourse on the competition between cities for global status (Kong et al., 2006). The market-oriented cultural industrialization was an unprecedented attempt by the Chinese government to reform the cultural system. Consequently, in the absence of indigenous, experience-based knowledge, the government had to rely on academic theories about (and policy blueprints of) other (global) cities and culture-based regional/ metropolitan development. Thus, a highly interactive network between the government and academia developed to facilitate the flow of expertise and collaboration in policy development. The International Forum on Cultural Industry in China, launched in 2003, and the 2006 International Forum on the Development of Culture Industry, which invited experts from Europe and North America – continents with the highest density of global cities – are testimony to the government's zeal in leveraging the existing discourse on building and sustaining global cities.

Cultural Industry in Beijing: Local Application of Global City Discourse

While discussions and debates within academia provided Chinese policy-makers with valuable inputs in developing a coherent global city building strategy based on the development of cultural enterprise, the challenge of adapting the discourse to the local context was surmounted by drawing on the structural similarities between cultural and scientific enterprise. Like science- and technology-based industries, creative/cultural industries are highly knowledge-intensive. Accordingly, emulating state interventions with regard to science and technology clustering, the government settled on a 'top-down' approach to stimulate the growth of the cultural sector. As a template for policy-making, the 'top-down' approach identifies two key areas of state intervention. First, the state articulates its conception of culture through a definition of the scope of cultural enterprise. Second, following the model of science and technology clustering, cultural industry bases are established, where the state can direct its strategic resources to promote clustering and the establishment of cultural value chains. These resources, enumerated in *A Number of Policies on Promoting the Development of Creative Culture Industry in Beijing*, published in 2006, include lowering the threshold for market entry and broadening market scope; encouraging private and foreign capital to be active in the creative culture industry; setting up special supporting funds; and granting 'green cards' (permits for residence) to creative talents. These are elaborated below.

First, clear delimitation of the scope of creative cultural enterprise constituted the first step in state planning and strategy. In the *Classification Criteria of Creative Culture Industry*, published by the Beijing municipal government in 2006, the creative culture industry is defined as an interconnected industry cluster that 'employs creation, invention and innovation as the fundamental means to provide the public with cultural experiences, and has the production of cultural content and creative product as its core contribution, and the consumption or realization of intellectual property as its main reason for transaction'. The creative culture industry is further divided into nine categories spanning the whole industrial value chain from creation to production and consumption. These categories are (1) arts and culture; (2) news and publishing; (3) broadcasting, television and film; (4) software, internet and computer services; (5) advertising and exhibitions; (6) art trading; (7) designing services; (8) tourism, leisure and entertainment; and (9) other auxiliary services.

In order to direct/control the flow of capital to the desired sectors of the cultural industry, the government drew up a Cultural Products Investment Index to distinguish projects that are encouraged, restricted or forbidden by the state. It also accelerated the creation of a uniform market admission policy, under which some restrictions on the private sector's investment in the cultural industry were dropped. To encourage private capital to its desired destinations, the government published the *Investment Guide for Beijing's Creative Culture Industry*. This guide listed the following eight categories as key areas for investment: arts performance; publishing and intellectual property trading; the making and trading of television programmes and films; animation and internet games research and development; advertising and exhibitions; the trading of antiques and art; design; and cultural tourism. To make explicit the terms of what is permitted and what is proscribed, the guide also classified the creative culture enterprises as encouraged, permitted, restricted or forbidden. For sectors or professions omitted in this guide, a 'not forbidden means permitted' rule is invariably applied. In other words, if a certain sector is not listed as 'forbidden', then it is open to private investment.

Second, following the science and technology model, numerous initiatives made up the core of official policy towards the creative culture industry. One such policy area entailed setting aside special funds in support of the industry. For example, each year since 2007, a Special Fund for the Development of Creative Culture Industry, worth CH¥500 million, is earmarked to be spent on supporting creative culture products, services and special projects. The fund is used to finance subsidies for interest on loans, special projects, government purchases and procurement and financial awards. In addition, a Special Fund for the Construction of Infrastructure of Creative Culture Clusters was set up. Over the span of three years from

2007 to 2010, this fund was envisaged to invest CH¥500 million into the construction of infrastructure and public facilities within the creative culture clusters to improve their physical environment.

A second major policy grants non-Beijing residents the coveted Beijing Resident Identity Card if they satisfy certain criteria. The Talent Development Index for the Four Major Economic Industries in Beijing issued annually by the Beijing municipal government, added the creative culture industry in 2006. Those creative culture professionals who satisfy the criteria as listed in this index, and who receive their employer's recommendation, become eligible for the Beijing Resident Identity Card after more than three years on an Employment-Residence Card.

A third major policy, the main focus of this chapter, is the construction of cultural infrastructure. The Beijing municipal government accorded priority to this in three ways. The first is exemplified in the construction of massive cultural facilities like the National Grand Theatre, the subject of Chapter 2. The second is concerned with the revitalization of former state-owned cultural enterprises such as Beijing Gehua Cultural Development Group. The third element of the strategy is to encourage competition among district governments in the development of creative clusters. The various districts are encouraged to develop the advantage of their respective creative clusters; successful ones are chosen by the municipal government as the city's creative culture base, to receive special funding and assistance.

In 2006, under the 11th Five-Year Plan, the Beijing municipal government announced the first batch of creative culture clusters and identified key projects that were to receive financing from the Special Fund for the Development of Creative Culture. These are listed in Box 7.1. As is

---

BOX 7.1   FIRST BATCH OF MUNICIPAL CREATIVE CULTURE CLUSTERS, BEIJING

Zhongguancun Creation Industry Pioneering Base
Beijing Digital Entertainment Industry Model Base
National New Media Industrial Base
Zhongguancun Science and Technology Industrial Zone (Yongheyuan)
China (Huairou) Television and Film Base
Beijing 798 (Dashanzi) Art Zone
Beijing DRC Industrial Design and Creation Industrial Base
Beijing Panjiayuan Antique and Art Trading Park
Songzhuang Original Art and Cartoon Industry Cluster
Zhongguancun Software Industrial Park

Source: Guangming Daily, 10 December (2006).

BOX 7.2   SECOND BATCH OF MUNICIPAL CREATIVE
CULTURE CLUSTERS, BEIJING

Dongcheng Cultural Zone
National New Media Industrial Base
China Film and Television Production Base
Sanchen Cartoon, Animation and Internet Games Industrial Base
Beijing Joy Valley Theme Park
New National Exhibition Centre
Deshengyuan Industrial Design and Creation Base
Chaoyang Park Cultural Zone

Source: *Guangming Daily*, 10 December (2006).

apparent, the range of activities is broad – science and technology found its way onto the list as well. Subsequently, another eight creative culture clusters were conceived and developed (Box 7.2).[1]

An examination of these creative culture bases/clusters reveals Beijing's predilection for three categories of creative clustering. The first focuses on the software, games and animation industries, which primarily employ modern technology to develop digital entertainment products. Examples include the Beijing Digital Entertainment Model Base, located in Shijingshan District, and Zhongguancun Creative Industry Pioneering Base, located in Haidian District. The second category of clusters employs the resources of traditional industry bases in art and design. The Beijing DRC Industrial Design and Creation Base and the 798 (Dashanzi) Art Zone in Chaoyang District are the flagship clusters in this category. A third category concentrates on the development of expertise and products in the conventional media sector. The new Beijing Television Station, the China Central Television Station and the spaces surrounding them are archetypes of enterprises within this category.

In the next section, this chapter focuses on one cluster, the 798 Art Zone, to illustrate how the strategic preference for cluster-based development translates into concrete policies on the ground, and to evaluate the effectiveness of such policies in realizing the goal of sustainable cultural development.

THE 798 ART ZONE

The state's development of cultural industry and its role in the construction of cultural space reflect its desire to stimulate Beijing's cultural capabilities in order to legitimize its claims to be a global city. Interestingly, however, while the proactive Chinese government relies on its top-down strategy for promoting the development of cultural industry, several cultural industry clusters exist in Beijing that exemplify the bottom-up model. The 798 Art Zone in Beijing remains the most visible of the clusters inspired by the bottom-up philosophy, while several others, such as the artists' village in Songzhuang and the Zhengdong Creation Park located next to the 798, are gradually gaining in prominence.

'Bottom-up' clusters are spontaneously formed and develop organically, driven by the synergies embedded in cultural networks. Within this formation, a cluster is, in addition to being a spatial phenomenon, a social structure held together by the dynamics of relationships between artists/entrepreneurs in the network. In contrast, the 'top-down' approach emphasizes primarily, if not exclusively, the spatial aspects of clustering. Accordingly, the construction of physical infrastructure and improvements to the physical landscape surrounding the clusters, made possible through the injection of public and private capital, gain precedence over the harnessing of the social (or soft) capital latent in networks. Table 7.1 summarizes the differences between spontaneous and state-sponsored cultural spaces.

Despite the dichotomy between 'top-down' and 'bottom-up', China's approach disrupts the seemingly neat division in attempting to reproduce the organic mechanisms of cluster development within a strategic framework designed and implemented by the state. Questions naturally arise about the effectiveness of such a strategy. Thus, the question – can state intervention facilitate rather than disrupt the organic growth and development of creative clusters? – becomes the focal point of interrogation. In the

Table 7.1   Spontaneous versus state-sponsored cultural spaces

	State-sponsored	Spontaneous
Purpose	To acquire the cultural credentials necessary for a global city; economic value creation by attracting private, commerce-oriented capital	Creation of artistic/cultural value; commercializability of products is secondary
Content	Construction of large-scale, contemporary physical infrastructure	Building artist networks
Driving force	Government initiatives	Collaborations embedded in the relationships among artists in a network

rest of this section, the experience of 798 – as a prime example of a spontaneously created cultural space picked by the government for redevelopment as a cultural industry park – is analysed and evaluated.

Background

The 798 Art Zone, also known as the Dashanzi Art District, is located in the northeast corner of Beijing on land that used to be an industrial area under the former Ministry of Electronic Industry. From the late 1950s to 1964, this area was the seat of the Ministry's 706, 707, 718, 751, 797 and 798 factories. Together, these factories were known as the 718 Joint Factory, or state-owned Beijing North China Wireless Electronics Joint Factory. At the time, these factories served as the Chinese government's base for manufacturing atomic bomb components. However, from the 1980s, this industry cluster experienced a steady decline. Cutbacks in production were drastic enough to reduce the industry to semi-operational status. As a result, the number of factory workers fell from more than 20 000 to less than 4000; over the same period a lot of the factory buildings fell into disuse. Nonetheless, an opportunity for the redesignation of these semi-defunct premises came with the rise of the high-tech industry in Beijing. The government incorporated this area into the Zhongguancun Science and Technology Industrial Zone in 1999 with a plan to re-establish it, after substantial renovation and refurbishment by 2005, as a science and technology park called the Zhongguancun Electronic City.

However, since 2000, 798's unique architectural style – the buildings were mostly in the German Bauhaus style, reflecting the East German contribution to its establishment in the 1950s – and low rent attracted artists from Beijing, the rest of China and overseas to set up studios here. Taking full advantage of the factory buildings' old style, these artists transformed the factory premises, with some modification, into unique spaces for creation and exhibition. As of 2005, a total of 103 arts bodies and businesses had made the 798 Art Zone home, with 59 of them engaged in artistic creation, exhibition and communication (accounting for nearly 60 per cent of the tenants), and 29 (accounting for nearly 30 per cent) engaged in design (including space design, advertising, furniture and interior design, fashion and image design). The remainder comprised businesses like bookstores, media and publication houses, restaurants and bars. There were a total of more than 300 artists, some of whom hailed from countries like France, the United States, Belgium, the Netherlands, Australia, South Korea, Singapore, Taiwan and so forth (Wang, W., 2006). Much of the growing popularity of 798 was attributable to the promotional impact of a series of large cultural festivals held between 2003 and 2005. Its public popularity and international visibility was further augmented by Beijing's selection as one of the world's 12 cultural cities by America's *Time* magazine in 2003.

Location, Clustering and Communities

The successful organic development of creative clusters depends on locational advantages, the presence of artistic heavyweights to create a gravitational field for other artists and the ability of the artists in the cluster to form networks and develop a sense of community. This subsection identifies the ways in which 798 possessed these preconditions that led to spontaneous growth.

First, in bottom-up models of art zone development, the strategic aspects of location – proximity to cities, low rents and the architecture of buildings – are critical in providing initial momentum. In the context of 798, sculptor Li Xiangqun observed, 'The factory buildings are very spacious, and they are not far from the city, plus, the rent is not high, so it is very suitable place for sculptors' (Zhou, H., 2006). In addition, 798 is in the vicinity of diplomatic enclaves and upscale neighbourhoods, providing it with a captive market for exhibitions and art/cultural products. Thus, while artists were attracted by the creative and economic potential of the area (large and aesthetically stimulating spaces and low rents), art galleries and foundations were subsequently lured by its commercial potential (the chance of establishing display and retail spaces in a place where both the creators and consumers of art were concentrated). While, on the one hand, these developments increased the diversity of tenants in 798, on the other hand, they also led to the transformation of what was primarily a creative space into a commercial platform oriented towards the showcasing of and trade in art.

Second, the 'neighbourhood' effect is an important factor in the formation of a successful cluster. While a strategically advantageous location appears to be a necessary condition for organic development of clusters, it is by no means sufficient. Locational advantages are by nature static, in the sense that they prepare the ground for clustering to take place. Thus, the 'art zone' potential of a location is merely latent; what drives its realization is the use of the location by famous artists. The presence of artistic heavyweights not only serves as a symbolic endorsement of the creative potential of the space but also lures other artists to settle in the 'neighbourhood' of established ones. In the case of the 798 Art Zone, the interest of artistic heavyweights to settle there may be traced as far back as 1996, when students and faculty members from the Department of Sculpture of the China Central Academy of Fine Arts rented a factory warehouse as a temporary studio. A batch of well-known artists followed suit. Some of these artists had graduated from the nation's top arts schools, some had studied arts abroad for many years and several were well-known artists from countries like Germany, France, Britain, Japan, Italy, Singapore and so forth. These famous contemporary artists included: Professor Li Xiangqun of the School of Arts of Tsinghua University, creator of the Deng Xiaoping statue in Guang'an and the statue of Bajin in the Gallery of Modern Literature; returnee artist Huang Rui, who studied in Japan and is also one of the founders of 'Star Arts Exhibition', a mouthpiece of contemporary Chinese art; photographer Xu Yong; and Robert Bernell, an American critic and promoter of contemporary Chinese art. In fact, the opening of Bernell's 'Timezone 8 Art Books' bookshop in 2002 is often regarded as the beginning of the formation of the 798 Art Zone. Bernell rented this bookstore to serve as the office of his English-language website providing information on contemporary Chinese art. This became an active promotional tool for contemporary Chinese art and popularized 798 among artists. Huang Rui, who returned from Japan, established his own personal studio in 798 on the basis of information on Bernell's website. Subsequently, the Tokyo Arts Gallery from Japan set up a gallery named Tokyo Arts Projects next to his studio.

After the artists moved in and established their studios, some came together to organize a series of exhibitions in an effort to draw in visitors and like-minded artists. In October 2002, the Tokyo Arts Gallery's exhibition, 'Beijing Afloat', drew in large crowds of visitors. Another landmark in 798's evolution was Xu Yong's '798 Space Gallery', which opened in April 2003. On account of its size – on opening, it was the largest exhibition space in the art zone – and its ambitious attempt at representing industrial space as a creative site, the gallery was featured as an icon of Beijing in a *Time* magazine article on world capitals. Further, promotional overtures by studios, especially a series of large-scale exhibitions held in 2003, such as 'Reconstruction 798', 'Blue Sky Exposure' and 'Exhibition of Contemporary Chinese and German Arts', in the 798 Art Zone – originally a preserve exclusively for artists – gradually became a popular public fixture.

The individual and group exhibitions exerted a powerful influence over other forms of artistic expression as well. The 'Yan Club', which brought in famous Beijing-based musicians and bands, moved in, showcasing 798's potential to be a creation and exhibition base for experimental music. Between 2002 and 2003, the number of art, fashion and lifestyle businesses such as art galleries, bars, boutiques and magazine stores jumped to about 40, while the number of art studios grew to more than 30. These developments distinguished the 798 Art Zone from other art clusters, which either specialize in a single genre or concentrate on a particular artistic function, and established it not only as a production space for creative culture but also a window to contemporary Chinese art and a platform for communication between artists from home and abroad.

Organic Growth of Cultural Networks: The Role of Crises and Grassroots Associations

Through mutual introduction, artists were led to 798. The pioneering artists were bonded by their common interest in contemporary art. Nonetheless, without the pooling of individual resources in the interest of communal enterprise, 798 would perhaps have remained a loosely organized interest group, lacking the deep interpersonal relations and dependencies that characterize a network. In this context, common adversity often provides the stimulus – by requiring a coordinated collective response – for a sense of community to develop, when members of a group identify their self-interest with the larger interest of the group. This sense of solidarity and the consequent evolution of trust and cooperation is what triggers organic artistic/cultural mobilization.

As the case of 798 illustrates, challenges to the continued existence of a network play a pivotal role in consolidating trust and cooperation among network members and fostering community identification, which are vital to the expansion of the network. Expansion renders problematic the group dynamic by diluting member relations and giving rise to conflicts over the distribution of scarce resources between existing and new members. In other words, expanding groups experience 'dis-economies of scale'. However, for 798, expansion was correlated with increasing solidarity and the cementing of communal identity because it was a network that had been baptized by fire. The 798 artist community had faced challenges together, and through the mobilization of the network's activists, a sense of 'revolutionary comradeship' had been established. This comradeship upgraded the rudimentary social relations into network relations.

Before proceeding to a discussion of the challenges that 798 and its creative community faced in its early days, a note is in order on the ability of localized cultural activism at the grassroots to mobilize resources beyond its initial spatial domain. In this multi-level mobilization, artists in the local network attract outsiders to join, thereby expanding the network and enriching the resource pool, with both tangible political and economic resources and the intangible asset of generating bodies of discourse that can pressurize the administrative apparatus and influence the political process. Thus, multi-level grassroots mobilization is strategically indispensable in dealing with both internal and external challenges to a network's sustainability and expansion. The ensuing discussion highlights the use of such a strategy by activists within the 798 network, as a response to the early crisis in its history.

The artists of 798 faced two challenges. First, contemporary art was still located at the far end of the spectrum of Chinese culture. To incorporate it into the mainstream, it was necessary to run promotional campaigns, building narratives to fire the public imagination. The second, perhaps more immediate, challenge was the imminent dismantling and recon- struction and redesignation of 798 in 2005. In fact, from the start, the Seven Star Group that owned the facility had made it clear to the tenants that the factory area had been earmarked to be part of the projected Zhongguancun Electronic City and needed to be dismantled by the end of 2005. Meanwhile, a Hong Kong real estate developer had struck a deal with the Seven Star Group to develop 798. The Seven Star Group's central priority lay in following the state's instructions to rehabilitate workers laid off when the factories had gone into disuse. Concerned that once the Art Zone took off, it would affect the group's plans for real estate develop- ment as part of the larger redevelopment project, Seven Star did not relish the prospect of an art network taking root and thriving in 798.

The 798 network was envisioned by its resident artists as a stronghold of contemporary Chinese arts. To promote the public visibility of the genre, the artists of 798 adopted a strategy of holding joint large-scale cultural festivals and exhibitions. Through these cultural promotions, they established 798 as an iconic cultural space within the popular imagination and promoted national, even global, recognition of local artists and their works. These efforts, though critical in raising 798's national and interna- tional profiles, ran counter to the Seven Star Group's vision for 798. In 2003, a group of artists led by Huang Rui staged 'Reconstruction 798', a large-scale exhibition designed to draw public attention to the art zone, which articulated the artists' conception of 798 as a creative base. The Seven Star Group countered by declaring that the artists were just tenants and, as such, they had no mandate to determine 798's future. Despite this, 'Reconstruction 798' triggered a movement that was accelerated by sub- sequent exhibitions and art festivals, which led to the local conflict over space use being framed, increasingly, as a national issue.

In the wake of the successful 2003 event, in April 2004, the art zone announced that it would hold a month-long Dashanzi Art Festival. Shortly after this announcement, the Seven Star Group declared its opposition to the festival on the grounds that the art festival had not been approved by relevant government agencies. In response, the organizers swiftly changed the event's name from 'First Dashanzi International Art Festival' to '2004 Dashanzi Art Zone Art Exhibition', a nomenclatural modification that was designed to circumvent the objection. In response, Seven Star put up placards announcing, 'The group has the right to seal off the art zone if the art festival is to be held', and proceeded to dig ditches in the art zone and ban taxis from entering the zone. As a result of the group's antagonism, the whole event was mired in chaos. Nevertheless, as a result, the sense of solidarity and camaraderie among the artists was strengthened.

Network members mobilized themselves to act against the threat to 798. Their instinct for self-preservation prompted mobilizing efforts to occupy both the national political ground and international media space. Critical to the success of artists' attempts to mobilize 'outsiders' to rally around their cause was their ability to create discourses that were sufficiently national (and, even, global) in content and appeal. In what follows, we discuss how the themes of architectural preservation and cultural development were popularized, politicized and incorporated into the national agenda.

During the 'Two Meetings' of 2004, as a deputy to the National People's Congress, sculptor Li Xiangqun presented the Beijing People's Congress with a bill named 'Preserve an Architectural Heritage of the Old Industry, Preserve a Thriving Art Zone', calling for the suspension of the planned dismantling of 798. The bill was well received by the Beijing municipal government. Accordingly, in March 2004, the Ministry of Construction issued a set of 'Guidelines on Strengthening the Preservation of Valuable Modern Architecture in Urban Areas', which highlighted the rare, 1950s Bauhaus-style architecture of 798's old factory buildings, uncommon in much of Asia. As such, the guidelines suggested, the buildings should be protected as an important part of the city's historical and cultural heritage. This reflects how the discourse on architectural preservation, in combination with a discourse on national pride, was used to generate substantial political capital.

Through the internet, Robert Bernell sent out a stream of reports on 798 and the development of Chinese contemporary art, which caught the attention of the international media. To a large degree, these reports were responsible for providing 798 with high international visibility and contributed to a recognition of Beijing as a global cultural heavyweight. A 2003 *Time* magazine report listing Beijing as one of 12 contemporary artistic cities of the world bears testimony to the growing media fascination with Chinese contemporary art, catalysed by the goings-on at 798, which Bernell made every attempt to publicize. Spurred on by the *Time* report and the international visibility it brought, a series of international events were held in 798 that duly received extensive media coverage. Influenced by rapidly building consensus in the global media on 798's status as the flagbearer of Chinese contemporary art, several international art foundations and galleries moved to establish their presence in the art zone. Prominent entrants included the Red Gate Gallery (one of Beijing's earliest foreign galleries) and the Ullens Foundation. Thus, successful mobilization of the international media around the discourse on 798 as a window to Chinese contemporary art facilitated the expansion of 798's network to provide it with increasing influence in the determination of its future.

Through the successful mobilization of political forces and the media, an originally local cultural subject had turned into one with national and even international ramifications. The development of the 798 Art Zone therefore became strategically important to the larger enterprise of positioning Beijing as a global city. Li Xiangqun pointed out, 'Of course, in terms of immediate economic return, nothing comes quicker than selling land. But in terms of a city's long-term development, a city's real attractiveness lies in the formation of a diverse culture' (personal interview, 5 July 2010). Academics also lent their voice to this end. Yang Dongping, an expert on urban cultural studies at University of Science and Technology Beijing, made the point that 'a city's soul and glamour are determined by the city's environment of humanism and by its cultural ecology. A city without culture is only a forest of concrete. So from this point of view, the contribution that 798 makes to Beijing is far larger than a landmark building' (Xu, P., 2004). The nation's intelligentsia joined in making the consensual point to the political elite that 798 played a pivotal role in representing Beijing to the world as a city with a 'soul'.

In sum, the above discussion illustrates how an essentially local mobilization of 798 artists to counter the Seven Star Group's philistine agenda harnessed political resources and mobilized the international media to transfer the local issue to national and international arenas. We have also illustrated how effective mobilization, at different levels, depends on the ability to create and articulate appropriate, level-specific discourse. Under pressure from this multi-level discourse, in 2006, the Beijing municipal government designated 798 as a Creation Industrial Park.

Mobilization and Organic Clustering: The 798 Experience

Mobilization at the local level reinforced the community spirit, which allowed the artists' network to cohere. The art zone came to be characterized by a sense of community, cultural pluralism and a creative learning atmosphere. At the same time, at the national and international levels, this mobilization established 798 as an indelible symbol of contemporary Chinese art. There was clear momentum at 798; it behoves us to explain why and how artists, galleries and cultural foundations continued to be attracted despite the lack of any significant investment in physical infrastructure. This subsection thus provides a brief overview of the accumulation of soft capital in 798.

As highlighted earlier, the conflict with the Seven Star Group rapidly fostered a community spirit among the artists, who had hitherto run their own studios or businesses individually and, to some degree, in isolation from one another. More importantly, the conflict also precipitated the identification of outsiders with the artist community. This public empathy and recognition conferred legitimacy on the claims and aspirations of the 798 community. Avant-garde artist Cang Xin remarked: 'Here we are regarded as artists. Before, we were called "vagrant". We had no identity and were seen as so-called unstable elements.' Artist Wu Xiaojun said, '798 is like a work-unit. In the past, if what we made were brought, let's just say to the roadside, they would be tossed away like trash. But here, at least we are recognized as artists' (*Southern Weekly*, 8 March 2007). Thus, the sense of belonging, the spirit of community within the network and outsiders' endorsement of the value of creative enterprise endowed resident artists with a sense of self-worth. This, in turn, contributed to a corresponding sense of distinction that membership in the network bestowed on the artist.

While the living, working and commercial environment at 798 are pull factors in promoting clustering, above all, the place is characterized by a plural, tolerant and free attitude: '798 is a vast grassland, a space with great tolerance, an ideal home for avant-garde artists to work' (Yang and Zhang, 2007). The artist Cang Xin considers 798 to be a paradise for creative stimulus and expression. Although the rent in 798 is slightly higher than in Dongcun, where he lived previously, 'The buildings are beautiful, and there are even security guards at the factory entrance.' He adds, '798 is relatively tolerant (as compared with Yuanmingyun and Dongcun)' (*Southern Weekly*, 8 March 2007). Before moving to 798, he had once been detained because of his art. Thus, he particularly values the freedom, openness, pluralism and tolerance that are deeply embedded in 798's ethic. Li Xiangqun asserted that on account of these virtues, 'it is easier to feel the pulse of contemporary artistic trends here than elsewhere' (Zhou, H., 2006).

In fact, rent in 798 has been steadily on the rise. Further, many small businesses around the art zone, such as coffee shops, bookstores and galleries, are not all profitable. Some are kept afloat by profits earned from the owner's other business outlets. However, this is no impediment to the operators' desire to continue doing business in this space. One interviewee noted:

I didn't come here to sell paintings. Business in Wangfujing is better than here. I came just because I like it here. This is a great place for creation and a day is incomplete unless I come here. Here you can meet with others in the arts community. You can even strike up a conversation with some visitors who share the same interests in the café. It feels very good.

For those who want to seek a career in the arts, 798 is seen as a place to fulfil their dream. A student who wanted to pursue his Master's degree in oil painting with the Central Academy of Fine Arts said, 'My dream is to secure a contract with a 798 art gallery and become a contract painter.' Even for artists in Taiwan who are optimistic about the prospect of the mainland art market and have plans to develop their careers in China, 798 is invariably their first choice because 'whether in terms of artists, or the general atmosphere, this place is unrivalled by other places. Open a gallery here and you can meet artists and like-minded folks. It's also a good place to learn' (Yi, 2006). Clearly, from the perspective of many artists, commercial concerns are trumped by the appeal of 798's ambience in their decision to settle here. This is why, despite the relatively high rents and a significant possibility of financial failure, artists and operators of art-related businesses continue to favour 798 as either a base or a location for an outlet.

State Intervention: The Nexus of Culture, Government and Commerce

Since its designation by the state as a creative cultural cluster in 2006, tremendous changes have taken place in 798. As discussed earlier, state intervention was guided by the desire to promote the industrialization of culture and cultural industry clustering, considered essential to the project of establishing Beijing's credentials as a global city. The industrialization of culture is inalienable from a desire to commercialize culture on a scale much larger than what already existed within 798. The impact of this desire and the actions undertaken to realize the same are analysed below.

Prior to 2006, the 798 Art Zone was plagued by infrastructural problems that compromised the material quality of living: lack of facilities; noise and acute air pollution; inadequate sanitation; and lax security. Despite extracting rents, the management provided the artists with little service. Further, the management's indifference to making material improvements to the artists' living conditions and, at times, its active obstruction of artistic events, took place in the midst of rental hikes at 798. This phenomenon is best attributed to demand-side pressures; in other words, the rapid growth of artist networks and the expansion of creative clusters produced an insatiable demand for space in the art zone. While many news reports on 798 cited the issue of rising rent, voicing anxiety that higher rents would disrupt the organic clustering process, the worry appeared unfounded (Xu, P., 2004; Zhou, H., 2006). As Huang Rui pointed out in his interview with *Xinjingbao*,

> Nobody left because of not being able to afford the rent (2 RMB/square metre every day in 2006). Some people rented their place while the rent was low, and now they are just subletting those places to make a profit. No painters or art galleries will pull out. In fact, there are many people who are on the waiting list to move in. To be fair, Seven Star Group's price is not too high. Besides, they also charge differently according to types of spaces and people. (Yi, 2006)

In addition to worries about high rents, sceptics also expressed concern that high levels of commercialization would be to the detriment of the creative ambience that had come to be the hallmark of 798. While conceding that the art galleries were getting more numerous and more active, indicating the growing influence of the commercial dimension of art over its creative dimension, Huang Rui remained optimistic. He maintained:

> What's most interesting about 798 is that it is not an entirely commercial area, nor is it an art gallery street. Without doubt, the influence of the art galleries is quite strong, and I think they will continue to grow. Indeed, more and more art galleries are holding commercial exhibitions. But in general I think these could be balanced out by other active art galleries which do not stage commercial exhibitions, such as the Evergreen Art Gallery, the Tokyo Art Gallery, the Southgate Space, etc. The activities of these galleries set a healthy direction for the development of the 798 Art Zone. Aside from reflections on social subjects, the Art Zone is also marked by the artists' individual artistic exploration and the general atmosphere of the zone is rich and dynamic. (Yi, 2006)

In 2006, the Beijing municipal government designated creative industries as strategically vital and earmarked CH¥500 million to help develop several creative industry parks, including the 798 Art Zone. As a result, 798's bottom-up development model encountered challenges to its ethos from an entirely different quarter. After being declared one of Beijing's creative industry clusters, the 798 Art Zone obviously could not maintain its self-sustaining status and develop independently as had hitherto been the case. A Beijing 798 Art Zone Development and Management Office was jointly set up by the Beijing municipal government, Chaoyang District, Jiuxianqiao Neighbourhood Community and the Seven Star Group to oversee 798's planning and management issues. In the context of this radical structural revamp, 798's potential to further evolve organically came into serious jeopardy.

To analyse changes brought about by state intervention, we first discuss the artists' expectations of the state's role, followed by an examination of official discourse about state intervention *vis-à-vis* the reality on the ground. Finally, the conflicts over space that resulted from state intervention and the transformation of cultural space are presented and analysed.

When asked what he thought of the government's intervention in 798's management, photographer Xu Yong had this to say: 'We are in a dilemma. On the one hand, we do hope that this place can be better managed, but on the other hand, we are also very concerned that too much management would undermine the art zone's vitality.' In his interview with *Xinjingbao*, Huang Rui pointed out:

> what the government should do is to provide assistance, or establish the development platform. The last thing we want from the government is policy guidelines, because artistic creation and art industry have their own characteristics. Furthermore, the Art Zone is already in pretty good shape and it draws attention from home and abroad. Maybe you can't sell a single piece of your paintings in other places, but in 798, there will be people to buy. So I think for now, it's better to leave the Art Zone to its own devices. (Yi, 2006)

Obviously, from the artists' point of view, creative autonomy is vital to 798's success. Thus, there is a strong preference for minimal state intervention that allows artists to retain control over creative space. Li Xiangqun made this point very clearly:

> It would seem to be a good thing that the government steps in. But the crux of the issue is that the government should try to focus on service rather than management. For example, nobody is responsible for providing public facilities in the art zone. There is even no WC. To build 798 into a mature creative industrial base, convenient public facilities and public services are indispensable. (Zhou, H., 2006)

He hoped the government could support improvements in the art zone's environment, without meddling in the affairs of the artist community, maintaining that a free and relaxed atmosphere is a precondition for the creative act.

Despite artists' wishes to the contrary, strong state intervention became inevitable after 798 was designated as a creative industrial base. On 28 March 2007, the 798 Art Zone Construction and Management Office was formally established with a mandate to coordinate, serve, guide and manage the development of the 798 Art Zone. To contribute to the global city building effort, the office was tasked with effecting environmental improvements, general brand promotion, industrial upgrading and tourism promotion, among others (*People's Daily*, overseas version, 9 April 2007).

At the top of the agenda was the improvement of the art zone's environment, which included 11 measures relating to the construction of infrastructure. These measures covered road improvement, building parking space, beautification and landscaping, electrical works upgrading, public security reinforcement, sanitation improvement, upgrading of fire control facilities and the provision of street lighting. Next, to create a better institutional environment, an association of resident artists in the art zone was to be established. The objective was to systematize communications between the artists and the government, thus institutionalizing and regulating 798's creative style. Above all, the most far-reaching decision was to take over the organization of the 798 Art Festival so that the event could be used to showcase Beijing's cultural industry and establish the city's global city credentials. The 798 Art Zone Construction and Management Office declared that the 2007 Beijing 798 Art Festival would continue to showcase the 798 Art Zone's avant-garde nature and provide a dynamic cultural window on contemporary China. With this as a basis, the office aimed to build 798 into an influential international art zone comprising high-end art galleries, foundations and museums. Given the strategic importance of 798 to the Chinese government's grand project to turn Beijing into a global city, it was clear that the state's ambitions would be realized only if it could exert control over the artist community. In this sense, strong state intervention was almost a foregone conclusion (Gao, J., 2007).

The government's strong intervention in cultural issues has begun to affect the course of 798's development (see Table 7.2 for a summary). The first impact of strong governmental intervention was on the open, plural and tolerant atmosphere that is 798's 'X-factor'. In particular, the state-sponsored artists' association, though ostensibly a channel for communication between the artists and the government, is at heart motivated by a desire to exercise control over the artists. Many of 798's artists use their work to express criticisms of social ills and domestic politics, which some government leaders have found irksome. In a society that is still under quite tight political control, this background context leads one to believe that the association will impose restrictions on 798's freedom of artistic expression.

The second impact was on the focus of the artist network, shifting from creation to cultural promotion and consumption. Art-related events, which in the past served to mobilize and expand 798's artistic network, have also changed. Before 2006, the art festivals were not only organized by the artists but also financed by funds raised by the artists themselves. After the management office was set up, with the support of government funding, exhibition professionals were hired to take over the organization and promotion of art festivals and other cultural events. On the

Table 7.2   798: Pre and post 2006

	Pre 2006	Post 2006
Major practitioners and purpose of practice	• Artists, collectors • Cultural creation	• State agencies, art retailers, foundations and galleries, international exhibition professionals • Display and trade of culture, cultural tourism
Discourse	• Construction of cultural space	• Industrialization/ commercialization of culture to build a global city
Mode of governance	• Grassroots mobilization • Horizontal; governance built on trust and cooperation	• Driven by state resources • Vertical governance based on bureaucratic hierarchy
Growth mechanism	• Organic, internal growth • Driven by a creative aesthetic	• Non-organic, external investment • Driven by commercial consumption forces

surface, this looked to be conducive to the development of art by freeing artists from the chores of administration and finance. But a deeper consideration of this division of labour suggests that the decision was made more for political and economic reasons than to support artistic activity. Economically, through the collective promotion of cultural brands and cultural tourism, the management office intended to further commercialize 798 with the goal of transforming it into, primarily, a space for cultural consumption. From the political angle, institutionalizing the organization, management and communication structures served the government's need to exercise control over 798's future development; the art zone's capacity to be a mouthpiece for Beijing's claims to global city status rendered it too valuable for the government to cede to the resident artist community discretion over its trajectory of growth.

A third change that has marked the transition of 798 from spontaneous network to institutional organization has had far-reaching implications. As a result of government intervention, a new culture network focused on helping Beijing to achieve global city status is beginning to replace the old artist-/creativity-oriented network. The members of this new network are government agencies and a new batch of cultural consumption bodies such as cultural service retailers, cultural sector professionals (especially exhibition professionals) and new investors in the culture sector (including art gallery foundations and cultural tourism businesses). While, on the surface, this expansion and 'pluralization' could be reconciled with 798's entrenched culture of diversity, deeper examination reveals that a fundamental shift has taken place. The participation and assimilation of these new cultural practitioners into 798's networks was made possible through government funding and therefore subject to the terms and control of government management. As the proportion of these members grew, the government, surreptitiously but surely, started establishing a stranglehold over the art zone. The old mode of governance, essentially horizontally structured, came to be supplanted gradually by a vertically structured, hierarchical form of bureaucratic management. As a consequence, the grassroots characteristics of 798 have come under serious threat of extinction.

There has been a steady trickle of the early generation of 798's artists out of the art zone. In 2006, the artist Huang Yue left 798 after his contract with the Seven Star Group expired. Further, the art zone's artists all expressed their dissatisfaction with the 798 Creative Culture Festival, which was organized by the management office in October 2006. Arguing that the festival jarred with the art zone's artistic atmosphere, and taking it as a foreboding of what was to come, some artists left 798 of their own accord and moved to neighbouring areas, such as Caochangdi, Jiuchang and Huantie. Cang Xin and several of his neighbours in 798 have already rented new studios in other places; they use their 798 studios only as exhibition space. Cang Xin's roommate Mogen moved everything to Huantie: '798 is more and more like a show place. It's full of small crafts and arts dealers. It's out of touch with us' (*Southern Weekly*, 8 March 2007).

CONCLUSION

The development strategy of Beijing's creative culture industry, as highlighted by the government's policy discourse, is modelled on that of the science and technology industry. Similar to its strategy of building science and technology parks, the government has sought to stimulate the development and clustering of the creative culture industry by building infrastructure and institutions. For all its good intentions and investments, the case of 798 illustrates how state intervention is welcomed by creative protagonists only insofar as it can improve facilities; its introduction of bureaucratic structures and hierarchies, and its emphasis on industrialization, consumption and tourism, have turned away artists engaged in the production of creative work. Thus, while the creative cultural industry grows at a miraculous pace, aided by strong government support and massive public investment in cultural infrastructure, and guided by the desire to project Beijing's claims in global city competition, question marks remain on the future of the creative dimension of contemporary Chinese culture.

The 798 cluster plays a bigger economic role today, but creative culture appears to have been adversely affected; the cluster's grassroots characteristics have been compromised. Drawn by its reputation, international tourists are pouring into 798. But the initial 'trickle out' of artists, art galleries and art collectors threatens to quickly become an exodus. The 798 Art Zone is becoming more popular – and less creative.

NOTE

1. Among these, it was expected that the output value of the Dongcheng Cultural Zone (Zhongguancun Science and Technology Park, Yonghe) would reach CH¥10 billion, and CH¥20 billion to CH¥30 billion in 2010. Around CH¥1 billion was invested in the Sanchen Cartoon, Animation and Internet Games Industrial Base over its first three years. The base's yearly output value was expected to reach CH¥3 billion and the output value of related industries will reach over CH¥10 billion. With 120 000 employed in it, the base was to become China's, or even the world's, largest animation and internet game research and development centre.

8. Remaking Shanghai's old industrial spaces: the growth and growth of creative precincts

INTRODUCTION

Shanghai was China's most modern city in the 1930s and 1940s. Following two decades of isolation, it renewed its acquaintance with the world in the late 1970s, in conjunction with the start of the country's Reform and Opening Up. Since then, the city's economy has grown at more than 20 per cent per annum for many years, and its physical landscape has undergone an impressive transformation. Old buildings in the city have either been restored or redeveloped as modern buildings, while the city has extended, at a great pace, into adjacent areas. Gilmore (2004) puts this transformation in perspective by pointing out that Shanghai has taken less than two decades to achieve a skyline that took five decades to create in New York.

This building of economic and physical muscle has enabled the city to seek cultural pursuits. As we showed in Chapter 3, large-scale investment in cultural mega-infrastructure has taken place, made possible only with economic growth and willingness to effect urban change. To an extent, Shanghai residents have responded: the city has a higher per capita cultural consumption than other Chinese cities (Ge et al., 2014). At the same time, Shanghai's cultural history has provided it with a multicultural personality and also allowed it to stockpile cultural assets and experience in managing international cultural connections. Thus, on multiple bases, the city has, along with Beijing, emerged as a frontrunner in the race to become China's showpiece cultural destination and the base for the country's creative industries (Zhang, J., 2007, p. 11).

Anticipating the centrality of knowledge industries in the future growth of its economy, the city has, since 2005, embarked on a strategy to promote high-tech and creative industries. The latter is of particular interest in this chapter and book. A review of the development of creative industries in Shanghai demonstrates a clear transition from organic growth to a growth orchestrated by the local government. Drawing from its cultural assets as highlighted earlier, and adopting and adapting the concept of creative clusters from the experience of other countries, the city adopted a place-oriented entrepreneurial strategy and began to construct 'creative parks', where 'creative workers and facilities' would agglomerate (Keane, 2011; O'Connor and Xin, 2006). In fact, in 2006, the Shanghai Economic Commission also published a *Guide to Key Points in the Development of Creative Industries in Shanghai* that articulated a detailed plan for the development of its creative industries. The cornerstone of this plan was a strategy of constructing creative industry parks by combining industrial restructuring with the reuse of obsolete industrial premises. These parks were envisaged to be spaces where creative enterprises and talented people would cluster. Guided by this vision, by the end of 2006, the city had established 75 creative parks and attracted more than 27000 creative workers from over 30 countries to work in those clusters (Shanghai Creative Industry Centre, 2007). By 2013, 119 creative parks had been created in total. Based on its market size and abundant human and cultural resources, Shanghai aimed to be conspicuous in the development of Asian cultural/creative industries. The city also had hopes that its hosting of the 2010 World Expo would offer an unprecedented opportunity to catapult Shanghai into the major league of creative industry players. In more specific terms, the city estimated in 2007 that the value added by the creative industries would reach 10 per cent of the city's GDP in 2010 (Cai, 2007). More to the point, the sum total of its ambitions would propel Shanghai to global city status.

In line with the central thrusts in this section of the book, this chapter interrogates how several of the very many cultural/creative clusters/parks[1] in Shanghai are variously organic or state-vaunted developments, and how the former become the latter with state intervention. The specific role of the state in the project of cultural or creative industry development through the cluster strategy is also examined. To do so, the remainder of the chapter is organized as follows. The next section focuses on Shanghai's creative industry and creative cluster strategies. This is followed by a detailed analysis of M50 (Moganshan Lu), Tianzifang and 1933 as case studies. The chapter then concludes with our observations about the value and perils of state intervention in organically evolving clusters, and the sustainability of state-initiated creative industry parks.

CREATIVE INDUSTRIES AND CREATIVE CLUSTERS DEVELOPMENT IN SHANGHAI

To understand the creation of creative parks or clusters in Shanghai, we paint the picture in the context of late 1990s Shanghai. It was a time when the city embarked on a major project of industrial restructuring to substitute the emphasis on manufacturing with a focus on providing financial, trade and other advanced services. Many energy-intensive, pollution-generating and inefficient factories and industrial premises were shut down. To accommodate these abandoned premises within the city's blueprint for urban development, most were initially released to developers for redevelopment as residential and commercial real estate, while some were transferred to the so-called urban industrial parks to host low energy-consuming and low pollution-generating manufacturers that would provide jobs for local residents. Several premises, in the transition period between being demolished and redeveloped were leased out for short terms to artists who refurbished these premises as their workshops. The 'artist as tenant' arrangement was purely market-driven; while artists were attracted by low rents and the prospect of occupying premises with a historical legacy, the owners of the premises benefited from the rental income and a reduced burden in managing and maintaining these premises.

By no means were these facilities without flaw. In fact, the pioneering group of artists faced numerous problems in adapting these industrial premises to function as creative spaces. Given the buildings' transient status, their upkeep and security was lax. Owners were uninterested in providing facilities and equipment to support the creative function. More importantly, owing to the duration of the lease contracts, artists remained under constant threat of eviction. Gradually, to respond to these problems, artists' organizations started to take form.

Taikang Lu (Road), Moganshan Lu and Suzhou Creek are among the most famous examples of such rudimentary, organic, creative clusters. The growth of these clusters in size and organization, coupled with Shanghai's unique city style and cultural foundations, attracted many artists/creative workers from other Chinese cities and even overseas. Nevertheless, in the early days of creative clustering, the local government's attitude towards the creative class was at best apathetic and at worst hostile. The administration's collaboration with real estate developers to demolish buildings in pursuing its urban renewal policy ensured that government objectives and artists' interests were in polar opposition to each other.

However, the increasing prominence of 'grassroots' creative clusters, combined with the influence of the discourse on competition for global city status (Kong, 2007), precipitated a marked shift in the government's stance towards creative clusters around 2004–05. As the aspirations to be counted as a global city grew, so did a consensus around the potential of creative industries in helping to realize those ambitions. Playing an increasingly proactive role in guiding the creative industry, the city established platforms for its holistic development and adopted more open policies to attract local and external creative workers and facilitate cultural concentration. The realignment in priorities is nowhere more apparent than in the tone and content of published documents like the *Eleventh Five-Year Programme for Creative Industries in Shanghai* and the *Guide to Key Points in the Development of Creative Industry in Shanghai*. The central target of this ambitious project that combines industrial restructuring, urban regeneration and the preservation of historic premises (Li, 2006) is to develop two main creative industry belts along the Huangpu River and Suzhou Creek and to have an equitable spatial distribution of creative enterprise among the city's districts, with each district specializing in its own niche.

The formal set of guidelines issued by central authorities for the development of the creative industry has also served to redraw and rationalize administrative jurisdictions and functions. While, on the one hand, it has arbitrated on differences between various wings of the government (such as the Propaganda Department and the Economic Commission) over attitudes towards the cultural industry and the logic for its development, on the other, it has institutionalized cooperation between levels of local government. The underlying basis of such cooperation is a principle of division of labour that allocates responsibilities for planning and coordinating to the city government while putting district administrations in change of implementation. A central aspect of city-level planning has been to identify districts' core cultural competencies through a detailed survey of each district's industrial foundations and cultural and heritage resources and accordingly allocate creative industrial sectors (Shanghai Creative Industry Centre, 2006). The district governments are tasked with initiating and executing creative cluster development projects. Our interviews with the secretary general of the Shanghai Creative Industries Centre (SCIC) (see next paragraph for an explanation) and district officers (18 October 2007) yielded several explanations for the districts' enthusiasm in performing their role as promoters of creative industry. While their subordinate status might imply that district authorities have no recourse but to follow central and city governments' policies, district officers have indicated their endorsement of creative clustering projects by citing the benefits that accrue locally. Such benefits include larger tax revenues, generation of local employment opportunities, the showcasing of the district and its officers and a broadening of the revenue base through receipts from the sale of local cultural products.

Another notable feature of the administrative apparatus behind creative industry development in Shanghai is the SCIC. Adapting several developed countries' experience to the city's particular circumstance, the Shanghai Economic Commission established this centre in 2005 to provide professional agency and consulting services to the government in charting road maps for the future growth of Shanghai's creative enterprises. A non-governmental agency, it nevertheless had good connections with the Economic Commission. Its board of directors includes representatives from the creative industries and government departments, as well as university professors. In addition to its consultative function, the centre monitors trends in domestic and foreign cultural markets and facilitates cultural exchange by arranging exhibitions and providing other platforms for communication between creative entrepreneurs, administrations and cultural markets. It also plays a critical role in coordinating the development of creative parks across districts to prevent niche overlap. In this capacity, the centre negotiates with and advises districts on their applications to the city government for permission to establish creative parks. Finally, the centre, through its website, disseminates information and provides an e-commerce platform for the creative industries and creative workers.

In addition to embodying the principles of government guidance and market orientation, the promotion of creative industries in Shanghai is characterized by its reliance on intermediaries (Shanghai Creative Industries Centre, 2007, p. 3) and by the administration's attempts to aid the developers of creative premises in circumventing regulations that, if rigidly construed, could inhibit the industry's growth. The increasing importance of intermediaries in creative industry development becomes apparent when we consider that several of them, such as SCIC, the Shanghai Design Centre, the Shanghai Creative Industry Association, the Shanghai Fashion Federation and the Shanghai Creative Industry Research Institute, have expanded their operational scope to establish themselves as important players in the creative industries. Finally, as an example of its support for the creative industries, the city encourages developers to adopt the approach of 'three invariables' in order to bypass the constraints of property rights and land-use zoning. In other words, the approach is to keep constant (hence 'invariables') three features of the existing system. First, property rights relations should remain unchanged, so that land does not need to go through the complicated process of market tendering. Second, the land use is unchanged, that is, the premises are still used by industry (although a vastly different kind of industry from the past), so there is no violation of land-use zoning regulations and thus no need to pay fees for land-use transformation. Third, the basic building structure should remain unchanged. This obviates the need to acquire a permit from the planning authorities. With this guidance from the city government, developers can develop creative industry parks with relative ease.

Such active state support has led to a proliferation of creative parks in Shanghai. As mentioned earlier, by 2007, the city had already established 75 creative industry parks to house creative parks of varied kinds, such as software services, digital entertainment, industrial design, advertisement design, architectural design, press and publication, consultation and planning services, visual arts and so on. Together, these parks have provided space and services to more than 3500 creative enterprises and employ 27000 creative industry workers (Shanghai Creative Industries Centre, 2007, p. 17).

The current scale of the creative industries in Shanghai, juxtaposed with its marginal status only slightly more than a decade ago, is testimony to the U-turn in the government's assessment of its economic value and consequent adoption of a proactive stance in promoting creative clustering. Based on the nature and timing of state intervention, two distinct categories of creative clusters can be identified. The first of these comprises the early, loosely structured artists' organizations, which were self-initiated, spontaneous responses to the logistical problems confronting a spatially concentrated creative community. State intervention, in terms of improving the physical environment in which these clusters operated and enhancing the quality of the infrastructure they had access to, took place only after these artists' organizations had matured. This bottom-up development is evident in the experiences of Tianzifang at Taikang Road and M50 at Moganshan Road. The second category of creative clusters, demonstrating a top-down approach from the start, is characterized by the active involvement of the state in the conception, design, operation and regulation of the cluster. An instance of this is the 1933 creative hub, where the state played an essential role at the beginning of the development process by carefully planning to build a suitable space for industrial development, providing the necessary services, improving the surrounding environment and then marketing it to creative enterprises and artists. The next three sections detail the evolution of these creative clusters as a way of identifying how intervention can influence the theory and practice of cluster development.

FROM MOGANSHAN ROAD TO M50

In the vicinity of Moganshan Road, spread over 35 acres, stand various types of industrial buildings constructed between the 1930s and the 1990s. These buildings, as representatives of a historical phase in the development of Shanghai's industrial architecture, have high cultural value. In 1999, these factories ceased operations, in line with the city's industrial restructuring policy. In the interim, between demolition and redevelopment, the manager of the defunct manufacturing enterprise leased out these premises temporarily in order, first, to use the rental income to settle redundant workers and second, to reduce the burden of managing and maintaining these obsolete buildings. Several artists, attracted by the historical aura of the space and the low rents, leased parts of these buildings. Thereafter, other artists, including some from abroad, such as ShanghART and BizArt, followed suit.

In 2001, the district government tendered out the land to a real estate developer for redevelopment as a residential community. Around the same time, the city government, under the aegis of its inner city industrial restructuring project, selected this site for an urban industrial park. As the future of Moganshan Road accumulated political and economic importance, the steady influx of artists sustained the early momentum towards creative agglomeration. M50 thus acquired visibility as a creative cluster in international cultural circles. The manufacturing enterprise had begun to notice that transforming these industrial premises into creative spaces enabled it to keep its right to use and manage the premises. From an economic standpoint, the stream of rental income sufficed to cover its operational costs. However, not only did this status quo conflict with the city's urban renewal's policy it also undermined the economic interests of the real estate developer.

The conflict of interests came to the boil in 2003 when the developer received approval for its redevelopment plan from the district authorities. Facing the prospect of losing their workshops and, more significantly, buildings of substantial historical worth, many artists in the area organized themselves against the redevelopment project. The artists who mobilized against the urban renewal and redevelopment plans acknowledged the difficulties of confronting the government and real estate developers. An involved artist indicated

> The frustration was there from the very beginning. We had to collect information to prove that those buildings had historical cultural value. However, we could not access the official material. They gave the reason that these materials belonged to secret archives. We spent a lot of time and energy to collect data through field surveys. We also needed to use various personal connections to contact and to persuade officers in several departments of the city and district government about the importance of preservation of the city's historical buildings. We were standing in a position opposite to that of the real estate developer. They always kept an eye on us. Initially, we were looking for help from university professors. Pessimistically, they said that the possibility to preserve those buildings was very low. Even after the government agreed to preserve those buildings, there was still uncertainty. We needed to spend a long time coordinating the different opinions of different authorities in the city and the

district government. Particularly, the planning department had its policy fixed with regard to this area's development; that is, to demolish all the buildings within 30 metres of the bank of Suzhou Creek. Under this policy, M50 would be demolished. In fact, in the process of negotiation between departments, several historical buildings were torn down by the developer. It was luck that preserved M50. (Personal interview, 17 October 2007)

Fortuitously for the artists, real estate values plummeted around the time on account of the severe acute respiratory syndrome (SARS) epidemic. As the renewal project got transferred to the backburner, the city had the time to reassess the redevelopment issue. In 2004, the Shanghai city government agreed to keep the historical buildings from being dismantled, naming the cluster Chunming Arts Industry Park. The following year, it became part of Shanghai's first batch of creative industry parks to be approved by the Economic Commission, changing its name to M50 Creative Park.

The government's rethink and reversal of policy on redevelopment was by no means sudden. While the artists' lobbying played a role, the key impetus was provided by the desire to compete for global city status and a review, in this context, of other cities' experiences with the development of their creative clusters. Our interviews with an artist and the secretary general of SCIC in October 2007 provide evidence for this thesis. Accordingly, the emphasis on creative industry development in two official plans for Shanghai's growth may be read to reveal an admission by the authorities of the backwardness of Shanghai's cultural credentials vis-à-vis other global cultural hot spots. As much as this realization has catalysed the city's development of its cultural and creative assets, the choice to locate this cultural (counter) revolution in old and defunct industrial spaces has been motivated by a desire to replicate the success that cities like London and New York have had in reinvigorating their urban wastelands by putting them to creative use.

The problems with initial government policy aside, the pioneering generation of M50 artists had to contend with a dilapidated physical environment. Most of the buildings were storage sheds holding abandoned equipment and raw materials that the tenants were required to clear themselves. The owners of the premises provided no logistical support with clearing the mess, improving the facilities or refurbishing the tenanted spaces. One of the interviewed artists mentioned that she was reluctant to enter and stay in this cluster and agreed to do so only after friends' continuous invitations. Only after the M50 had established its reputation in Shanghai did the enterprise/owner start to provide services to its tenants and attend to the state of disrepair.

The management of the M50 admitted that it was only after it realized the value of historical buildings and the contributions of creative industry that it made efforts to support the creative workers and to learn how to operate a creative cluster. Since then, it has hired several young graduates and cultivated their abilities to manage the cultural and creative industry. Perhaps the greatest change in the management of M50 has been the attitudinal transformation of owners and managers towards creative workers and industries. To use a metaphor, the creative industry is now seen less as a golden egg and more as the goose that lays it. Thus, the management is committed to sustaining the creative industry as a long-run investment rather than being guided by short-term profiteering motives. To underscore this commitment, the management restricts the expansion of commercial space in the premises despite the potential for higher rents. However, ultimately, M50 is an economic project (and not a purely creative one) where artistic merit might be subordinated to competitive advantage (a synonym here for marketability). Thus, rents have been on an upward trend in response to market-based pressures. Justifying the increase in rents, the manager said in an interview

> It is for promoting M50's long-term competitiveness. The aim of rent increase is to keep the dynamics of the creative park – to introduce new creative workers while eliminating those are not competitive. (Personal interview, 18 October 2007)

At this stage of M50's development, another dimension bears scrutiny: the dynamics of inter-artist relations in the cluster and their contribution to the local cultural community. Interviews with the artists show that relations between artists have changed with the shift in the government's stance on M50. In the early days of the cluster, the threat of redevelopment and the adverse working conditions served as a rallying ground for the first few batches of artists and helped to form a sort of 'revolutionary bond' (*geming qinggan*). They worked and lived together, not unlike a big family, and developed a sense of community, supporting one another. These relationships were crucial in driving the cluster's initial organic phase of growth. However, an increase in the scale of the community – M50's increasing reputation attracted many new artists and enterprises to become part of the cluster – corresponded with a dilution in the sense of community affiliation. While the size of the cluster might clearly impede the maintenance of a cohesive identity, another reason has been forwarded to explain the decline in cohesion of the network of artists and entrepreneurs in M50. As the owners and governments have scaled up efforts to improve the physical infrastructure and provide requisite services to the occupants, the consequent depersonalization of space and easy access to services that previously demanded communal intervention and effort have resulted in the dissipation of the 'revolutionary' emotions. On account of the disparate circumstances of the early settlers and the new arrivals, interviewees also reported a 'generation' gap in terms of relationships between them (personal interview with artist, 17 October 2007).

The expansion of M50 has benefited the local community by providing job opportunities, such as cleaners and security guards for the galleries and workshops in the cluster. Interviews with members of the local community suggest that these jobs are considered better than factory work; as such, the local community has been welcoming of the creative class working at M50 (personal interview, 14 July 2008).

Artist interviews suggest that the community is amenable to the government playing a larger role in the future development of the cluster. According to one artist, while the organic model had been successful in ensuring early growth for the cluster, it might become ineffective once the cluster grows beyond a critical size. The importance of public investment in removing infrastructural bottlenecks (including inadequate transportation facilities, insufficient dining facilities and pollution in the Suzhou River) was also used to highlight the need for state intervention. However, better infrastructure comes at a cost; another artist remarked that regulations designed for efficient cluster management have increased in the wake of government involvement (personal interviews, 17 October 2007).

In sum, the M50 creative cluster represents the crystallization of artists' initiatives to secure a creative communal space. Driven by the initial, organically derived dynamic energy, M50 acquired an international reputation and global cultural connections. It also generated economic opportunities for the local community and the local creative class, in particular. However, the steady expansion of the cluster limits the effectiveness of the organic model. As more artists, shops, art dealers and tourists started using the space, the trend towards increased government intervention – both in terms of infrastructure investment and increased regulation – seems set to continue. Against the backdrop of these changes, a complicated, efficiency- and regulation-inflected network of relationships has already started to replace the simpler, highly cohesive network of interactions characterized by intense creative learning and exchange. As the scale of M50 expands further, and as the government starts playing a more proactive role, it faces the challenge of retaining its creative energy.

TIANZIFANG AT TAIKANG ROAD

The Taikang Road area had previously been dotted with many alley factories (that is, small factories along narrow alleys, interspersed with residences) manufacturing paper cartons, monosodium glutamate, plastic houseware, cutlery and hand tools. The built environment of the neigh-bourhood comprised a mixture of factories and residences, many of them old and in a state of disrepair. Under the industrial restructuring schemes of the 1980s, many of these factories were gradually abandoned. The neighbourhood also had to contend with infrastructural deficits and an unappealing facade. Under its urban renewal mandate, the city govern-ment had planned to tender out the premises to real estate developers to be transformed into modern functional spaces. As in the case of M50, before being demolished, the premises were leased out to temporary users. The cheap rent and the premises' historical association with famous masters Zhang Daqian and Xu Beihong – who had once lived here – encouraged several artists to set up their workshops in these premises.

As the cluster developed and its reputation as a creative centre grew, it generated a momentum for the influx of more creative workers, includ-ing artists from other parts of China and abroad. Newcomers obtained space by renting nearby residential premises and refurbishing them into studios, workshops or souvenir shops. This pattern of spatial colonization by artists kept pushing the scale and boundaries of this cluster. In 2001, a well-known resident artist named the cluster Tianzifang, after a famous ancient painter, thus designating it as a congregational place for cultural workers, artists and designers. Tianzifang has since become the brand of this cluster. In 2005, Tianzifang, along with M50, was approved by the Economic Commission as part of the first batch of creative industry parks. In 2009, the city designated it as a cultural industry park, affirming its contributions to cultural industry development. Currently, it is the city's largest visual arts centre, with more than 160 specialized creative industry enterprises and workshops.

Tianzifang is another example of a cluster that developed organically from the initiatives of, and interactions between, creative workers. In the initial period of its growth, there was no government involvement to support the cluster. The emergence of space for creative activities in a site earmarked for redevelopment was even antithetical to the urban renewal policy. Accordingly, it required an alliance of artists, historical preservation workers and local residents to fight against the redevelop-ment projects conceived by the local state and property developers. The common opposition to the philistine tendencies of the state contributed to infusing the early generation of artists in the cluster with a kind of *geming qinggan* [revolutionary bond]. Consequently, as with M50, a close-knit network, characterized by a strong sense of communal identity and intense artistic exchange, started to form. However, as mentioned earlier, the limited factory space entailed that the growth of the creative cluster spilled over to residential areas in the vicinity. In many instances, the inhabitants of the residential premises leased the ground floor of their homes to creative workers and moved upstairs. It was also common to lease out the whole building and move out to other parts of the city with lower rents. The rent around the Taikang Road area was determined by market demand and supply. As the cluster matured, the dynamics of demand ensured frequent, upward rent revisions, leading to a high replacement rate of tenants (personal interview, 14 July 2008).

While both M50 and Tianzifang owe their early development to organic growth, the latter is distinguished by the close interactions between the settler artist community and local inhabitants. The intermixing of residents and artists generated unique benefits; connections between cultural and commercial activities were fostered and a creative ambience pervaded the area, rather than being restricted to the confines of the cluster. Put another way, the boundaries between creative and conventional spaces were blurred. The local non-creative community benefited from this development model as well. While rent collected from artists and entrepreneurs augmented local income, the creative industry generated employment opportunities for residents. The Tianzifang model of creative industry development has provided an alternative approach for the rejuvenation of an old urban community in Shanghai based on a symbiotic relationship between the creative industry/community and peripheral communities.

As observed in the case of M50, the increase in the scale of the creative industry in Tianzifang, combined with the government's recently acquired commitment to cultural development, has resulted in the attenuation of personal bonds and creative exchanges between creative workers in the cluster. Tianzifang faces an additional challenge in trying to sustain its early conception of creative work as a collaborative, rather than competitive, enterprise. As mentioned earlier, escalating rental costs have contributed to a high artist turnover in the cluster. Short tenancy periods imply transient connections and expedient relationships, which have replaced the cooperative interactions of the cluster's early development phase. Relationship gaps between generations of artists also mirror those observed in M50. One of the artists interviewed expressed his resignation about the changing relationship structures thus:

> I only expect that there are no conflicts between us; to entertain the possibility of developing a cooperative relationship is futile. (Personal interview, 29 June 2008)

Tianzifang's similarities with M50 are also reflected in the role that the state played in its development. Over time, state intervention has evolved from being peripheral to proactive, in line with state rethinking on the importance of the creative industries. Only after Tianzifang was announced as one of Shanghai's first creative industry parks did local government invest in infrastructure and improve the environment, repairing drainage, restoring or replacing pipelines, building public lavatories, providing street lighting and so on. It also established an administrative body – the Administrative Committee of Taikang Art Street – in April 2008. The committee provides comprehensive services for new enterprises or artists, including business registration, repair and refurbishment of workshops and so on (Wu, M., 2006). On a deeper level, the establishment of this administrative body implies that the operation of the creative cluster has been bureaucratized and its orientation commercialized. The foundations of the tight connections and dense interactions characterizing organic cluster learning, on which the early development of Tianzifang rested, are also being shaken by commercial considerations in the administration of space.

Despite the many similarities identified between Tianzifang and M50, there are notable differences, attributable to the urban topography of the two areas. While M50 developed in large, abandoned industrial spaces, Tianzifang's journey as a creative park started from alley factories. As mentioned earlier, alley factories are considerably smaller and are interspersed with residential premises. This difference in landscapes entailed that while the growth of M50 was more or less spatially contained, the development of Tianzifang has largely been an instance of unstructured spatial expansion. Both models have their unique merits and liabilities. While development confined by rigid spatial parameters can increase creative density, prevent the diffusion of creative energy and foster stronger creative linkages between members of the cluster, creative clusters characterized by fluid boundaries can give rise to stronger ties between creative enterprise and local community and, hence, have a greater sustainability quotient. Tianzifang's experience suggests that such hybrid landscapes might also boost the diversity of cultural activities carried on within the cluster.

THE 1933 OLD MILLFUN

The 1933 Old Millfun building is a refurbished slaughterhouse, with more than 30 000 square metres of floor space. The building is characterized by five floors of maze-like, concrete corridors and a beam-less structure. When built in 1933, it was the most advanced slaughterhouse in China. In 1969, the building was used as a pharmaceutical manufacturing plant.

The plant was shut down in 2002 and the buildings abandoned until 2006, when its architectural and historical value was noticed. The redevelopment that followed was undertaken by the Shanghai Creative Industry Investment Co. (SCII). After two years' refurbishment, 1933 came alive in 2008 with shops, restaurants, bars, clothing outlets, creative offices and concert spaces. The top level of the main building has been transformed into a large open space used for concerts, exhibitions and corporate events like product launches. However, although 1933 witnessed an increase in the number of its tenants between 2008 and 2009, an overwhelming amount of space was still unoccupied in late 2009. Five years later, in 2014, spaces are largely occupied and visitors are not generally lacking but creative production is minimal.

The redevelopment of 1933 was the product of a state initiative undertaken by a significant injection of public funds through the SCII – a joint venture of the Shanghai Automotive Asset Management Co. (SAAM) and the Shanghai Creative Centre.[2] SAAM is a public enterprise; the Shanghai Creative Centre is an agency that was set up, under the direction of the Shanghai Economic Commission, to provide the impetus for creative industry development. The landed assets belong to the Shanghai Jin Jiang International Group. The Shanghai Economic Commission functioned to coordinate the efforts of the three parties in developing 1933 as a creative hub (interview with a member of staff of the Shanghai Creative Centre, 18 October 2007). The state was active in conceiving, designing and implementing the project and retained control over its operation thereafter. To further its cultural ambitions, the plan for 1933's reuse aimed to redevelop the old building into a leading design and innovation, cultural, educational and entertainment hub. In conjunction with this flagship project, the Hongkou District government has also planned community development projects over a two-square-kilometre area in the vicinity. The drive to attract creative enterprises to register and operate in the district is further evident in such incentives as tax breaks offered to creative industries.

Based on our observations, in the late 2000s and early 2010s, most of the space in 1933 was used for commercial purposes by various kinds of creative businesses. Our interview with a newcomer who entered 1933 in early 2009 provides insights into the way the space is used. This creative firm, specializing in high-quality household utensils, is owned by an American-born Chinese who aims to fuse European design and Chinese cultural elements to establish an upscale household utensils brand for the Chinese market. However, the products are neither designed nor produced in Shanghai. Thus, 1933 serves as an exhibition and marketing space. The designers do not work here; they only visit for short periods to respond to the products' publicity needs. This case may be considered a barometer for space use in 1933, and indicates that while the premises have the potential to develop as a hub for commercial activity surrounding creative products, they are unlikely to succeed in becoming creative spaces.

The emphasis on the commercial dimension of creative work is further emphasized in the local government's efforts to establish an enterprise-friendly business environment by providing tax incentives and relaxing zoning regulations. The previously mentioned 'three invariables' approach has its conceptual origins in the operational design for 1933. These considerations make it clear that 1933's development adopted the essence of the entrepreneurial strategy in pursuing a proactive, market-driven approach for economic growth via cultural investments. While the clarity of vision backed by government zeal and resources might have the twin effects of urban conservation and the agglomeration of creative enterprise, it is unlikely that an organic creative network will be established in the near future. The rent structure at 1933 further militates against this possibility. Higher than those at either M50 or Tianzifang – the exhibition space at the top level of the main building costs close to half a million renminbi for one night – they serve commercially viable creative industries rather than make creative work commercially viable (personal interview, 13 July 2008). In addition, the lack of emphasis on creative production and on support for the local creative community inhibits 1933 from developing into a creative park in the substantive sense from its current status as a corporate social space for creative industry elites.

The fissures between 1933 and the local community is another obstacle to its sustainability. Though the local government has invested resources to improve the physical environment of the surrounding areas, the connections between 1933 and the surrounding community remain weak. With the exception of leading the renovation of a nearby hotel, residents have not had the opportunity to interact with the creative enterprises in 1933. As it stands, 1933 is itself struggling to survive, which makes it even harder for it to take care of its surrounding community.

It is clear that the development pattern of 1933 is markedly distinct from that of M50 and Tianzifang. Borne of state initiative and efforts, 1933 lacks the creative energy that drove the organic development of creative enterprise in M50 and Tianzifang. Further, the design and operation of 1933 demonstrate a commercial bias that is at variance with the creative orientation in the other two examples of creative clusters. An additional contrast lies in the clusters' links to the local community. Of the three cases, 1933 has the weakest relationship. As such, while it may have the potential (at present seemingly unrealized) to contribute to the growth of Shanghai's creative enterprises by providing a platform for creative talents to display their products before a global clientele, it has not contributed significantly to the promotion of local creativity.

CONCLUSION

The case studies discussed in this chapter highlight the variations in creative cluster development patterns in Shanghai. Though they are all characterized by a reuse of old industrial premises as creative spaces, they differ in several aspects, including the nature and timing of state interventions in their development; organization of and relationships within the cluster; links with the local community; and characteristics of cluster occupants. These differences are summarized in Table 8.1.

This chapter has highlighted how Shanghai's creative clusters have broadly navigated along two distinct routes in their development. In the first, artists responded circumstantially to the temporary availability of historically valuable, defunct industrial spaces by organizing themselves spontaneously as creative communities. Transforming urban spaces into sites of creative activity, these associations of creative workers benefited from the close creative interactions among occupants and, as such, developed organically into clusters with substantive creative content. Their growing popularity triggered a steady influx of artists and creative entrepreneurs, which either increased creative density (as in the case of M50) or creative dissemination (as in the case of Tianzifang). As the clusters became more prominent, government policy, initially hostile, turned supportive. This rethink, to a large extent, was prompted by the recognition of the clusters' potential to provide bases for the next phase of the city's economic growth and their capacity to augment the city's cultural credentials. While state support, in the form of investments to improve infrastructure, has led to a better physical environment for the creative workers, it has also altered the networks of creative relations within the clusters and led to the dissipation of creative energy, as witnessed in M50 and Tianzifang. In sum, such bottom-up approaches have not only been instrumental in urban heritage conservation but also infused the old industrial spaces with a new industrial element and contributed to their becoming a field for creative industry.

The second approach is characterized by active state involvement in converting abandoned industrial premises into creative parks over all stages of the transformation process, from conception to construction and operation. The resulting creative spaces have a strong commercial orientation and serve to provide platforms for the showcasing and marketing of creative/cultural products, as the study of 1933 illustrates. However,

Table 8.1   Comparing M50, Tianzifang and 1933

	Criterion	M50	Tianzifang	1933
1	Initiators	Creative workers	Creative workers	Local government and enterprises
2	State intervention	• No intervention at the beginning • Intervention after the cluster had developed	• No intervention at the beginning • Intervention after the cluster had developed	Active involvement from the early stages
3	Impetus and basis for organization within clusters	Spontaneous, creative	Spontaneous, creative	Formal, commercial
4	Development type	Organic pattern	Organic pattern	Planned and implemented by the state
5	Main users	Creative workers (for production)	Creative workers (for production)	Creative enterprises (for exhibitions, corporate events or product launches)
6	Domicile status of creative class	Resident	Resident	Visits for short periods of time for commercial purpose
7	Interactions with local community	Moderate	Close	Minimal

the emphasis on the commercial aspects of the creative industry obscures more substantive creative functions and alienates the local creative community, in particular. This estrangement of the cluster from the local community is exacerbated by the fact that creative workers and other cultural elites regard such spaces as corporate meeting points rather than as spaces for creative domicile. Accordingly, there are question marks on the sustainability of such clusters.

Thus, notwithstanding the manner in which intervention occurs, the city government plays a large role in directing the development of the creative industry. The policies and strategies adopted by the city authorities shape the content of Shanghai's creative clusters and influence the trajectories of their development. Currently, the city pays more attention to the economic dimension of creative industries in the name of honing global competitiveness. An underlying ideology of playing 'catch up' with other cities in the developed world has precipitated a top-down, entrepreneurial approach in the construction and operation of creative parks focusing mainly on creative business and the market value of creative output. Such an approach has its merits. It is conceivable that reusing old urban spaces as creative bases can generate positive publicity locally and abroad and, combined with astute marketing, result in the rapid agglomeration of creative workers in these spaces. By the spatial dispersion of such clusters, the state can hope to popularize the creative industry and imbue the general population with a creative instinct. In addition, the state can better coordinate the development of creative industry in various districts by ensuring, through planning and regulation, that niche overlap between creative parks does not happen.

On the other hand, the state's heavy-handedness in directing the growth of the creative industry might endanger the creative potential of the city in the long run. As illustrated by the case studies, greater state intervention has impeded the organic growth of the clusters by eroding creative vigour and creative cohesion among members of the cluster. State investments in the improvement of physical conditions have invariably been accompanied by a stronger regulatory framework for the artists; both have the potential to alter traditional creative networks in the cluster and dissipate the organic creative energy generated by the linkages. Facility improvements in the cluster can also increase the space costs and, accordingly, rent. Thus, market competitiveness might become the new ethic of creativity and naturally select in favour of creative output and enterprises that are commercially viable, consigning alternative forms of creative expression to extinction. Excessive marketing of creative hubs to culture consumers has its own pitfalls; mass cultural tourism can generate negative externalities and destabilize creative worker habitats by disrupting the creative process.

Moreover, and ironically, large investments in developing creative parks can militate against the sustainability of the creative industry in Shanghai and, hence, the city's aspiration to be a great cultural destination. The discussion on 1933 shows that such scenarios can engender a preoccupation with financial bottom lines, to the detriment of creative activity. Thus, the management will opt to lease out available space to businesses with the capacity to pay higher rent than artists. This might lead to the cluster being operated mainly as a centre of cultural consumption rather than for artistic creation. The key to the success of creative enterprise lies in the ability of the cluster management to strike the right balance between the needs of the creative class and the need for steady consumption demand. From Shanghai's point of view, if it is to emerge as a regional, or even global, cultural player, the ability to retain the creation and production function of cultural enterprise is essential. As the situation stands, however, it has been criticized for being a city that is concerned only with the consumption of creative products, not with nurturing the production of creative output (Wei, 2006).

Yet another concern about the nexus of state intervention and the sustainability of creative enterprises is raised by the scale of the state's moral support for creative park development. Its generous patronage of the creative industries has caused a mushrooming of creative park development projects; the city had approved 75 creative parks by 2007, and several other projects brandishing the name of creative park appeared in the market without official patronage. By 2013, 119 official cultural parks (52) and creative parks (87) had been established. However, many of these projects are not truly for promoting the creative industry; rather, they are real estate development projects masquerading as creative parks. As well intentioned as the state's support might be, it has contributed to the creative industry project becoming a fad without any substantive content (Cai, 2007). Developers, in the pursuit of costless publicity and government incentives, have been quick to climb on the bandwagon and indiscriminately tag their projects as creative parks. This has led to a situation where creative parks are mass produced and rapidly proliferating. Creative parks have become the most uncreative products.

Another criticism of the state's inability to harness the complementarities between cultural activity and creative industry arises with regard to its attempts to keep the domains apart, both in theory and in practice. While the city government designated several design and digital industries as creative industries to be administered by the city's Economic Department, the Propaganda Department has jurisdiction over cultural activities. However, creative industry and cultural activity may not be as dichotomous as the state makes them out to be. Accordingly, the evolution of the creative industry confronts the issue of managing overlaps with cultural activity. Invariably, the output of the creative industry will have some cultural content; thus, the question of which department has regulatory oversight of this content becomes pertinent. Jurisdictional disputes between the economy and propaganda divisions have arisen in the past, indicating that boundaries between creative enterprise and cultural activity are, unsurprisingly, ambiguous. The lack of definitional clarity also affects creative firms' ability to design products with cultural crossover components. Further, distributing control across two government departments over creative industry output that is a cultural hybrid imposes administrative costs on the industry. A solution to the problem in the context of Shanghai (and China in general) has been, and remains, elusive. While a clear definition of the domains of the creative industry may be generated by fiat, its conceptual basis would necessarily be arbitrary. Hence, creative freedom and even the point of creative enterprise would be compromised. On the other hand, eliminating the distribution altogether would attenuate the state's capacity to regulate the contents of the products of the creative industry.

Finally, further study is needed to evaluate whether the city's efforts – by reusing its old urban space to construct creative parks – have been able to promote its international cultural linkages and standing as a global city. So far, M50 and Tianzifang have attracted some external creative workers and foreign tourists. However, the galleries in these clusters mostly exhibit works of contemporary Chinese artists rather than those of foreign artists. In this regard, the clusters are still spaces for local artists, and have not yet become an important global creative locus.

NOTES

1. In general, we use the term 'creative cluster' in this chapter to refer to the concept generally used in academic literature, while the term 'creative park' refers specifically to the equivalent phenomenon in Shanghai as established by the city government.
2. SAAM is also the investor in another of Shanghai's creative parks – the Bridge 8.

9. Factories and animal depots: the 'new' old spaces for the arts in Hong Kong

INTRODUCTION

Hong Kong, as we highlighted in Chapter 4, is not usually associated with thriving arts and cultural activities, and is better known instead as a place of commerce, finance and economic bustle. The West Kowloon Cultural District was meant to help redress the imbalance, but the long drawn-out impasses with the project discussed in Chapter 4 did little to improve the situation. It is in this context that we turn to other kinds of spaces used by artists and cultural groups in Hong Kong, spaces made visible not because of their iconic architecture, monument status or renowned architects but because they are ordinary spaces made into clusters of cultural activities, either wrapped up in the warp and woof of ordinary life (at Fotan) or made possible through reuse of abandoned facilities (at Cattle Depot). Unlike Beijing and Shanghai, where municipal intervention in such spaces was characterized by initial apathy or hostility but turned later to proactive development, the situation in Hong Kong is vastly different. In one case (Fotan), there has been a persistent lack of interest, which has enabled sustained organic development. In another case (Cattle Depot), the governance of culture and urban space is fractured; the partial and splintered effort at integrating culture into the neoliberal fabric of Hong Kong as 'Asia's World City' sees little by way of positive results, and appears to be no more successful than its slaughterhouse counterpart in Shanghai, discussed in Chapter 8.

FOTAN: AN UNLIKELY ARTS CLUSTER IN AN UNLIKELY CITY

In the light industrial district of Fotan, a suburb of the Sha Tin District in the New Territories of Hong Kong, a number of art studios scattered across several factory buildings bear a quiet reputation as an organic part of Hong Kong's local arts scene. Numbering between 80 and 100 studios and well over 200 artists in 2010–11, the area comprising factory buildings began sporting a handful of arts studios around the year 2000. Among the pioneers were Lam Tung Pang, Tozer Pak and their classmates from the nearby Chinese University of Hong Kong (CUHK), all in search of cheap space where they could practise their art. As students, they could ill afford studio rentals. They turned to their mentor at CUHK, Victor Lui Chun Kwong. The fine arts professor bought a floor of units in an industrial building in Fotan and began renting them out to his students. It was a time when the property market in Hong Kong was slow, and factory spaces were emptying out as manufacturing shifted to the cheaper southern provinces of China. The units in factory buildings like Wah Lok and Wah Luen in Fotan became very affordably priced. Rumour has it that the professor bought several units within three hours, and rented them out to his students in as quick a time. Not long after, in 2003, as severe acute respiratory syndrome (SARS) claimed lives in various cities around the world, including Hong Kong, the property market in the city dropped still further. The professor bought more units and rented them out to still more students. Others followed suit, purchasing and renting space from grateful landlords and owners whose units would otherwise have stayed empty. Today, Fotan has, by far, one of the most organically evolved spaces for the arts in the city, developing beyond the official gaze, which has been trained on mega-projects and cultural infrastructure.

Just as Hong Kong is an unlikely city for organic development of the arts, so Fotan is an unlikely place to find an arts cluster. Artists are located amid surviving industries, so unlike many other arts clusters in Asia where the cluster is exclusively used by artists and related workers (such as theatre groups, galleries, photographers and the like), artists here are located alongside commercial storage businesses, food processing factories, garment and textile wholesalers and computer peripheral manufacturers. This means that the artists are simultaneously dispersed and clustered – dispersed throughout the several factory buildings in Fotan, but concentrated in the Fotan industrial estate. This departs from the situation of 798 in Beijing and M50 in Shanghai, where factories have all completely exited and entire factory buildings have been taken over exclusively by cultural/creative workers.

Incongruous Sustainability

Anyone traipsing past factories producing roast meat and fishballs, hardware stores and factories involved in woodwork and metalwork, before meeting an artist in his or her paint or sculpture studio, might well wonder at the sustainability of this unlikely arts cluster. Such sustainability may be questioned on numerous fronts: (a) cultural sustainability, that is, the ability to support the development of indigenous art and the evolution of a local idiom (Kong, 2009b) and the maintenance of conditions necessary for cultural workers to engage in their cultural work; (b) social sustainability, or the sense of support and community that comes with social interactions within the cluster and in the vicinity; and (c) economic sustainability, or the economic viability of the cluster.

On each of these counts, Fotan turns in a healthy report card. The artists at Fotan are optimistic about the cluster's cultural sustainability, despite some less-than-ideal conditions. Their optimism is derived from the geography of Fotan, particularly two aspects of the physical environment. The first is the physical space: the high roofs and spacious units allow for big pieces of work, features not easily available in crowded Hong Kong (personal interview, 12 February 2009). While the conditions of support for artistic work are more usually thought of in social, cultural and political terms (for example, a vibrant social milieu, a deep cultural heritage, open political conditions), the Fotan artists remind us that a very fundamental condition for sustaining certain types of artistic work is having appropriate physical space. In this respect, the factory buildings offer a related advantage: there are huge industrial lifts that allow the artists' materials to be easily transported to their studios (personal interview, 15 January 2010). The second aspect of Fotan's geography that the artists value, and that plays an important role in its cultural sustainability, is its relative location. Its proximity to existing light industries has provided a much-needed source of material for the artists. Many who do woodwork speak about the ability to purchase materials like wood from the nearby hardware store. The electrical stores in the vicinity have also served some of the artists well, with one learning his welding skills from the workers there (personal interview, 17 January 2010). More than the practical value of this proximity, the very grittiness of the physical space is what makes the place interesting for artists. As one gallery owner explained:

> We are in this industrial space, and the first time you arrive, most people will be like, what the hell is this? It is dirty, it is smelly, it smells like fishballs on one floor, it smells like barbequed pork on the top, and they are like . . . what is this space? But it is always these kinds of places that tend to be one of the best spaces for artists to be creative and do their thing. And you know beautiful things come out of it. (Personal interview, 17 February 2009)

For artists to be able to do their art, a very basic condition is to have the right kinds of space in locations that are interesting and that provide easy access to materials. This is so fundamental that it is not often remembered. In Fotan, these fundamental conditions of artistic and cultural sustainability are addressed.

A big part of the sustainability of Fotan is in the nature of the social ties experienced by those in this cluster, making the cluster socially sustainable. Part of the density of networks is due, first, to the pre-existing ties among the artists (by virtue of their links with the CUHK). Indeed, at the beginning and for a few years thereafter, it was estimated that more than half of the artists who had units in Fotan were graduates, students or faculty from the university. Many were friends, and either shared a studio or rented/bought units in close proximity to one another. Second, the linkages are not only within the cluster. Fotan's proximity to CUHK ensures continuing ties between the arts community at Fotan and the fine arts faculty and enrolled students there. The artistic interactions and sense of support serve as continuing encouragement to the Fotan community. Third, the ability to meet new artists in one place, and many of them at that, provides opportunities to interact, share ideas and learn new things. Fourth, the interactions are not confined only to artists. The sense of community is more broadly felt because of friendly ties with non-artists in the vicinity, such as the security guards who know in detail what the artists do and in which units they may be found, as well as the building managers, who make extra efforts to keep the place clean and make it more salubrious for the artists as the numbers grow, including cleaning the lobby and improving the image of the buildings. Fifth, particular activities have been helpful in generating opportunities for interaction. This includes the arrival of galleries in Fotan and the organization of Fotanian, a near-annual event since the first small-scale and informal beginnings in 2001, in which the artists open their studios to the public over several days. As one artist observed, the opening of galleries in Fotan has created the opportunity for 'some connection with different studios', as artists bring their work to the galleries. More significantly, Fotanian has enhanced the interaction among studios, as artists invite one another to visit their work spaces. While not everyone will participate, the numbers that do are significant. In 2008, 34 studios and more than 160 artists took part, a big growth from the original three or four studios in 2001. Indeed, the event affords the opportunity to bring artists, art lovers and the curious public to the cluster and, in thus acknowledging its existence, endorses its place in Hong Kong's art world. Sixth, perhaps the evidence of a mature community is the fact that not everyone feels the need to be constantly in touch with other Fotan artists to feel like they belong to a community and share a certain sense of identity. A full-time engineer who works on her art at Fotan on weekday evenings and weekends explains that the time is precious for her, so she spends most of her time in Fotan on her art and only occasionally interacts with other artists. Nevertheless, she explains that the fact of there being artists and friends close by is sufficient to make the place feel like an art community. This is a sense of an 'imagined community', as Ben Anderson famously described it, and 'existence value', as economists term it. The former term is well known to mean a community that is not (and cannot be) based on everyday face-to-face interaction among members, but is based instead on an 'image of . . . communion' (Anderson, 1991, p. 224). The latter term conveys a sense that utility comes from simply knowing a resource exists. In this case, even the fact that 'there are artists in Fotan who have never spoken to artists from other studios because they don't want to disturb others' does not diminish the knowledge and sentiment that there is a 'group of like-minded people in this community' (personal interview, 13 January 2009). The fact that the number of artists has simply grown over the years also means that even if people are not consciously looking for fellow artists to interact with in their studios, they will still run into each other, such as in the lift lobby or in the food stalls or hardware stalls nearby. The serendipitous encounters are as important in the development of a sense of community.

The many positive perspectives notwithstanding, the social sustainability of the cluster is not unchallenged. Two factors put a limit on the upbeat experiences discussed above. The first is the lack of pre-existing ties for some, and the second is the lack of a common space. While the strength of social ties in Fotan is in part built on pre-existing relationships, this factor is also its weakness. There are artists who commented on being an 'outsider', that is, not a university-mate of other artists, while those from overseas feel welcome but nevertheless not part of the network. Artists also comment on the lack of a common space, the existence of which could enhance interactions even more. In sum, some combination of a grounded (real) as well as imagined community is important to the social sustainability of such clusters. The former is facilitated greatly by pre-existing ties and highlights the important contributions to companionship and friendship that make the cluster socially sustainable. Even without the former, the latter is significant, for the sense that there are artists close by, working away in the solitude of their studios and the dark of the night, spurs the artists' morale, encouraging them in their pursuits. In this sense, the cluster that generates such a sense of imagined community is one that is socially sustainable.

Much as clusters thrive when the specific nature of artistic activity is supported (cultural sustainability), and important though it is to have healthy social interactions and/or an imagined community (social sustainability), another key dimension of sustainability is the economic viability of the clusters. As with M50, rents have been growing at Fotan as a condition of the growing popularity of the sites and the fluctuating property market. As the original reason that prompted rental of these units – their cheapness – became eroded, some artists began to move away, to other industrial areas such as Tsuen Wan or Chai Wan. In their place, richer artists and 'yuppies' moved into Fotan, which, in the view of one of the earliest pioneers, began to 'change the dynamics of the artist community' (personal interview, 13 January 2009). Another pioneer artist believes that the later artists also relocated to Fotan because they were attracted by the increasing popularity of the site and saw an opportunity to exhibit their works, in addition to producing them there. This motivation differed from that of the earlier artists, who were not so much driven by exhibition and commercial opportunities. The opening of galleries in Fotan elicited mixed reactions. To some, particularly the newer artists, the presence of galleries enabled the sale of their works. On the other hand, some other artists believed that the galleries would further contribute to rental hikes in the district since they operated as businesses, and landlords would be inclined to price the units higher with them. This would ultimately be unhelpful to artists looking for affordable spaces. In these ways, Hong Kong's Fotan demonstrates the same dilemmas that emerged in Shanghai's M50, between, on the one hand, economic opportunities and viability and, on the other, cultural sustainability.

Two key differences, however, emerge between the two sites, rooted in geography and governance. Unlike M50, located centrally by the Suzhou Creek in Shanghai's Puxi area, Fotan is relatively isolated in the New Territories. Fotan's location has simultaneously kept it from becoming more commercialized (thus retaining more of the original artists than in M50), while also attracting some moderate commercial activity (though not to the same extent as in the Shanghai site). In other words, the geography of Fotan has helped it strike a balance between original authenticity and the seemingly inevitable commercialization that comes with greater popularity and rental hikes.

A second difference is related to the governance of the space. In the case of M50, the municipal authorities recognized the growing popularity of the site and took it over, adopting the old factory spaces as one of the creative parks in Shanghai. The name M50 was a new christening – part of the rebranding that came with the transformation of an organic cluster into one governed by the municipality. Like M50, Fotan began without deliberate planning, and followed a natural evolutionary path over time. Unlike M50, however, the authorities have not adopted the site. Indeed, the use of factory space for artistic activities remains something the authorities turn a blind eye to. As one tenant reveals, there cannot but be awareness of the alternative uses (artistic and even residential) to which some of the spaces have been put, but the authorities have not sought to enforce regulations. Others are less sanguine, and worry about whether their 'illegal' use of the space might be discovered. Nevertheless, the evidence suggests that there are no attempts to regulate. This situation may be aided by the fact that the site has not been adopted as part of Hong Kong's creative industry agenda, which has focused very much on design, film, television, music, animation, digital entertainment and such, rather than the fine arts (Hong Kong Special Administrative Region, 2013). In this way, the official economic imperative has not exerted its agenda on the site, which has allowed it to remain relatively organic in form and evolutionary direction. The absence of an official economic imperative and thus the lack of new governance from the authorities has helped the cluster retain its independent direction, thus far, with positive implications for its sustainability.

CATTLE DEPOT ARTIST VILLAGE

In contrast to Fotan, the Cattle Depot Artist Village demonstrates how a site with much potential to contribute to the sustainable development of arts and culture in Hong Kong does not deliver for a variety of reasons. Here, clustering generates neither a grounded nor an imagined community. The interactions, collaborations and shared sense of purpose are somewhat partial and periodic rather than wholesome and sustained. Heritage is a liability, imposing (un)reasonable constraints on activities and behaviour, ceding the advantage it could have generated. Finally, the governance of culture and urban space is fractured. Responsibilities overlap, with different agencies adopting different stances and evidently little inter-agency coordination. Together, they contribute to a wasted opportunity, rendering this former slaughterhouse no more successful than its Shanghai counterpart.

The origins of the 1.7-hectare Cattle Depot Artist Village, as its name implies, lie in its past as a cattle slaughterhouse, the oldest in the former British colony. First constructed in 1908 in Kowloon's Ma Tau Kok Road, it went into disuse in 1999 and was then reopened in 2001 as Cattle Depot Artist Village. The site is labelled a third-grade historical monument,[1] and is made up of five blocks of red-bricked, mainly single-storey buildings. The original 32 arts practitioners (six arts groups and about ten individual artists) occupying Cattle Depot were resettled from Oil Street, where they had occupied a government general supply depot for about a year. In the early 2010s, only about 15 of the 19 units at Cattle Depot had been occupied on one-year leases, housing performing arts groups, visual arts exhibition venues run by non-profit arts organizations and some individual artists. Activities include alternative theatre, multimedia performances, new media production and installation arts, arts education, arts criticism, arts policy research and international cultural exchange.

Various artists in Cattle Depot have expressed satisfaction with their unique heritage site, extolling its spaciousness in highly built-up Hong Kong. One artist describes the sense of liveability, using words such as 'relaxing', 'more healthy', 'like having a vacation'. The heritage value of the site also appeals to a sense of pride for some occupants. Yet, this positive evaluation of the environment quickly gives way to a recognition of the practical difficulties of occupying a heritage site, for Cattle Depot's facilities were not made for arts use. Tenants shared how they had to do much on their own to improve the place, from putting in partitions between units to prevent rain from getting indoors, to renovating space at their own expense into a black box, including putting in lighting, audio systems and stage controls. They also had to put up with frequent blackouts prior to 2002, disrupting performances, and had to live with restrictions on putting nails into and repainting walls.

Even while these inconveniences could be tolerated, tenants complained about other less comprehensible prohibitions, for example, on the placement of plants outside the units in the shared public space within the compounds of the complex. Even sculptures – works of the artists – are not allowed, nor may theatre groups perform. Photography is prohibited. 'How can the place come alive with a spirit of art, if everything has to be kept indoors, and preferably behind doors?', one artist asks. It is difficult to understand these restrictions except to see them as the actions of over-zealous implementers, giving the very heritage conditions that provide the site meaning a constraining rather than enhancing role.

For Cattle Depot to exist as a socially sustainable site, two dimensions of its social existence need to be addressed. The first is the internal dynamics within the cluster; the second is its relationships with the society and community beyond it. Relationships within the cluster are partial and uneven. Whereas some report interactions with neighbours in the cluster, others complain that other tenants appear 'invisible', returning only once every week or two, often keeping to themselves. In fact, some space had been sublet to groups for storing props, which reduced the possibilities for interaction. Further, the policy not to accept new tenants in the late 2000s and early 2010s was implemented at a time when old ones had moved out, which did nothing to help enliven the place. The policy reflects the underlying official attitude – a lack of certainty as to future plans for the place, with inertia resulting. Below the official surface, however, some new artists have obtained space by sharing units with the original lessees. Such subletting thus circumvents the effects of official (in)action. Since March 2012, the place has been open to new tenants again, but only from one day to three months per rental, renewable only to a maximum of six months (Commissioner for Heritage's Office, 2013), discouraging the establishment of a 'home base' for arts groups and ensuring that longer-term relationships are difficult to forge.

In the latter half of the 2000s, as a reaction against official policy, five of the units at Cattle Depot formed a group to liaise with the authorities. The idea was first mooted in 2006 when the Arts Development Council (ADC) wanted to turn Cattle Depot into a performing arts space and to move all the visual arts groups and individuals to a new project in Shek Kip Mei (the Jockey Club Creative Arts Centre). The tenants did not want to move. In the face of an increasingly aggressive approach by the ADC, five of the groups got together to present their case to the ADC. The five – named G5 – comprised two visual arts groups, one multimedia group and two theatre groups. The internal dynamics strengthened as a result of facing a common 'enemy', and the members of the group have since extended their cooperation to take on other causes, such as an attempt to secure a collective grant for their activities, to secure a 'live' rental system to allow the inflow of new tenants, to set up a board to oversee the management of the artist village and to run an arts festival, turning themselves into the Cattle Depot Arts Festival Association. Some of these efforts have given the groups a sense of purpose, even if they have yet to fully rejuvenate the cultural and artistic life of the village.

With regard to the interface with the larger community and society, a recurrent view among tenants is that the arts space needs to be an integral part of community life and rhythm, to be part of the warp and woof of Hong Kong social and cultural life. Unfortunately, its relationship with the immediate surrounding community is not healthy. As one artist put it: 'Their image of this place is not good. People living across the street have no idea what kind of space this is. They think we are the scum of society.' This may be rooted in the fact that the surrounding housing is low-cost, high-rise housing catering to the lower socioeconomic classes for whom, in general, the arts mean little. For the site to be socially sustainable, it is imperative that it is able to attract people who value its existence and appreciate its offerings. While those who are especially interested in the arts – the 'culturally interested', as one artist put it – do sometimes visit, it is 'not yet a space for passers-by'. Indeed, another artist describes it as 'a bit dead', acknowledging the need to make the place 'more lively and vibrant'. This has been achieved to some extent through an event called October Contemporary, a month-long event first held in 2007 to promote contemporary visual art in Hong Kong. Eight of Hong Kong's leading art spaces and institutions worked together to present talks, workshops, exhibitions and performances under an overarching theme. Three of the groups at Cattle Depot participated; some of the events were held there as well. There has also been a book fair, which has helped to draw in crowds. As one artist put it, 'That was the first time that Cattle Depot was really used in a way that it should be used, and that was quite nice.' While successful for the duration of the event, the momentum and liveliness is unfortunately not sustained throughout the year, for as long as the space is treated as private space, with security guards at the entrance and the requirement that visitors show their IDs and sign in at the door for the best part of the year, the space is unlikely to be particularly welcoming. Thus, despite ideas such as October Contemporary, the Cattle Depot Arts Festival and the book fair, the artist village generally does not project a sense of inclusivity, nor will the artists find sustainability and encouragement for their art from a 'general public'. This state of affairs is expressed in quite depressing terms by one of the artists:

> I drew 19 crows on the wall . . . some of them are facing out, just like some of the artists are moving out. And why I drew 19 crows is because we have 19 units here. I choose crows because it is a metaphor. From the word crows, if you take down the 'r', you can see cows. And crows, you have a feeling that it is related to dying, going to die I mean. Because the government, they won't extend here, I think it is not sustainable, you can't see good prospects here. The exhibition . . . I took a big corner and just drew some crows on the wall, and I placed some blue pigment on the floor. The blue pigment, though the colour is very beautiful, it is poison. (Personal interview, 20 February 2009)

In evaluating the challenges to the sustainability of Cattle Depot Artist Village, it seems impossible to ignore the fact that the lack of clarity of official responsibility, the broken chain of governance and the lack of will has hampered the realization of the site's potential. One of the members of G5 explained how the Government Property Agency (GPA) manages the site, just as it does all other vacant government properties, treating it as workshop space for the artists and refusing to open it to the public. On the other hand, the government agency responsible for arts and culture – the Home Affairs Bureau – sees it as an artist village, but does not have direct oversight of the compound. The Tourism Commission, for its part, has put up a sign outside labelling the site 'Cattle Depot Artist Village', contradicting the GPA's refusal to allow the artist community to put up a permanent banner stating the same because it is not supposed to be an artist village! A temporary sign is allowed, and the request has to be repeated every two months. Reflecting this stance, official maps of Hong Kong label the site 'Cattle Depot Quarantine Centre'. The case thus demonstrates clearly how a site with much potential to support the sustainable development of arts and culture in Hong Kong cannot deliver better because the governance of culture and urban space is fractured.

CONCLUSION

Hong Kong's branding campaign to be 'Asia's World City', its cultural economy ambitions and its long drawn-out efforts to develop the West Kowloon Cultural District all add up to the need to see a broader base of arts and cultural activities develop. A city cannot be said to have a vibrant arts and cultural scene while relying only on 'starchitecture' (monumental, iconic building projects by celebrity architects) in the form of theatres and museums. 'Grassroots' cultural spaces are as important: Fotan and Cattle Depot demonstrate the promises and challenges in the development of such spaces in Hong Kong.

Fotan draws to our attention three characteristics of arts clusters that shape their development and sustainability: their genesis, geography and governance. First, Fotan's genesis has linked it inexorably to pre-existing sets of relationships; its sustainability is encouraged and supported by these social ties, which often go beyond professional acquaintanceship; there is a sense of community among the artists, many of whom have known one another before (re)locating to the cluster. Here, Fotan demonstrates that the spontaneous social relationships and strong reciprocal bonds described by the German scholar Tönnies in his concept of *Gemeinschaft* are important in this arts cluster's sustainability. Their significance stems not from resultant interdependencies, creative synergies or externalities but simply from the moral and social support that artists (young ones especially) appreciate as they pursue what is, at the end of the day, an individual journey in artistic discovery and development. The pre-existing relationships ease 'entry' into the cluster, facilitate comfortable social interactions and build a sense of community. Yet, precisely because social relations are more significant for moral support than for active collaboration in artistic work, clustering is also important for the arts even if the artists do not get together (frequently or at all) because the idea/knowledge that there are others nearby who are walking the same journey is moral support enough. This is the imagined community of artists and the existence value that they appreciate. This understanding helps us depart from the received wisdom about clustering, where the assumed benefits are about strong interactions and ties that lead to externalities and more creative, innovative and productive outcomes. For artists engaged largely in individual creative endeavours, the close linkages and interdependencies that might be important in business and industry clusters are less important, but the commonality of purpose and moral support feature more significantly.

Next, the geography of the cluster is crucially important in influencing its development and sustainability. This refers to location and physical space. Location influences the cluster's openness and accessibility and hence sustainability. Physical space influences (even determines) the kind of artistic work that can be accomplished, and hence the very nature of the artistic/cultural work undertaken.

Finally, the governance of a cluster determines whether it is able to develop organically or whether it is subject to multiple external forces (friendly or otherwise to the development of art and space). Fotan has not been co-opted into the government's creative industry agenda and has thus maintained its status as an organically evolved cluster, largely sustained because of affordable rents, suitable space and a supportive milieu (whether in terms of actual friendly relations among the artists and their neighbours or as an imagined community among the artists). The artists are loosely organized, if at all, usually during the open studios season known as Fotanian. Otherwise, there are no committees, no external agencies to interface with and no pressure to become something else according to a preconceived script about what a 'cultural/creative cluster' should look like or be. This general freedom to evolve and develop, if sustained, augurs well for the natural maturation of the cluster.

The same cannot be said for Cattle Depot Artist Village, however. Relationships both within and without the cluster are sporadic and minimal. Interactions within the community hardly take place, and there is poor recognition externally among immediate neighbours. There is thus a lack of palpable vibrancy within Cattle Depot Artist Village; the prospects for the site to generate social capital and be socially sustainable do not seem strong. The need to counter external forces – official pressures – has helped to draw some constituents together for collective action, but the outcome in terms of cultural development is weak. Classic cluster theory, which suggests the power of geographical propinquity to generate fruitful relationships among constituents, yielding externalities, is not borne out in this case. Clustering in and of itself does not necessarily provide conditions for supporting mutual growth and sustainable development.

Second, the case of Cattle Depot shows that despite the potential to draw on the cultural capital that heritage bestows, heritage can be a liability rather than the asset it is assumed to be. Because it exacts unreasonable detracted constraints on activities and behaviour (as in Cattle Depot), the heritage location has detracted from the project's success. The lessons that may be drawn from this analysis relate to the need for sensitive management of the environment and appropriate harnessing of the past.

Finally, the governance of culture and urban space plays a critical role in contributing to the sustainability of cultural and social life. The case of Cattle Depot demonstrates clearly how a site with much potential to contribute to the sustainable development of arts and culture in Hong Kong cannot deliver better because the governance of culture and urban space is fractured. Responsibilities overlap, with different agencies adopting different stances, with evidently little inter-agency coordination.

Ensuring the sustainability of cultural and social life in global cities is deeply rooted in efforts to ensure the sustainability of cultural spaces. The organic development of a cluster (Fotan) has led to better management, more engagement and more evidence of cultural productivity than a cluster (Cattle Depot) that has been fostered through government action. However, that is not to say that there is no merit in concerted governmental efforts in cultural planning. Rather, a more engaged and open approach, coupled with a greater understanding of the specific needs of the community and a clear vision of the developmental path of specific clusters, could go a long way towards developing cultural spaces that are well utilized and that contribute to the cultural and social sustainability of the city. Cases from other cities addressed in this book demonstrate that there may sometimes be merit in official intervention, if such action is moderate and/or well targeted.

NOTE

1. This refers to 'buildings of some merit', where 'preservation in some form would be desirable and alternative means could be considered if preservation is not practicable' (Antiquities and Monuments Office, Hong Kong).

10. Reusing old factory spaces in Taipei: the challenges of developing cultural parks

INTRODUCTION

In facing the pressure of globalization and competition between cities, Taipei has embraced the concept of a cultural and creative city and come to regard the creative industry as an essential element for its development (Florida, 2002a, 2005; Kong et al., 2006). The city has made efforts to construct and provide cultural space for the creative class, offer diverse cultural events to residents and promote the city's image. It has diligently tried to enhance its cultural capital by presenting, remoulding or creating venues with their own character and identity. By promoting the city's creative industry, the goal is to promote cultural consumption among its people, consolidate the citizenry's identity and cultivate the city's image by creating its own cultural characteristics (Hsing and Chou, 2003).

Like other Asian cities, Taipei also intends to capitalize on the cultural heritage in its old urban spaces. Publicly owned and abandoned factory spaces in the city centre have been regarded as suitable sites in which to establish creative clusters. Between 2001 and 2003, the Council for Cultural Affairs held symposia and seminars to collect opinions from various sources and to build consensus in promoting cultural/creative development. Since then, a series of policies have been implemented. However, various stakeholders, such as artists, scholars, city planners and creative enterprises, have voiced disagreement with the state on various aspects of the development process. Some felt that the creative parks should promote the growth of the creative network and support creative production by providing affordable space to creative workers (Lui, W.-T., 2004). Others suggested that it was more important to support the development of the creative industry by using the premises as a platform for interaction between the creative class, enterprises and cultural consumers (Huang, 2008). Another group of scholars pointed out that the space should be opened to the public as a cultural venue to enrich urban cultural life, or used to host international cultural activities for the purpose of promoting Taipei's global city status. Some emphasized the importance of conserving Taipei's industrial heritage (Hsia, 2006), while others observed that the emphasis on developing cultural parks has resulted in a lack of clear objectives for the cultural parks policy (Han and Liu, 2006, 2008; Wang, P., 2009).

In the case of Taipei's creative clusters, we found that the thinking and policy in reusing Taipei's old urban space to support the creative industry has shifted over time. Initially, the space was reused purely as creative space for artists. Later, the creative park came to serve as a multi-purpose platform, gathering the creative class, residents and art consumers. This evolution reminds us that the concept of reusing urban spaces by developing them into creative parks is not simply about a delimited space but about the location of creative production, interaction and consumption in a city, and about the dynamic process of the competition between various actors in a city's spatial structure. It is worth exploring the process of dynamic development and the functional transformation of those creative parks by answering the following questions: What were the forces leading to the transformation of function? How did the state intervene in the development process of these creative clusters? What is the influence on this city's long-term creativity and the effects in facilitating the city's cultural/creative class or creative industry? Does it contribute to promoting the city's global city status?

To understand how the development of creative clusters in Taipei compares with that in the other cities described in this book, we must pay some attention to Taipei's peculiar characteristics. On the one hand, its social atmosphere is relatively free and loose. This facilitates the transmission of ideas and news through the creative class, with minimal constraints placed on the content and display of their creations. On the other hand, the state's ability to push through its policies on cultural or creative industry development is weak and often stalled by opposition. Understanding these contexts might help give a clearer picture of how the state intervenes in the development of creative clusters. Issues discussed include the development patterns or strategies that have been selected (such as entrepreneurial, creative or progressive strategies), the investments in physical environment and facilities made in reusing old urban space, the priorities in allocating resources and the restrictions encountered in implementing cultural policy. In addition, this chapter discusses how these factors have influenced the development of this city's creative clusters, and their impacts on the spatial distribution of creative activities (production, social interaction and consumption). In order to explore these issues and to evaluate the sustainability of Taipei's creative parks, the study reviews the development process of Taipei's creative parks and analyses the interactions between the state, enterprises, creative workers and communities during the process.

In addition to introducing the general background of the reuse of Taipei's old industrial space in support of its creative industry, this chapter selects three cases to describe the development of Taipei's cultural/creative parks. The cases are selected to compare projects initiated by different groups, namely, creative workers, commercial enterprise and the city government, respectively. They are the Huashan Park, initiated by the cultural community; the Jianguo Beer Factory, initiated and operated by the Taiwan Tobacco & Liquor Corporation; and the Sungshan Cigarette Factory, initiated by the city government. Through the analysis and comparison of these cases, the roles played by the state, creative workers and local residents, and their interactions within the process of park evolution, are examined. This chapter then concludes with the estimated contributions of these creative parks to artists, the creative industry and local residents. It discusses the outcomes of efforts to promote the city's creative abilities or cultural influences.

The case studies also reveal the mechanisms of governance and evaluate the possible effects of a creative cluster policy that has been criticized by several scholars. For instance, Griffiths (2006) indicated that the 'instrumentalization' of culture might have the effect of marginalizing or displacing local cultural distinctiveness, weakening connections between cultural production and consumption and damaging the long-term viability of local cultural organizations. Other issues that have been highlighted by researchers include the difficulty of measuring cultural policy effects and the unresolved problems relating to governance mechanisms (see Barnes et al., 2006; Bayliss, 2007; McCann, 2007; Ponzini and Rossi, 2010; Ward, 2007).

JIANGUO BREWERY CULTURAL PARK

The Jianguo Brewery was built in 1919. At that time, together with the Sapporo and Shanghai breweries, it was one of the three largest breweries in East Asia. It was the oldest brewery in Taiwan and occupied a land area of more than 50000 square metres in the city centre. The brewery still houses antique pieces of equipment, or some might say 'works of art', that are now very rare around the world. Furthermore, the buildings in the factory are a specimen of Taiwanese architectural history as the red bricks used in the red chamber are identical to those used in the office of the president.

This section describes the efforts to maintain this industrial heritage and develop it into a cultural park. In the late 1990s, new breweries built in the suburbs and their efficiency in mass production meant that the old machinery and equipment in the Jianguo factory had become obsolete. In addition, the quick development of the downtown area around the brewery, and the desire of nearby residents to improve the quality of their living environment, meant that the factory faced additional pressure to terminate production. Under these circumstances, the owner (Taiwan Tobacco & Liquor Corporation, a government-owned company) planned to close down the factory and sell the site.

However, the workers and trade union felt strongly that they should keep Taiwan's first brewery open. They thus made efforts to keep the factory in operation, including lobbying the decision-makers of the corporation and the government bureau, coordinating with other social groups to raise the issue of industrial heritage and interacting with the local community to obtain their support.

In 1998, the trade union, with support from local scholars and local cultural organizations (mainly the Yaoshan Cultural Foundation[1]) put forward a plan for the 'live' preservation of the first Taiwanese brewery. In 2000, the city's Cultural Bureau accepted this idea and marked the site, its buildings, production line, machines and equipment as industrial heritage. The first brewery was successfully retained. Its historical value was enhanced when some of the old machines and equipment were maintained in order to preserve the first production line in the history of the Taiwanese beer industry. Together with some other historical buildings and structures, the park became a 'live' cultural asset or industrial heritage (Hsia, 2006). Other areas of the park were redeveloped under an approved plan, with the aim of establishing it as a multi-functional cultural park, incorporating elements of production, commerce, culture, tourism and leisure. The construction of the park was completed and it was reopened in 2006. It was renamed as the Jianguo Brewery Cultural Park in 2007. In the same year, the park was used as a venue in Taipei's art festival, when several artists, including international arts groups, were invited to the brewery to perform their creative works.

The impetus for activism mainly came from three groups. The first was the local cultural organizations that lobbied for the preservation of the historical buildings. The second was the trade union of the brewery workers and staff who were hoping to keep the factory and production lines open. The third was the residents from surrounding communities who wanted to shut down the factory and redevelop the site to provide space for public use. To satisfy the requirements of these three groups, the site was developed into a cultural park showcasing beer production culture, while providing space for culture, entertainment and tourism, including a sightseeing tour of the beer production facilities, dining and cultural activities. The development plan also satisfied the neighbouring residents' demand, with two hectares of land allocated for building a junior middle school, strengthening local infrastructure and supplementing public space for the community's needs.

The park has now become an important sightseeing and leisure space for citizens. Its 346 warehouses have become some of the most popular places for beer and dinner at night (particularly on weekends) and an attraction for many local residents and tourists. The venue has thrived despite its lack of artistic ambience. In fact, the venue has failed to deliver on its promise to become a centre for creative arts production. Initially, it was anticipated that the cultural park would become a venue for artists to interact, exchange ideas and exhibit their creative works, or even a space for creating new works. However, since the 2007 art festival, only a few arts and cultural activities have been held here. The activities that have taken place include a beer culture festival and a wine exhibition. The operator of the park, the Taiwan Tobacco & Liquor Corporation, undertakes these 'cultural activities' mainly for the purpose of marketing wine production and promoting its brewery as a sightseeing destination in order to achieve the necessary profits. Our interviews with numerous artists and an officer from the city government Cultural Bureau revealed that the park has not been able to attract creative activities for three reasons.[2] First, there are many different types of creative space available elsewhere in the city, such as the international artist village, which are better positioned to attract artists and creative workers. Second, there is an incompatibility between the requirements of artistic creation and the environment needed for sightseeing or entertainment. The park does not present an ideal environment for those undertaking creative works as many tourists present a source of disturbance. Third, creative workers did not actively participate in the development process and, as a result, the park design plan did not take into account their needs when allocating creative space. It is ironic that despite the 'live' preservation of the first Taiwanese brewery being initiated by local cultural organizations, the artists and creative workers did not feature effectively in the process of planning and decision-making and the demands for creative and exhibition space were not integrated into the park's main functions. In planning the park's development, the local authorities also favoured the requirements of the local communities and the trade union representing the brewery workers. In its eagerness to satisfy the requirements of these main stakeholders, the local government failed to consider the needs of the creative cluster, and therefore also lost the opportunity for potential international cultural interactions.

This case study reveals that the direction and contents of a creative park development are influenced enormously by the state's attitude and the interactions between main stakeholders at the material time. The main goal of the operational organization also shapes the development of the creative park. In this case, the Taiwan Tobacco & Liquor Corporation was mainly concerned with pursuing profits.

HUASHAN 1914 CREATIVE PARK

The Huashan Creative Park is located at the core of the city. Its distance to the main train station is less than one kilometre. A large part of the site was occupied by the Taipei Brewery, while the other part of the site was land made available after the railroad was moved underground. Built in 1914, the Taipei Brewery was one of Taiwan's largest liquor producers throughout the 1920s. However, the dense housing development of the neighbouring area, and the issue of water pollution in the process of liquor production, caused the company to close down the factory in April 1987 and move it to the suburbs.

With its excellent location, large size (7.36 hectares) and high market value, the parcel attracted great interest from many parties, including government departments, local communities and even real estate developers. In 1992, the Legislative Yuan (the National Congress of Taiwan) decided to build the new Congress building on this site. However, the new building project was soon shelved due to negative public opinion over the huge price tag attached to the reconstruction. As a result, the site was left abandoned for many years.

In 1997, a local artist group discovered the intriguing but abandoned premises. The group restored a small part of the factory and used it for their experimental performances. With its open spaces, high ceilings and attractive architectural style, the place soon caught the attention of local artists and the community. Artists from across Taipei visited and used the factory as an inspirational work space. The place developed into a creative cluster, a close-knit network of interaction and learning. At the same time, the place also caught the attention of local law enforcement over the issue of trespassing and the noise that the artists made at night.

Eventually, several artists borrowed the premises temporarily to host an international art event. After this event, the artists came up with a proposal to reuse the old urban space as cultural and creative space. In order to get this proposal accepted by decision-makers, they connected with artists, urban planners and cultural scholars. They put in a joint request to retain the old buildings and transform the site into a cultural and creative park, for supporting local cultural and creative activities and for hosting large-scale international cultural events. The proposal was approved by the Cultural Bureau of Taiwan Provincial Government in 1998, following which the landowner, the Tobacco & Liquor Bureau, entrusted the premises to the Cultural Bureau. From then on, the Taipei Brewery was replaced by the Huashan Art and Cultural Special Zone. However, the Cultural Bureau did not take over the operations of the park. In 1999, it requested that an NGO, the Association of Culture Environment Reform Taiwan, be responsible for the operation and management of the special zone. The Huashan Creative Park provided space to artists for their creative works and gradually became a full-fledged arts centre, with works and performances in all fields of experimental and modern arts. It became the first large abandoned industrial site that was reused to form a creative cluster in Taiwan.

In 2002, the central government officially listed the cultural/creative industry as one of the country's important development plans. As one of its policies, it adopted the concept of the creative park to achieve the multiple functions of clustering, promoting interactions, circulating ideas and mutual learning – providing a platform for fostering creative industry development. The Council for Cultural Affairs[3] began to analyse user demand and construct creative parks. The Huashan Creative Park was regarded as its flagship project. The city's planning authorities quickly completed the legal zoning readjustment and issued the necessary permits to bring it into force in 2003. It was anticipated that the creative park construction could push forward the redevelopment of the local community, strengthen the diverse urban lifestyle and vitality of the local community. One of the interviewees indicated:

> We expected that reusing the old urban space could extend the city's cultural assets and through the creativity, produce new motivation and force for the city's development. (personal interview with an officer of planning development, 12 August 2009)

In 2004, the Council entrusted the creative park to the care of L'Orangerie International Art Consultant Co. to expand Huashan's creative repertoire beyond the experimental arts. L'Orangerie organized many different types of performances and activities, including concerts, cultural festivals, arts expositions, creative markets (*chuangxin shiji* – space for creative workers (or dealers) to sell their creative products) and art exhibitions at both local and international levels, as well as graduation exhibitions put up by students of design and art. In July 2004, the council set its sights higher and prepared an ambitious plan titled 'New Star of Taiwan's Culture and Arts', which proposed to cluster creative industries, government offices, a pop music centre and other cultural facilities together in the Huashan base. Using a building technique where new structures are added to the top of heritage structures, the plan meant to develop Huashan Park into a comprehensive cultural facility. Unfortunately, the idea was not supported by the cultural and creative class. The planning process lacked a forum for public discussion and did not obtain feedback from people directly involved in culture and the arts. In particular, more than 20 000 square metres of land was set aside for administration and office space in the proposed plan, more than the proposed space for creative use. This led to criticism that the council had lost sight of the main function of the creative park. Artists and cultural groups united in the Alliance for Promoting Creative Huashan to request that the state hold a forum to openly discuss the direction and contents of the Huashan Cultural Park. They expected that, through the forum, a common consensus could be established and a solely bureaucratic decision could be avoided. However, the Cultural Bureau did not respond to the request. In October 2004, the alliance, together with the Association of Culture Environment Reform Taiwan, carried out protest activities to put pressure on the government. Tension was thus generated between the cultural administration and the local creative class.

In the beginning of 2005, the Council for Cultural Affairs took back management responsibilities and declared that it would operate the park itself. It closed the park thereafter to carry out renovation and improvement works on the facilities, including the restoration of historical buildings and the renewal of the power supply, telecommunications, water, drainage, fire prevention and air-conditioning systems. The park was reopened at the end of 2005. However, due to the lack of support from local creative workers and artists, the park has not hosted many cultural activities. Only a few local residents have used the space for their community activities (Wang, P., 2009). The development of the creative park in Taiwan thus lags behind that in other cities in the region.

The minister of cultural affairs was replaced in early 2006. The new minister made great efforts to repair the relationship of the government with the creative class. The council soon set up an advisory committee and a management group to discuss and redefine the developmental focus of the park. Finally, it was determined that the park should provide space for creative incubation, performance promotion and cultural product consumption. The state would not interfere in its operations and high-rise offices would not be built for administrative purposes. Instead, the right to operate the park would be given over to cultural or creative people through the mechanism of open tender. From then on, the direction and contents of the park were confirmed and the creative class once again worked hand in hand with the state in promoting the development of the creative park. In 2007, the Taiwan Cultural-Creative Development Co. won the contract to operate the park for 15 years, with a possible ten-year extension, and took on responsibility for renovating the historical buildings within the park. The new management team soon renamed the park Huashan 1914. According to the requirements of the contract, the company would have to complete the construction and restoration works before the end of 2010. The main operational principle is to promote Huashan as an essential platform for the exhibition of creative achievements, as a place for the exchange of ideas and as a transaction field for creative products. The aim is to enable the citizens to realize and enjoy a diverse cultural and creative lifestyle. It is meant to be a national-level public space, and an important base for the development of the creative industry. The management team was contracted to enhance the cultural characteristics of the site by supporting the development of the creative industry and establishing a harmonious environment in which artistic, cultural, creative and production activities may coexist. The park will therefore become a space of cultural vigour and creative production. The management team also expects to develop the park into a famous creative base in the Asia-Pacific region.

In reviewing the development history of this park, we were aware that the creative environment had been established before 2005. However, in the period 2005–07, until the Taiwan Cultural-Creative Development Co. was selected as the operational team, the state's intervention resulted in a tense relationship between itself and artists or creative workers. This poor relationship caused a delay in Huashan's development and resulted in the loss of many opportunities to compete as a top-notch cultural centre in Asia. From 2005 to 2009, the development of Huashan remained stagnant (Wang, P., 2009), as the company spent two more years renovating the historical buildings and improving the physical environment. During this period, Huashan did not contribute to the promotion of Taipei's status as a global cultural city.

Since it took over at the end of 2007, the new management team indeed put in substantial efforts to develop the creative park. The creative environment has been gradually established; the number of creative people who use the space has been growing ever since. The place has gradually attracted back various types of artists and creative people, including those in the fields of performing arts, music, drama, dance and film. In 2010, the park joined the public museums in the Taipei area as an important cultural venue and hosting ground for Taiwan's main cultural activities, such as music festivals, performances, exhibitions and a student design expo. In addition to providing space to the creative class, it also succeeds in connecting a unique architectural past with the modern arts.

From the aspect of reusing old urban space, the site of Huashan, a valuable site located in the city centre, has always been the target of various interesting groups who need to contend for space, such as creative workers, government departments, local communities and even real estate developers. The expectations surrounding this space changed over time. Even as the site was set aside to be developed into a cultural/creative park, the developmental focus and the main stakeholders also changed several times during the process. In the early stages, the space was used mainly by experimental artists for their creative works. Thereafter, the intervention of the central state restructured the operations and finally resulted in distrust, conflict and tense relations with the creative class. Even when the state invested more resources, the lack of support from creative people resulted in the stagnation of the park's development. It was not until the state and the creative class resolved their differences and decided to work together again at the end of 2007 that the park gradually improved to function with real cultural and creative contents. Since then, users have increased and extended the park's functions, from production space to space for exhibitions, interactions with fellow users, cultural consumption and leisure (Huashan Creative Park, 2005–09). During weekends, the park also hosts a creative market, which provides space for creative workers (or dealers) to sell their creative products. In this way, Huashan has also become public space for cultural consumption.

We can observe that the state (in the form of cultural bureaucrats) had to go beyond satisfying the demands of artists or creative workers. It also needed to consider the effective use of this valuable site and the public demand for access to the space. As the development of a successful creative industry is deemed key to the competitiveness of today's global cities, the state faced the additional pressure of time in expanding Huashan Park. The reuse of this old urban space was thus influenced by various dynamics. It was the outcome of numerous interactions and discussions among many stakeholders.[4] The strength of the relationships among the stakeholders also varied, alternating between conflict and harmony. Therefore, the approach taken by the state in its intervention was restricted by the complex interactions between stakeholders. In the case of Huashan, cultural officers had to learn to interact with different interest groups on the task of planning and constructing a cultural/creative park. Ultimately, the main gist of the state's intervention lay in transforming the old urban space into an open, public space where the people of the city could enjoy diverse cultural and creative activities.

In selecting an organization to operate the park, the state established the mechanism of an open tender so that it could monitor the competition between various interested parties. The organization that eventually obtained the right to operate Huashan for 15 years had to pay an amount of NT$20 million per year to the state as rent and for the right of operation. Although the use of an open tender has the advantage of avoiding or reducing disputes that might arise, this approach still has its weaknesses. Today, the question of whether a private company operating the park might be more concerned about profitability than cultural development remains unanswered. However, the signs are that the park's main focus has shifted from creating cultural production space to creating exhibition and consumption space.

There are many who would agree that Huashan might not be very suitable for the production of creative works as its central location, with the convenience of nearby transport and its proximity to the city's main electronic products market, would attract many tourists and disturb the working artists. This site may be more suitable as a place for interaction among artists, the exchange of ideas, the exhibition of creative products and as a place for cultural consumption. The cultural activities held here are targeted more towards Taiwanese people; most of the visitors are Taipei residents, rather than an international audience, as had been the plan before 2005.

Unfortunately, during this process of transformation, the networks previously established among different artists were lost or failed to continue to grow along with the park (Huang, 2007). Despite this, the issue is whether Huashan still maintains its function of providing space for artists or creative workers for the exchange and exhibition of their creative works. The state also needs to ensure that creative networks will not be lost due to the change in Huashan's main focus.

Interviews with local artists revealed that most of them hoped that this park could still provide space for creative activities. However, in response to the question of whether the space at Huashan was necessary for their creative works, the answer was no. They indicated that although Huashan did not provide space for their creative works, they could still find affordable space in Taipei, and their creative networks were still found in Taipei, including some at Huashan. Whether they would use the space (either for production or for exhibition) at Huashan would depend on the cost and the services provided by Huashan compared with other places in Taipei. In other words, there were no compelling geographical or financial reasons for artists to use Huashan, and the social networks there do not amount to either a real, grounded community or an imagined one (as in Fotan in Hong Kong).

In conclusion, Huashan has been transformed from a creative cluster to a multi-functional base for the creative industry. At an early stage, it was an essential place for artists undertaking their creative works. During that time, the park managed to aggregate a large number of creative workers and developed a dense creative network. It contributed to the city's cultural and arts development, providing a locus and opportunity for the creative class in various fields to interact and cooperate. Later, as the state intervened by investing resources to improve the physical environment, the park changed its focus. Its latest development plan covers the three aspects of cultural industry creation, circulation and consumption. Whether these aspects may be achieved and sustained in the longer run requires further observation of the park's future development.

THE SUNGSHAN TOBACCO FACTORY PARK

The Sungshan Tobacco Factory was built in 1937 as the first specialized tobacco factory in Taiwan. In order to build the best and biggest tobacco factory in Asia, the Japanese colonial government sent a team to Europe and the United States to learn the intricacies involved in building a modern tobacco factory. It used the concept of 'industrial village' to build the factory. In addition to production space, the factory was also set up with comprehensive living facilities for its workers, such as a staff dormitory, bathing room, medical treatment and nursing room, pharmacy and nursery, among others. Its architectural design was succinct and elegant. It began its operations in 1939 with 1200 workers, as a model of industrial excellence at that time. After World War II, the Taiwanese government took over the plant and continued with the production of tobacco. From then until 1987, the factory played an essential role in the Taiwanese tobacco industry, with an annual production value of more than NT$20 billion (the exchange rate in 2014 was about NT$30 to $US1). The plant closed down at the end of 1988, with the decline of the tobacco industry and under pressure from the development of neighbouring communities.

After the plant closed down, the city had to tackle the issue of reusing the space while preserving the buildings for their historical value. The city government held a series of symposia in 2000 to discuss the site's reutilization in view of cultural preservation and the sustainability of urban development. The parties involved in the symposia (artists, designers, scholars and officers, local communities) eventually proposed building a cultural park as well as a stadium at the site. In the same year, the Council for Cultural Affairs (the central government's department) also proposed a plan to set up a cultural park at the site, with the aim of preserving the historical buildings and ecological environment, and opening up the space for the public. This resulted in both levels of government (the central government and the city government) fighting to acquire the valuable land and, along with it, the right to redevelop the Sungshan Tobacco Factory.

In 2001, the city government designated the site as a historical site, including the office, the workshop, boiler room, warehouses, the lotus pond and transport track; it announced that these historical premises would be developed into a cultural park. The following year, the Executive Yuan (the central government) agreed to the city's proposal to build a cultural park there. It also approved the city's proposal to build a baseball stadium at the other end of the site.

The city government's proposal aims to provide a public park and complex by integrating cultural with sporting functions. But such a plan has received its fair share of opposition. For instance, several local NGOs insisted on developing an ecological park instead of a ball park. The site has an exquisite landscape and is the largest green space found in eastern Taipei. After the factory was built, a large number of trees were planted in the factory district. It also has a large pond, forming an aquatic and wetland environment. After the factory closed down, the site remained as a part artificial and part natural ecological environment. These NGOs argued that the Sungshan Tobacco Factory was a priceless natural ecological treasure in the city centre and that it would be myopic to destroy this ecological park. It all boiled down to a difference in values and opinions between the government, which wanted a historical, cultural and sporting leisure space, and the NGOs, who wanted to preserve the ecological environment.

Having paid off the previous owner of the land, a state-owned enterprise, the city government now owned the site. However, it did not want to develop the park itself, but instead held an open tender to select a private developer. In order to attract developers, the city government allowed for a limited list of commercial entities to be developed in the park. In 2006, the city signed a contract with a real estate developer to build a ball park with attached commercial facilities. However, the public believed that the development was in actual fact a commercial real estate project under the guise of a culture and ball park. According to the developer's plan, the attached commercial facilities (hotel and shopping mall) were larger than the stadium, and the commercial buildings were more conspicuous than the ball park. As a result, several NGOs opposed the development project.

With opposition halting the ball park project, the plan to privatize the development of the cultural park and its operation was also unsuccessful. The city government's plan to use the site for exhibitions, performances and public interactions, as well as to offer affordable space to creative workers, did not attract any willing developers due to the high risk and low return rate of the project. In order to simplify the cultural park's development and accelerate the renovation of the historical buildings, the city government revised its strategy in 2007 and decided to contract out only the operation of the cultural park, thus removing from the investor the burden of repairing and maintaining the park's historical heritage. According to the readjusted plan, the park would be divided into two zones. Zone 'A' occupied six hectares and covered all the historical buildings. The government had budgeted for renovation works on the buildings in this zone, with renovations completed by the end of 2010. The city also worked with the Ministry of Economic Affairs to develop the 'Taiwan Design Hall' in this zone. The hall has been completed and opened in April 2011, in time to host the 2011 International Design Alliance (IDA) Congress. The hall is being positioned as an integrated platform for the promotion of creative design and operated by a central government agency, the Taiwan Design Centre (TDC), established in 2003. Its main mission is to improve the originality and creativity of Taiwanese designers, to promote international design exchanges, to increase the market competitiveness of Taiwanese industries and to help enterprises build up their own brand (Taiwan Design Centre, 2014). Under the operation of TDC, the hall has been used as a creative workshop that concentrates the display and selling of creative work in one place, with the aim of developing it into an essential base for the cultural and creative industry and achieving the effect of clustering by attracting designers, artists and other creative workers. It has also been developed as a platform for international cultural interaction and connecting to global creative industries.

The other zone, known as Zone 'B', occupies a site 1.2 hectares in size and does not have any historical buildings on it. The city used the mechanism of BOT (build, operate and transfer) to select a developer to demolish the obsolete warehouses and construct new buildings that would complement the historical buildings in Zone 'A'. The development project must provide physical locations for the cultural and creative industries; create a diversified platform to allow artists and consumers to closely interact; and facilitate opportunities for cultural and creative industries in three stages of development: start-up/R&D, publication/manufacturing and sales. The project includes the construction of a 14-storey building, and is authorized to run for a total of 50 years (inclusive of the building phase) (Taipei New Horizon, 2013). The building was completed in May 2013 and has been operated by a private company since then. According to the operator, all the space of the building has been leased out, even though there are complaints about the high rents.[5]

In summary, the proposed development of this park has drawn criticism from various fronts; those who disputed the development of the ball park were especially vocal. It resulted in many years of delay, from the time the decision to reuse the place was made to the time of actual physical development. The disagreement between the city government and the NGOs stemmed from differences in values, particularly in the development process, where only a small space was allocated for creative works. It is highly likely that, as with Huashan, the amount of space provided would not draw the creative class. They will keep working on their creative projects in the larger Taipei area, finding the space they need at an affordable price. Their interaction networks are still based in Taipei, although not necessarily at the Huashan and Songshan Parks.

It is worth observing that after the direction and focus of the Songshan Park was decided by the city government, the BOT approach was used to redevelop and operate the cultural park. The adoption of this approach was due to the financial burden and the limitations of the city government's manpower resources. Although such an approach might allow the government to capitalize on the resources and vigour of the private sector, it opened up the difficult dilemma between the pursuit of profits or support for creative activities. A large amount of resources had to be invested to repair and maintain the historical buildings, a deterrent to most private developers considering rates of return and risk. After the government readjusted its strategy and took upon itself the burden of renovating the historical buildings, it became much easier to find a private sector organization willing to construct and operate the creative industry's development base. Unfortunately, although that made it easier to attract investors, it also provoked criticism regarding the main purpose of the cultural park's development. They questioned if the main aim of the investment was to satisfy the private developer's rate of return or to support the growth of creative/cultural activities. Ultimately, whether the pros gained with private sector involvement outweigh the cons is still an issue that has to be considered thoroughly.

After Songshan's 2001 appointment by the Taipei city government as the city's 99th Cultural Heritage Site and its renaming as the Songshan Cultural and Creative Park, it took ten years for the debates to play out and for the site to be readied for use again. On 15 November 2011, it was finally officially opened to the public. It is now positioned as the 'Creative Hub of Taipei', with the objective to 'nurture creative talents and energy' (Songshan Cultural and Creative Park website). Its webpage declares that it is 'not designed with a commercial focus, but rather, its mission is to kindle creativity and innovation and to be in synch with the interdisciplinary developmental trend observed in today's industries'. It is 'not just a platform for showcasing creativity and innovation'. Rather, it strives to be a hub for inspiring and nurturing the spirits of creativity by organizing various artistic, cultural and creativity events, including presentations of design, visual arts and cross-disciplinary events. Whether it will 'truly become a comprehensive multi-faceted creative center' remains to be seen.

CONCLUSION

These Taipei case studies demonstrate how old urban spaces have the potential to be reused as bases for cultural/creative industry development. They present an opportunity for altering the course of a city's cultural development and the restructuring of the city's landscape. In so doing, they attract the attention of the general public, which has its own sense of what the space could be used for, as well as arouse the interest of the creative community, who might force the government to pay more attention to their space needs. In responding to public demand, the cases described in this chapter reveal that reusing old urban space often entails the renewal of space to support the activities of surrounding communities. Regardless of the future of these creative bases, they have managed to change the local landscape and urban functions, and provided local residents with a more diverse choice of cultural and leisure opportunities.

The cases also demonstrate that the state plays an essential role in the developmental process of the creative parks. The development requires government involvement and investment: offering up the premises for development (land and buildings); initiating the redevelopment plan for the creative park and the surrounding communities; and investing resources for the improvement of infrastructure or renovation of historical buildings. However, the degree of state intervention and the approach used affects the direction and outcome of the creative park's development, including the types of creative activities carried out in the park. In the case of Huashan Park, the state changed its level of involvement from none (managed by artists) to full involvement in the park's development and operation, and then back to minimal involvement by opening the park to private investment. However, selecting the operator through competitive tender meant the spatial use cost rose sharply due to the cost-benefit considerations of the private operator. This has reduced the affordability of studio space at Huashan Park for artists or creative workers.

The characteristics of the executive organization will also affect a creative park's developmental direction and outcomes. Although the Jianguo Brewery Cultural Park achieved its aim of the 'live' preservation of the first Taiwanese brewery, in the hands of a profit-making enterprise, it has gradually become a place for sightseeing, tourism and leisure rather than a place for creative work. The case of Huashan is even more telling. In its early development, it was initiated and managed by the artists or creative workers. At that time, a creative network formed, with close interactions between creative workers from various fields. Later, the central government intervened and took over the park. Due to the disputes that occurred between the state and the creative class, the government's development plan could not be implemented. Finally, in order to repair its relations with the creative class, the state revised its plan and decided to develop Huashan as a creative platform and multi-functional space for cultural activities, emphasizing that the park would be developed into a cultural leisure space belonging to citizens. This unique development process, however, caused the existing creative network in the park to disintegrate and shift to other places in Taipei. Finally, the development of the Songshan Cultural Park was driven by the city government, which intended to build a ball park and cultural park at the same site. This combination was not welcomed by the creative community; the city government experienced criticism and resistance from several NGOs. As a result, the project was delayed for ten years before it was opened to the public. Whether it has truly developed into a creative cluster, fulfilling its stated mission, remains to be seen.

These case studies all serve to show that the main contributions of the government in the development of a creative industry are in offering vacated public space to creative people and playing the role of facilitator through infrastructural support. Too much intervention or the setting of multiple goals in cluster development may not truly help the creative industry. However, when it comes to promoting the city's creativity, it is not enough simply to rely on governmental efforts. It is also important to take into account interactions with the creative class and other stakeholder groups in undertaking a cultural park development project. The case of Huashan shows that the failure to integrate opinions from the creative class resulted in the government's inability to push through with the development of a creative park, despite the fact that the plan had visionary prospects and great ambition.

This chapter shows that the cultural activities eventually carried out at each of these parks were mainly consumed by the local community and Taiwanese citizens. Although these cultural parks were initially planned as a platform for international cultural interactions and for connections to global creative industries, and although many foreign tourists have visited these parks, they have not yet built up sufficient influence to become an important base for international cultural activities. This indicates that the investments put into the cultural parks have not yet yielded significant returns in promoting Taipei's status as a world-class cultural city. The main achievement of these clusters so far has been the enrichment of local residents' cultural life. This is not to be belittled, except that, at times, the main achievement seems more to be about enhancing leisure and entertainment opportunities for local residents than about truly enriching their enjoyment of arts and culture or enlarging the opportunities for arts and cultural workers to develop their creative work.

Finally, the chapter also shows that the spatial proximity afforded by clusters is not a necessary condition for artists or creative workers in their production process. Their 'production' sites are by no means limited or fixed to a specific locus, such as within the premises of cultural parks. More importantly, creative workers need a place that has abundant cultural assets (the city), along with an environment that is able to support and stimulate creative workers. They need affordable production space (studios) for carrying out their creative work. They also need places to display their products, to interact with other creative workers and to collect or obtain related information in their field. They require a space where they can sell their creative products and attract visits from the general populace. This space should be in a convenient location within a comfortable environment. This type of space is not easily created by any individual or artist group. It needs the government to intervene by reusing public premises and resources to establish a cultural park and generate a creative atmosphere that attracts creative workers and cultural consumers. Through the cases examined in this chapter, what becomes clear is that, perhaps, in the context of Taipei, spaces of cultural production are best left to be discovered and developed organically, while the government's contribution to the community might best be focused on the development of sites for exhibition and consumption. The notion of 'cultural parks', thus redefined, might achieve a better score on the cultural cities report card.

NOTES

1. Yaoshan Cultural Foundation is an NGO that aims to elevate Taiwanese cultural life and promote international artistic and cultural exchange.
2. Interviews with four artists on 11 November, 22 November, 23 November and 11 December 2008. The same opinion was also obtained from the interview with a cultural officer of the city government Cultural Bureau on 16 January 2009.
3. The Council for Cultural Affairs was reorganized and renamed the Ministry of Culture on 20 May 2012.
4. Compare Lui Win Ting's (2004) study, which postulated that Huashan was formed as a result of three forces: cultural regulation, cultural creation and cultural economy.
5. See the website http://udn.com/NEWS/FINANCE/FIN1/8784590.shtml (accessed 24 July 2014).

11. From education to enterprise in Singapore: converting old schools to new artistic and aesthetic use

INTRODUCTION

Particularly in the first decade of the twenty-first century, a range of related ideas surrounding the 'creative economies' were adopted by numerous government agencies in Singapore, signalling the optimism with which they approached the sector. Official discourse included references to creative/cultural industries, creative manpower, creative workforce, creative clusters, creative town and cultural capital. As we explained in Chapter 5, the economic potential of culture and the arts was championed by numerous political leaders, including and perhaps particularly by the then Minister for Information and the Arts, George Yeo. Agencies such as the Economic Development Board and, later, the Ministry of Information, Communications and the Arts (MICA), as well as the Economic Review Committee (ERC) of 2002 were active in promoting this potential. Official documents such as those we introduced in Chapter 5 (for example, *Report of the Advisory Council on Culture and the Arts* (1989), *Investing in Singapore's Cultural Capital* by the Ministry of Information and the Arts (2002) and *Creative Industries Development Strategy* by the Economic Review Committee (2002)) serve as reminders of the context within which we must examine the use of space for cultural and creative activities.

While we have examined the urban strategy in terms of the construction of large performance spaces and cultural monuments, we turn in this chapter to an examination of spaces that may be characterized as 'everyday spaces' for those in the cultural and creative community, spaces that we foreshadowed at the end of Chapter 5, such as that for rehearsals, workshops, storerooms, office space and spaces that, simply, artists can call 'home'. We focus particularly on the clustering of such spaces (cultural/creative clusters) and examine the resulting interactions, networks and collaborations. Ironically, 'creative clusters' are most commonly non-spatial in the official discourse in Singapore or at best aspatial, used as the defining nomenclature for industrial groups. Three 'creative clusters' are identified in official categories: 'arts and culture', 'design' and 'media'.

This aspatial use of 'cluster' does not imply that there are no spatial clusters in Singapore, whether conceptually or empirically. In official discourse, the idea of a creative cluster appears in the concept of a 'creative town', an idea contained in the Renaissance City 2.0 initiative.[1] The idea was that Community Development Councils[2] (CDCs) would work to develop 'Creative Towns', to be piloted first with a selected township. This town would serve as a developmental model for a 'vibrant, creative, culturally rich, entrepreneurial and technologically savvy community'. This prototype would then be fine-tuned and eventually adopted by the rest of the CDCs to evolve a creative and connected Singapore. The 'Creative Towns' proposal was endorsed during the Mayors'[3] Committee Meeting on 19 August 2002. A multi-agency taskforce involving private, public and people sectors was then set up to prototype the 'Creative Towns' concept at a selected township in order to

> unleash the latent creativity and passion in each individual; integrate arts, culture, business, design, and technology into community planning and revitalization efforts; enhance the ideas-generating capacity and entrepreneurship qualities of the community; increase cultural awareness among people; and promote community bonding, local pride and participation through arts and cultural events, and the employment of the newest infocomm and media technologies. (Economic Review Committee, 2002, p. 17)

The programme was eventually rolled out in 2005 under the name 'Creative Community Singapore'. Comprising a S$10 million fund to be disbursed over three years, the programme was implemented nationwide instead of, as was the original plan, piloted with a selected town. The CDCs are still involved. However, the cluster concept is more dissipated now, with the 'Creative Community Singapore' programme intended to nurture creative projects at the community level and build capabilities for supporting the development of the creative industries through seed-funding creative projects from the people, private and public sectors, and through providing facilitation, co-branding and marketing assistance to these projects to maximize benefits to the community.

Although in official discourse clusters and the concept of the 'creative town' have morphed into a 'creative community' initiative, the phenomenon of creative clusters can in fact be found in different ways in Singapore, even though the 'cluster' terminology is not used in relation to them. The most apparent example is the National Arts Council's (NAC) Arts Housing Scheme, in which old buildings (such as old schools and shophouses) are identified and converted into suitable housing for arts use.

Unlike the situation in the other cities covered in this book, old factory spaces are comparatively rare in Singapore, as industries remake themselves in existing spaces or as the bulldozer razes through defunct factory spaces in the land-scarce city-state. The old buildings in Singapore to be recycled have generally been old schools and old shophouses. Old school buildings have become available as the reduced fertility rate has resulted in the shrinking of the school-going population, and as newer and better-equipped facilities replace older ones, or relocation takes place for various reasons. The old shophouses have secured heritage and conservation status and have the potential for reuse (Kong, 2011).

In NAC's Arts Housing Scheme, premises may house a single arts group or may be multi-tenanted, with several arts groups and artists of the same or different art forms. In 2010, it was reported that NAC operated 43 properties under the scheme, comprising five multi-tenanted arts centres, 36 single-tenanted buildings and two co-located spaces in community buildings (Marine Parade Community Club and Ulu Pandan Community Club). Some are stand-alone buildings, such as in Telok Ayer Street (Telok Ayer Performing Arts Centre) and the Substation, while others constitute what might be characterized as 'arts belts' of several arts housing properties in close proximity to one another (on the same street). The most prominent arts belts are at Waterloo Street, Chinatown, Little India and Telok Kurau; they have been identified through collaborative and strategic site planning by the Urban Redevelopment Authority (URA) with NAC. Over the ten years from 1990 to 2010, NAC reported that the scheme benefited 135 artists and arts groups, including the 68 arts groups and 28 artists who were at that point resident (National Arts Council, 2010).

The scheme was first implemented in 1985 to provide affordable space for arts and cultural activities, in order to support the development of the arts in Singapore. A revision to the scheme was announced in 2010. The original scheme was designed so that buildings were leased to selected artists and non-profit arts groups at highly subsidized rates. Tenants pay 10 per cent of the rental charged by Singapore Land Authority, while NAC pays the remaining 90 per cent. The premises may be used for offices, studios, administrative, rehearsal or performance space. The scheme is open to all registered arts organizations. The criteria for the selection of the groups include good track record, managerial strength, artistic standard, level of activity and growth potential. In addition, groups are assessed on their need for housing, the merit of planned activities and commitment to organizational and artistic development. While motivated by a desire to support the arts, the Arts Housing Scheme only partially met the needs for proper working and rehearsal facilities. The buildings were old and deteriorated. The period of tenancy was short (three years) with no certainty of renewal, which made it difficult for performing arts groups to undertake refurbishment, at relatively high costs. The buildings made available were unsuitable in that rehearsals held concurrently by different groups became a source of irritation to one another. The simple solution of air-conditioning to filter out noise pollution was not possible because the old buildings did not have an adequate utility supply and risked being overloaded (Iau, 1988, pp. 37–8). Despite these problems, some housing was better than none. At the same time, there were not enough buildings to house the groups looking for accommodation. Since 1988, many more buildings have been refurbished, though it was reported in 1995 that even when the economic situation was good, and even while sponsorship for the arts had gone up, sponsors were more willing to support concerts and plays than the arts housing programme, which they saw to be less high-profile. This posed problems for arts groups that needed sponsorship to customize renovations to suit the interiors of buildings to their own needs (*The Straits Times*, 4 November 1995). Needless to say, with the Asian economic crisis in the late 1990s, housing the arts was not a top priority for many potential sponsors.

In 2010, a new framework was announced for arts spaces. It was motivated by the large growth in new arts companies and societies (from 2000 to 2009, about 520 new arts companies and societies had been formed; National Arts Council, 2010) and in response to feedback that the properties and housing scheme were inadequate, that new working arrangements of artists and arts groups had evolved and new types of spaces in creative clusters and community facilities had emerged. The revised scheme was more targeted, moving away from a one-size-fits-all approach. There would be three targeted schemes, introduced in a phased manner from 2011 to 2014: the Incubation Scheme for new, young artists, arts companies, associations and societies, community/amateur arts groups, established for no longer than three years; the Scheme for Developing Artists and Arts Groups, targeted at those established for more than three years; and the Arts Centre Scheme, targeted at mature, established groups that had the capacity to champion a sector or an art form, and were able to operate facilities to benefit the wider community, including shared facilities. The rental grant was marked to 80 per cent of the market rental, with a maximum cap. Those under the Incubation Scheme and the Scheme for Developing Artists and Arts Groups would not have to contribute to a separate sinking fund, while those under the Arts Centre Scheme would have to contribute 10 per cent of market rental towards the sinking fund, representing an increase of 5 per cent from the rate in 2010. Beyond the three schemes, NAC would also look into matching artists and groups with communities so that there might be co-location with community or commercial spaces. It would also look into the possibility of storage facilities through private sector arrangements, that is, a privately operated facility open to artists and arts groups for storage, props rental/exchange and props-making (National Arts Council, 2010).

The transition to the new scheme is under way, and the jury is out as to how much more successfully it will address the needs of artists and arts groups, and how, from a larger perspective, they contribute to the cultural life in Singapore. We now examine one of the clusters that came about because of the NAC Arts Housing Scheme, discussing the ways in which the cluster functions, in comparison to the stated ideals. The Telok Kurau Studios is unusual among NAC arts clusters as it houses only visual artists, as compared to the more multi-disciplinary nature of other clusters (Table 11.1). We shall examine how it has performed in relation to NAC's vision for arts clusters/belts, as articulated for one of the arts belts (the Little India (Kerbau Road) arts belt). Specifically, the intra-cluster dynamics as touted in much of the literature on clusters is assumed here: 'the diversity of arts groups housed here presents a good opportunity for exchange of ideas and learning from each other' (National Arts Council, 2014). The idea of knowledge-sharing (whether tacit or codified) to enhance artistic creativity is thus part of the explicit impetus for clustering artist(e)s together. It is also envisaged that the arts will help to revitalize forgotten areas.

By way of comparison, we also present an analysis of a second cluster, developed under different conditions for different types of creative/cultural groups. We examine the now defunct Old School, housing multi-disciplinary, multi-genre artists and groups, which operated on leased properties from the government, with a master tenant bringing together numerous tenants/talents, developed on a business model. Like Telok Kurau Studios, Old School operated on a former school site; but unlike Telok Kurau Studios, it drew on this history and heritage in its branding and usage of the site.

TELOK KURAU STUDIOS

Originally Telok Kurau South Primary School (1960–84), the buildings were turned over for use by the LaSalle-SIA College of the Arts until it moved out in 1996. In February 1997, the first artist tenants began to move in even as NAC brought in electrical supply. Today, there are two societies (the Singapore Colour Photography Society and the Singapore Watercolour Society) and 27 artists using the premises. The artists include

Table 11.1   Key NAC 'arts belts' and their occupants (as of June 2014)

Location	Occupants	Remarks
Waterloo Street	Sculpture Square, Action Theatre (a theatre group), the Singapore Calligraphy Centre, the Young Musicians' Society (YMS) Arts Centre and the Dance Ensemble Singapore	Nearby are the Selegie Arts Centre (with photography), the Singapore Art Museum, the Nanyang Academy of Fine Arts and the Stamford Arts Centre
Chinatown (Smith Street and Trengganu Street)	Arts groups that specialize in Cantonese Opera, Beijing Opera, Teochew Opera, music, theatre, calligraphy, as well as literature: Chinese Theatre Circle, the first non-profit professional performing Chinese Opera company in Singapore; Ping Sheh, or the Singapore Amateur Beijing Opera Society; Xin Sheng Poets' Society; Toy Factory Theatre Ensemble, a bilingual theatre company; Er Woo Amateur Musical and Dance Society (for Teochew Opera); and Shicheng Calligraphy and Seal-Carving Society; Harmonica Aficionados Society; and TAS Theatre (for Beijing Opera)	
Little India (Kerbau Road)	Bhaskar's Arts Academy (Indian); Sri Warisan Som Said (Malay); Dramaplus Arts, Wild Rice Ltd and Spell #7 (contemporary performance groups); Plastique Kinetic Worms (contemporary art space); I Theatre; and Maya Dance Theatre Ltd	From traditional to avant-garde
Telok Kurau	All visual arts occupants: two societies and 27 artists	

well-established award winners as well as up-and-coming younger ones, working in various media – watercolours, acrylic, charcoal, oils, sculpture and others. Some have been there from the beginning; others are more recent additions. While none live there, some do work through the night and occasionally stay over as their art engrosses them. Each unit of about 45 to 50 square metres is rented to artists for only S$100 per month (10 per cent of the actual rent) (prior to the new scheme described above), while NAC pays the rest to the Singapore Land Authority. There is an exhibition space, opened in 1998, to allow the artists to showcase their work. A management committee is elected from among the occupants, and an arts administrator is appointed whose role is to maintain the building, handle the office administration and help with organizing exhibitions.

Official discourse about the cluster comfortably adopts the logic and language of cluster theory. For example, at the 2007 10th anniversary exhibition, a commemorative magazine was produced, which captured some of the works of artists in the Telok Kurau Studios and contained key messages from the Chairman, Edmund Cheng, and the Director of Visual Arts and Resource Development, Lim Chwee Seng, of NAC. These messages reinforced the hopes expressed about arts clusters. Specifically, Cheng wrote that the 'Telok Kurau Studios [had] grown into a centre for *synergistic, creative relationships* where new and interesting Singapore art is conceived, developed and *shared amongst its established tenants*' (TKS, 2007, p. 3, emphasis added). Similarly, Lim suggested that Telok Kurau Studios was a reminder that 'arts housing is not just a space for the production of work but also an incubatory space *where artists can engage each other through practice and discourse*' (TKS, 2007, p. 5, emphasis added). Whether their language about engagement and productive relationships constituted rhetoric necessary for the occasion, sincere hopes to be realized or honest evaluation of the cluster's achievements, the seemingly inevitable conclusion had to be drawn that productive relationships must develop when a group of artists with similar interests are housed in a cluster.

In reality, how has the visual arts cluster at Telok Kurau Studios gathered meaning for the resident artists? Based on our observations and interviews with the artists, we conclude that productive relationships are neither inevitable nor invariable in clusters. Rather, in this cluster, reputation (cultural capital), repose (environment) and rents (economic value) seem much more important in constituting the identity and value of the cluster, defining and supporting its continued existence. On the other hand, social relations seem devoid of trust, understanding and mutual support.

Reputation, Repose and Rents: The Value of a Cluster

In cluster literature, social networks, tacit knowledge and trust relationships are valorized. The social capital (Fukuyama, 1995) derived is believed to constitute and/or enhance relationships to the extent that individuals and firms are more prepared to undertake risky ventures and reorganize their relations in support of mutual goals. Although there is nothing explicitly spatial about this, such social network relationships are said to be easier to maintain when participants are located in close proximity to one another (Gordon and McCann, 2000; Simmie, 2004, p. 1098). Geographical propinquity thus stimulates productivity.

However, in a cluster where the 'business' is art, and in a national context where the area is small, do these assumptions hold? We illustrate below how social relations are weak and trust is all but non-existent in Telok Kurau Studios, although it remains an important site in the visual arts landscape in Singapore. The accrual of cultural capital (reputation), the environmental effect (repose) and the economic realities (rents) supersede social networks and trust relationships in making the art cluster viable and valuable.

The identity of the Telok Kurau cluster, its national significance and its draw for artists are premised on its reputation as the site of concentration of nationally (and, arguably, internationally) well-regarded artists. When asked the key reasons why artists would want to locate at Telok Kurau Studios, one artist says, 'I think it is the prestige. There are a lot of big names here' (personal interview, 7 March 2008). Indeed, several of the artists readily named Cultural Medallion winners who have studios there. The Cultural Medallion is Singapore's highest award for artists; among the award winners in Telok Kurau Studios are Chng Seok Tin, the late Chua Ek Kay, Goh Beng Kwan, Lim Tze Peng, the late Anthony Poon, Tan Kian Por, Tan Swie Hian, Teo Eng Seng and Thomas Yeo. There are also Young Artist Award winners, UOB Painting of the Year Award winners and other accolades, which 'give a certain lustre' to the place (personal interview with artist, 22 February 2008). The congregation of individuals who have achieved high standing in the visual arts world makes Telok Kurau 'our so-called national studios' (personal interview, 7 March 2008), likened to the national studios of China and France (personal interview, 22 February 2008). In this sense, the reputational effect is what keeps the cluster going, generating a momentum for the addition of new artists and keeping the pioneers in place.

A second way in which the cluster gathers meaning for the artists is in the atmosphere and environment of the setting – one of repose, quiet, relative isolation and solitude. Several artists expressed gratitude that there should be affordable space made available where they could concentrate on their work. As one artist put it, 'I can keep the windows and door closed and quietly concentrate on my work. Because for art, we have to sit down and think about it, and not just go and do it any old how' (personal interview,

7 March 2008). Having the studio also allows separation between work and home: 'When my children were very young, I worked at home. But my children took my brushes and cut off the hair! That's why I found it very hard. And then sometimes, when I was halfway through a painting, they wanted me to play with them' (personal interview, 7 March 2008).

A third reason why the artists have found the cluster to be attractive is because of the affordable rents. As one artist put it, 'Even though the space is quite small and not ideal – it does not allow me to produce big works of art, like in New York – the rents are cheap and you can't get this anywhere else in Singapore. So I exercise my creativity and work with the physical constraints because the finances work well here' (personal interview, 7 March 2008). The economic realities thus prevail and, indeed, shape (the type of) artistic work.

Cultural capital, environmental effects and economic realities are not often qualities that are foregrounded in the academic literature or policy documents as reasons for the establishment, existence and persistence of arts clusters. They certainly do not feature as benefits of clusters. Instead, relationships (social networks, tacit knowledge and trust relationships) are celebrated as positive and powerful rewards for co-location. The experience in Telok Kurau Studios disputes the often presumed benefits of agglomeration – networks and relations.

Rivalry in Relationships

Not only is the optimism and received wisdom about social relationships in clusters not borne out in the empirical case of the Telok Kurau Studios but, with the exception of one voice, the reverse is true. The exceptional case is that of an artist whose teacher also has a studio in the cluster and who feels he continues to learn from his mentor. All other artists interviewed spoke (with varying degrees of candour) about the hostilities that mark the relationships within the cluster. As one artist put it, 'For ten years at Telok Kurau, there have been fights, fights, fights' (personal interview, 17 March 2008). The unhappiness is palpable in the words of another artist:

> What does he do? He sues fellow artists, uses the government, uses the media, uses big names! Don't offend him for he knows a lot of rich and powerful people and if you offend him, he'll sue you. He sued ten artists in the past and now he is suing one writer, and don't know what next. What to do? The media supports him, the authorities support him. (personal interview, 7 March 2008)

The lack of dense and mutually supportive intra-cluster relationships and the glaring absence of cooperation are manifest in various ways:

in complaints, in officious rather than humane relationships, and in a reluctance to engage in or the sheer absence of collaborative artistic endeavours. For example, one artist elaborates on a complaint against him when his spouse (also an artist in Telok Kurau) and children stayed over:

> We don't live here, but sometimes we stay overnight when my wife has a project going and I have painting to do. Then people complained – two studios complained about how we all stayed here and slept here and lived here! (personal interview, 7 March 2008)

Another artist offered by way of example two instances in which he felt the cluster was characterized by officious relationships rather than those thick relations of trust that enable support of mutual goals:

> Recently, I was sick. I had lymphoma, and only just got well. When I got sick, I told the committee but the committee didn't care, didn't tell the NAC, which we're under. Because of chemotherapy, my hand was numb, I wasn't able to sign my name. They sent me a letter to remind me about the utilities payment but never mentioned anything about my illness. They even cc-ed the letter to NAC, to let NAC know that I owed money for the utilities. But since 1997, I have never been late with any payments. NAC knows that. (personal interview, 7 March 2008)

> This year's committee chairman came to tell me that because I have a lot of students, they want me to pay more for utilities, because they say my students use the toilet often. But I told them I won't pay because I don't go out and recruit these students, they come to me . . . But the committee insisted that I have a lot of students who use a lot of water. That's just ridiculous. So I told them, if you want, you should hire someone to sit at the toilet door and collect money. (personal interview, 7 March 2008)

Given such experiences, it is unsurprising that there are hardly any artistic interactions and cooperative efforts. As one artist observed:

> I don't see any exchange or interaction in Telok Kurau. It's very sad. Maybe it's the arts circle or maybe it's Telok Kurau. They very seldom really sit down to discuss . . . I find it very difficult. We have nearly 30 artists; we have nine committee members. When we want to organize any talks or any activities or any exhibitions, we have very little support. They don't come in to help you. I have to work a lot as a volunteer. The administrator also helps. We get very little support . . . I find it very disappointing. It's very hard. There are those who might know about art theory, art movements in the world, what's happening recently, this and that. They might have new ideas, but they don't share. Some of the good artists, they don't share. Everybody is like this! (personal interview, 22 February 2008)

The fact that visual artistic work is largely an individualistic enterprise (certainly by comparison to the performing arts) and that there is intellectual property involved in the creative work may be part of the reason for the lack of more sharing, cooperation and collaboration, and for the more atomistic experience in a visual arts cluster such as Telok Kurau. This raises the question of whether, in this field of art, cluster logic cannot prevail and collaborations cannot ensue even if common interests intersect and relationships develop. The artists themselves believe in the possibility, even if in reality there has been little cooperation. As one artist lamented:

> there can be value in the cluster, for example, exhibitions can be done collectively, and shared experience can make the event better. Unfortunately, this positive benefit has not been realized. (personal interview, 22 February 2008)

This view is echoed by another artist, though his view of a more hierarchical approach would not be the only model nor indeed the most appropriate one for this group of artists, more than several of whom have been lauded in their own right and who may not see themselves as working to someone else's lead:

> This place will be better if we could cooperate. Cooperate and listen to one leader, one art director. Then we can work and follow the lead, have shows and work towards them, like the New York schools. But here, we fight, fight, fight. Mine is better, no, special arts is better, or must be Cultural Medallion winner, or watercolour is out. (personal interview, 7 March 2008)

That cooperation of this sort, with an art director setting the direction, may be difficult is evident in one artist's assessment of what the root cause of the problem is – rivalry:

> This is because I am a threat to them. My wife and I are from [name of school]. It is famous and has produced some of the best artists. But we get no official support because the official support goes to the same few ones. Still, I leave them alone or they might come and sue me. (personal interview, 7 March 2008)

Beyond perceived personal jealousies, there can sometimes be real conflicts of interest:

> We are in the same trade, and sometimes you don't even know when you have offended them. It's conflict of interest. If I secure this project, it's mine, and someone else doesn't get it, so there's hatred and such. (personal interview, 7 March 2008)

Evidence suggests, therefore, that there is no causal relationship between geographical propinquity and the development of positive social relations. Indeed, the close proximity puts strains on relationships, which might not be as immediate or as apparent if it were not for co-location. It is not difficult, when suspending for one moment the somewhat hypnotic grip of cluster logic, to see that there is really no reason to believe that physical proximity should be determinate on the development of mutual understanding, tacit knowledge, social networking and a conducive environment for innovation and expressions of creativity. As the case of Telok Kurau Studios demonstrates, the opposite may sometimes be true, that proximity brings its own tensions and conflicts.

A Significant Node in Singapore's Cultural Landscape

Rather than a cluster in danger of demise, Telok Kurau continues to be a well-known site in Singapore's visual arts landscape. Despite the quarrels, artists are reluctant to give up their space in Telok Kurau, 'even if they don't fully utilize it' (personal interview, 22 February 2008). One such artist explains that he is not always at Telok Kurau because he has more than one studio, and the other location is more vibrant. His reluctance to give up the Telok Kurau space is practical: the rent is cheap and he needs two studios for his two different genres of work (sculpture and painting). Even those whom fellow artists believe have not contributed significantly to the art scene continue to stay; NAC has difficulty moving them out because '[t]hey will appeal. They will get somebody to write them a letter, to appeal for them to stay' (personal interview, 22 February 2008). The cluster thus has a sustaining momentum.

If geographical propinquity does not in itself generate fruitful relationships among the artists, and this in turn yields no accruing externalities, socially or culturally, why then does the cluster have a sustaining momentum? In this case, reputation, repose and rents go a long way to explain the continued stability of the cluster. The concentration of well-known, often award-winning, artists in Telok Kurau has created a reputational effect so that the whole is greater than the sum of the parts. Artists (perceive that they) derive cultural capital from location in the cluster. The environment is conducive for quiet contemplation and solitary work, which the artists value. The pragmatic economic benefits of cheap rents, conditions made possible by NAC, help to win the day.

OLD SCHOOL

Unlike Telok Kurau Studios, Old School was a privately organized creative hub located at 11 Mount Sophia. The premises used to house the Methodist Girls' School (from 1925 to 1992), the Singapore Hotel Association Training and Educational Centre (SHATEC, from 1993 to 2001) and St Francis Methodist School (from 1995 to 2001). The site was left vacant for several years after SHATEC and St Francis Methodist School moved away. In May 2007, the Singapore Land Authority (SLA) awarded the site to 11 @ Mount Sophia Pte Ltd, a private enterprise established by a group of five individuals: three directors who provided the investment capital, one creative director and one publicist. Together, the group wished to establish a creative hub characterized by multi-genre and multi-disciplinary creative arts.

Old School retained the former school buildings and, some would say, much of its charm and vibrant energy. Its nearly 140 000 square feet of space comprised a mix of buildings and open spaces that had clearly originated as school grounds made for young people to run around on. From the start, SLA made it clear that the premises would be leased on a two-year basis (2007–09) with an additional one-year option, and that the temporary use would have to give way to residential development, for which the area was zoned in the 2008 Master Plan. Rent at around S$36 000 per month, payable to SLA, was high compared to that available under NAC Arts Housing, but a steal for the location in the heart of the city and the size, when compared to commercial rates. Perhaps this was what allowed the company to spend an initial S$2.5 million to renovate the premises, install electricity and water, and generally make the area usable and pleasant, despite knowing that the lease was short.

Old School closed down in June 2012 after five successful years. Closure did not come about because of a lack of activity or a failed commercial enterprise; in fact, there were many efforts to protest its closure and appeals to the authorities to reconsider (*The Straits Times*, 23 October 2011, 11 November 2011). As it was, Old School outlasted the two-plus-one-year lease originally stipulated, as the authorities allowed the lease to be extended twice beyond 2010 to June 2012. Nevertheless, in December 2011, the master tenant of Old School was informed by SLA that the lease would not be extended any further beyond June 2012. In January 2012, Old School's management tried to negotiate for a further extension, but was turned down by the URA in March 2012 (*The Straits Times*, 23 October 2011, 14 April 2012). From early 2012, some of the tenants started moving out (*Wall Street Journal*, 23 November 2011). The site was put up for sale in the first half of 2013 by the URA to private developers, the only concession being that two buildings had to be conserved and the site must be sold without any building demolished, so that developers would have the option to retain any building for their use. The site attracted nine bids from various private developers. The bid was eventually won by a consortium consisting of Hoi Hup Realty, Sunway Developments and SC Wong Holdings, at S$442.3 million (*The Straits Times*, 13 September 2013). The premises were completely closed and sealed off in September 2013, and the buildings demolished by April 2014. Meanwhile, many Old School tenants have moved elsewhere, testimony to the fact that, as individual businesses, artists, designers, architects and so forth, they were viable (sometimes more than viable), and that Old School had the potential to thrive and grow.[4]

Officially opened in December 2007, Old School housed over 30 tenants by the time it was fully occupied. Tenants were from different backgrounds and worked in different genres. As one of the members of the founding group explained: 'As long as they are creative, they have a place here. They could be in design, they could be in production, they could be in gaming, they could be multimedia' (personal interview, 21 February 2008). Tenants included Osage Gallery, an international art gallery (with a presence in Hong Kong, Shanghai and Beijing); famous Singapore artists Baet Yeok Kuan, Lim Poh Teck and the late Chua Ek Kay; a well-known photography duo who run their practice under Mark Law & Wee Khim Photography; and one of Singapore's most famous fashion designers, Wykidd Song's atelier WK Design. Old School was also home to Sinema Old School, the self-described 'indie space' for supporting a 'cozy cinematic experience with 136 sofa-style plush leather seats and state-of-the-art projection and sound system' (Sinema, 2009). Other well-known tenants included Works Design, the studio fronted by Theseus Chan, the man behind the successful CDG Guerilla Store in Singapore. Mikoishi Studio, an international gaming production house, also set up in Old School.

These activities and tenants reflect the multi-genre, multi-disciplinary character that its founders intended. However, they did not entirely fulfil the conditions that the URA had initially set out, as interviews with the founding members revealed. Zoned for residential use, the temporary, interim lease was to fill a space that might otherwise have simply stood empty. As part of the creative industry initiative, the URA played its part by designating the space for arts, drama and music use. The founding group were certain that as a private entity, they would not be profitable if they kept to the straight and narrow definition of 'arts, drama and music' as delineated by the URA. From the planning authority's perspective, a list of creative activities failed the 'arts' test – film was not considered as part of the arts; nor were production houses (for music or film), design or publishing. To fulfil the criteria, effort was made to bring in galleries (such as the regional player Osage). Further, Old School adopted the Philharmonic Orchestra, the Philharmonic Chamber Choir and re:mix (a music group), offering them rent-free rehearsal space, though the groups would be responsible for utilities and expected to put on a charity event once a year. In this way, the founding group demonstrated their efforts at fulfilling the criteria, while simultaneously 'flouting' them by bringing in fashion design, film, gaming, architecture and so forth. They recognized that the URA had 'backed up' in allowing the project to proceed as long as a certain proportion of the space was for 'arts, drama and music'.

How did the founding group succeed in attracting numerous famous artists, designers and other creatives to set up in Old School? What was it that led the tenants to speak so positively about the 'creative vibes' and the 'creative juices' that flowed? What attracted the tenants and how did it become a 'buzzing place' – 'very chill' – and the 'hot spot' in creative clusters, with the potential to be 'Singapore's equivalent of Paris's Montmartre', to use the words of various tenants? What lessons might city authorities learn from this case, and how well might the experience and ideas travel?

First, the founding group approached the development of Old School as a business from the start, with a product to sell. As a business with a short time frame for achieving success (given the short lease), the founding group recognized that it was critical to have clarity of concept, positioning and branding. As the publicist in the group explained, it was crucial to 'define what the space would be', 'who it should attract as tenants' and 'what sort of crowd it would attract' (personal interview, 21 February 2008). Based on the brand definition, 'we started to develop the look and feel of the place, the tonality of the place, the corporate identity, our marketing, our press messaging, our public messaging, what kinds of collaborations we should be after' (personal interview, 21 February 2008). They further elaborated that they did not want to create a 'Disneyfied, highly curated space' but a 'very villagey' kind of place where people interacted freely and did not feel constrained (personal interview, 21 February 2008). The clear vision ensured that they chose their tenants carefully. The selection was very much an exercise in composition, which laid the foundation for a place with 'creative vibes' and 'a lot of creative juice' (personal interview, 13 March 2008):

> We were careful about selecting our tenants. They have to come from the creative arts space. And we wanted a nice mix, so when people applied, we said yes or no based on whether we thought there was a good complement. No,

we've got too many design studios. Now, we want production houses. No, we don't have a gaming studio, can we find a gaming studio. It was that sort of discussion that we had. (Personal interview, 21 February 2008)

Similarly, the types of events hosted at Old School were part of the effort to 'brand' the place and establish its 'tonality'. As Old School established itself, it was quickly able to attract the likes of Fendi and Burberry to host corporate events there. These events brought in visitors to Old School of the 'type' that fit the 'tonality' and 'chimed with the vibes' (personal interview, 28 March 2008).

Of course, not all businesses succeed, so the question remains as to why Old School managed to attract talents and tenants in the creative industries, create a buzz and draw in visitors. In particular, as many tenants described, the place was run down, 'really in quite a bad shape' and, in fact, a 'total mess' when the master tenant first took possession of the site and started trying to attract subtenants. The state was such that 'nobody wanted it'. The change in three months was remarkable. Our observations and interviews suggest seven significant factors.

First, an analogy might be drawn with the ways in which malls attract tenants. The ability to pull in a major anchor tenant whose prestige and name recognition draws in other tenants finds a parallel here. Several tenants pointed to the first couple of 'big name' tenants whose presence drew in other creative workers. These draws included well-known photography duo Mark Law and Wee Khim, and 2006 President's Design Award winner Theseus Chan. Once these tenants moved in, many others decided to follow suit before long. One tenant was very clear about Chan's reputation and his concomitant expectations: 'Because Theseus was around, we knew that he was going to be very particular about how the place looked, and the original state was not going to last long, so we took the space because we happened to trust that, and know him, and know the guys in the other block, Wee Khim and Mark Law.' As another interviewee shared:

> As the prospective tenants came and we started sharing with them that so-and-so is here, they said 'oh wow, I want to be there too'. And that is exactly what people who haven't gotten space here have told us, 'oh my god, I want to be here, all the coolest people, all the edgy people who do good work, all the famous people are here'. (Personal interview, 21 February 2008)

The reputational effect that was apparent in the case of Telok Kurau Studios also played a key role in the development of Old School. In this case, it was instrumental in bringing in tenants. In the case of Telok Kurau, it led to tenants staying put despite unpleasant relations.

Second, unlike Telok Kurau that housed only visual artists (albeit of different media), Old School was insistently multi-disciplinary, multi-genre and multimedia. This was part of the vision and part of the attraction for its tenants. Rather than rivalry among those working in the same field, as in the case of Telok Kurau, the potential for collaboration was real across different genres, disciplines and media:

> No discipline is in the box anymore today. When you look at fashion, there is art in there because you can see artists collaborating with fashion designers on their clothes. There is music, there are shows that are curated to music. There is soundscape, there is lightscape, there is landscape. The fact that we have Philharmonic Orchestra here, together with Sinema, has already given them an idea where they want to present silent movies but as the silent movies play, the Philharmonic Orchestra will play music to the film. That is collaboration. (Personal interview, 18 February 2008)

A third factor was the way in which the founding group managed the place, as a 'sort of white cube where they could do whatever they wanted in the office', 'come to work in shorts and tee shirts, in their Havaianas, that's the kind of environment they want. They don't want to be restrictive. If they want to ponder and think about a concept, they can sit on the corridor and look at the trees and just be inspired, and that is what they like' (personal interview, 21 February 2008). Tenants appreciated that the place had a relaxed and open ambience, and did not feel 'corporate', 'sterile' or 'stultified' (personal interview, 11 March 2008). This contrasts with some of the restrictions in NAC Arts Housing (Kong, 2009b) and the experience in Cattle Depot in Hong Kong, as discussed in Chapter 9.

Fourth, specific attention was paid to what might draw visitors to the site. Weaving in amenities for consumers, particularly eateries, was another part of the business thinking, recognizing the tenants' need for somewhere to eat and have coffee, and also to attract visitors. Thus, restaurants, bistros and cafés were brought in, from the now well-regarded Wild Rocket, serving Italian food, to Bistro Gaga, Milk Bar and Recess. They offered tenants a place to gather and socialize; it was not uncommon to observe neighbouring tenants gathering for drinks in the evenings. The dinner crowd also added a buzz to Old School, as a food-loving Singapore public found reason to visit.

Of course, a fifth factor was critical – the location – which predisposed it to a downtown crowd. The central city location also enabled easy access for clients of the creative businesses. Equally important for some of the tenants was the proximity to the cultural precinct in the central city, which allowed them to be in touch with other cultural and creative activities with ease. At the same time, the uniqueness of this location bears mention, described by one of the tenants as 'in the city but not quite in the city', a reference to its hilltop location, granting it a certain tranquility in the midst of the urban bustle. The physical environment, with its greenery, the 'nice canopy of trees', the spacious grounds and the high ceilings were all valued (see also Kong, 2009b for similar sentiments expressed by tenants in another Singapore cluster, Wessex Estate). This sixth factor is reminiscent of the appreciation for Beijing's 798, though in that case it was the Bauhaus architecture that mattered. The combined effect of the two factors of location and physical environment prompted one tenant to sum it up pointedly thus: 'the magic of it is just here'. Alas, in anticipation of the closure once the lease ran out, a tenant lamented how 'all will be lost and cannot be recreated elsewhere' (personal interview, 12 March 2008).

Finally, the founding group drew on the symbolism associated with the former school, and marketed it accordingly. In so doing, it was effective in appealing to those who valued heritage and social memory; particularly, it appealed to generations of schoolgirls who had studied at Methodist Girls' School. For example, in its toponymic selection, it chose to name a café 'Recess', evoking memories of the well-loved time in between classes, and another 'Milk Bar', again reminiscent of younger days. We observed during our fieldwork that the space was rented out for a wedding with a 'schooldays' theme, featuring a 'tuckshop'-style reception.

The outcome was a hive of activity, with tenants enthused by the creative buzz and visitors adding to the tonality. Indeed, this was no nine-to-five site. Many worked late, including designers and architects rushing their projects late into the night and musicians in the adopted groups arriving to rehearse only after their day jobs. All this amounted to a vibrant environment even in the wee hours of the morning. As an artist commented: 'There was one night when I worked till 3 am. I thought the place would be deserted, but when I went to the carpark, everyone was still here. Lights were still on everywhere; people were still working. The people here work very hard, especially the designers. And knowing that everyone is working makes you want to work even harder!' (personal interview, 18 January 2008).

All this came to a close in June 2012. As we complete this manuscript, the site stands only as a pile of rubble, buildings largely demolished, tenants relocated, with piling equipment soon to move in.

CONCLUSION

In this chapter, we have introduced Singapore's Arts Housing Scheme as the government's policy to house artists and arts groups in old buildings, in the form of arts clusters or arts belts. We have also introduced government formulations of creative industry and creative cluster initiatives. The Arts Housing Scheme appears similar in concept to the textbook cultural creative cluster in one respect: it co-locates artists, with such clustering believed to produce conditions that enhance collaboration and spark creativity. However, the highly subsidized arts belts (targeted primarily at amateur artists and arts groups in need of subsidy) differ from those creative clusters populated by creative businesses and characterized by cultural entrepreneurship and cultural consumption (such as in Shanghai's creative parks). On the other hand, the official 'creative clusters' in Singapore are actually industry groups rather than spatial entities.

The case studies examined in this chapter illustrate the parallel universes that the two clusters examined seem to occupy. Indeed, this is noted by the artists who have studios at both clusters. Telok Kurau Studios is mono-disciplinary: it houses only visual artists; Old School was insistently multi-disciplinary and multi-genre. Telok Kurau Studios is government-initiated; Old School was the product of a group of visionary individuals. Telok Kurau Studios is managed by NAC as part of its Arts Housing Scheme, and its role is to provide subsidized arts housing to artists and arts groups; Old School was managed by private enterprise, and its bottom line was profit-driven. Telok Kurau Studios is characterized by in-fighting, resentments and antipathies; Old School was characterized by friendly relations and collaborations. Telok Kurau Studios feels somewhat boring, with artists either absent or holed up in their own studios behind closed doors; Old School was abuzz with activity at all hours of the day and night, and exuded creative vibes. Telok Kurau Studios has not made anything of the site, while Old School tried in numerous ways to draw on the history, heritage and symbolism of the site. Telok Kurau Studios seems to be culturally productive, but socially unengaged, environmentally bland and economically dependent on subsidies; Old School was dynamic, culturally productive, socially engaging, environmentally pleasing and economically viable. Yet, Telok Kurau Studios continues to stand and retain its artists and arts groups, while Old School has been demolished, its tenants mostly relocated to other parts of Singapore.

What lessons are to be learned from these cases? It would be naive to generalize that government-initiated schemes are inferior to industry-led initiatives. There are common factors in both clusters that point to their salience in the lives of clusters, regardless of whether the initial impetus is public or private sector. For one, we learn that the reputation effect is a powerful attraction and retention force for individuals and groups, and that this effect can transcend antipathies within a cluster. Further, the physical environment of a cluster – the place – matters, whether it is the quiet, relative isolation and solitude of Telok Kurau Studios or the canopy of green on a hillock in the city centre, and yet not in the city, as Old School has been described. We learn here that geography matters.

At the same time, there are also divergent conditions in the two clusters examined in this chapter that point to potentially more generalizable lessons. First, multi-disciplinary clusters generate opportunities for collaboration where monolithic clusters grapple with rivalries. This differentiates creative clusters from industry clusters, where externalities accrue from co-location among firms manufacturing the same product. Second, visionary leadership, with a strong sense of the desired 'tonality' of a cluster, leads to the formation of one that is carefully assembled – a judicious, if not artistic, orchestration and composition, as opposed to an assemblage that comes out of bureaucratic ordering. A well-composed cluster is alive, vibrant and buzzing; an ill-composed one lacks cultural inspiration, fails to support the development of professional and personal networks and is deficient in community engagement. Third, the ability to draw on the heritage of the site brings added advantage in the building of new activities and the making of new symbolisms. Failing to do so misses an opportunity.

Telok Kurau Studios has lasted more than a decade. Ironically, Old School is a pile of rubble. Which, eventually, is the successful cluster?

NOTES

1. Renaissance City 2.0 was introduced in 2005, following the Renaissance City Project (RCP I) first introduced in 1999. Whereas RCP I was about strengthening the National Arts Council and National Heritage Board's budgets so that they could develop Singapore's cultural 'software', RCP II was part of a broader Creative Industries Development Strategy, emphasizing an industry approach in the development of arts and culture (Renaissance City Plan III, 2008, p. 8).
2. The Community Development Council (CDC) is the local administration of a district. It initiates, plans and manages community programmes to promote community bonding and social cohesion, and provides social assistance services delegated from the government ministries. There are five CDCs in Singapore (http://www.cdc.org.sg/1160984256463/aboutus.html).
3. Each CDC is headed by a mayor.
4. Just some examples will illustrate the point. Paprika Global, a creative agency, has relocated to One Sims Lane. Visual artists Baet Yeok Kuan and Lim Poh Teck have studios at Telok Kurau Studios, while Milke Photographie is at Spottiswoode Park. Sinema has moved to Joo Seng Road. The 2902 Gallery relocated to Queen Street. Elixr (a boutique graphic design house) is now at Tembeling Road. Sparch Architects relocated to Murray Street. And so forth.

12. Culture, globalization and urban landscapes

REFLECTIONS

In this final chapter, we step back from the rich tapestry woven from ethnographic material amassed for each city and the grounded analysis of site-specific contexts and developments to reflect more broadly about culture, urban landscapes and global cities. We take stock of what the specific cases tell us about cultural mega-projects and cultural clusters in cities, but, on an even larger canvas, we draw lessons more generally about urban governance, community engagement, cultural capital and city identities.

Before we pull together and assess the learning points drawn from the case studies, we remind ourselves of the ambitions of the cities in question, recollecting why it is important that analyses of the Asian context as (only partially) represented by these cities are critical to the task of rethinking some of our existing theoretical knowledge, so often derived from observations of the Western world. The already evident importance of some of these cities on the world stage and the growing significance of others make it imperative that we understand their developments. Insights from their particularities must inform theoretical apparatuses for understanding the role of culture and the impact of globalization on urban landscapes, as well as the ways in which urban landscapes (re)shape cultural developments and ground global flows of ideas, expertise and strategies about the city.

PAYING HEED TO CITIES IN ASIA

'Beijing is without any doubt already a global city,' declares Wang Feng (2013, p. 5) in a paper on Beijing as a 'globally fluent' city, though the rise is acknowledged to be as yet incomplete. Wang traces the 'ambition and determination' to both the central and municipal governments, identifying Beijing's strong 'legacy and position as China's political and cultural center' as a key factor supporting its rise, as well as the 'massive investment in infrastructure to support business and innovation activities'. Wang nevertheless recognizes that there are other conditions that are still absent: a leadership that keeps an open mind, rather than a 'selectively open' one (Wang, F., 2013, p. 9); a liveability and vibrancy that is much loved by the city's residents; and a larger proportion of visitors and foreign migrants (as opposed to domestic migrants) than is currently apparent.

Many other assessments of this nature have appeared. In 2014, in the A.T. Kearney Global Cities Index (only one of numerous such indices, and included here for illustrative purposes and not because it is necessarily superior) Beijing is ranked eighth among the world's most global cities, its highest ranking since the index was introduced in 2008. As reported in *The China Daily* (16 April 2014), Beijing 'scored an overall 3.5 in five categories, including business activity, human capital, information exchange, cultural experience and political engagement. It stood out from other Chinese cities in terms of the number of Fortune 500 companies, international schools, broadband subscribers and museums.' But a cautionary note was sounded: given Beijing's air pollution problems, many companies, and with them their employees, were looking to move out of Beijing, which could dent Beijing's standing as a global city. This kind of mixed assessment is typical of appraisal of China's capital city, pointing to its growing importance on the world stage amid some abiding challenges.

And what of Shanghai? In 1999, *Time* magazine labelled Shanghai a rival to New York City as the 'Center of the World' in the twenty-first century (Yatsko, 2001, p. 9). Others think 'not yet'. Writing in 2000, Fulong Wu (2000, p. 1359) declared that Shanghai was 'still not comparable with a truly global city' though Shahid Yusuf and Wu Weiping (2002, p. 1213), two years later, believed it to be a 'regional aspirant' with 'reasonable long-term prospects'. In 2014, it featured at number 18 in the A.T. Kearney Global City Index.

Whatever others may think, Shanghai itself has clear and overt aspirations to be part of the race for global city status. Certainly, Shanghai's history in the 1920s as a financial and cultural centre means that it has a past that it can hearken back to. The city's determination today is described as that of 'seeking revenge' – to regain its status as a leader among cities in the world (Lu, H., 2002, p. 171). It is also aggressively using as reference points cities like London, seeking after 'multinational investment, tourist income and a flowering of the arts' (Wu, C.-T., 2002, p. 168). In 2003, it proclaimed publicly its goal to increase the expatriate population to 5 per cent of the metropolitan total, a level recognized as standard for global cities (Farrer, 2005). This aspiration is expressed by many individuals in the city who have a role in helping it realize its ambitions. Yatsko (2001, p. 11), for example, reports the personal conviction of a deputy director at the foreign affairs department of the Shanghai Foreign Economic and Trade Commission in 1996: 'Shanghai,' the young woman said, 'won't be a center just for China – that's too small. It will be a leader in the world.'

As with Beijing, pervasive evidence exists of Shanghai's multifold efforts to situate itself prominently in the global urban hierarchy. There are mushrooming skyscrapers, massive redevelopment and relocation of residents and new infrastructure projects. Old neighbourhoods have been flattened; elevated highways, extension bridges, roads, a light rail system, digital telecommunication lines, a new international airport and cultural complexes have all been constructed. On the eastern side of the Huangpu River, Pudong's new financial district, Lujiazui, bristles with shining edifices housing financial and business services that form the backbone of the city's quest for global city status. On the western side of the river in Puxi, old factories have been moved out and replaced with commercial buildings. Neon lights and billboards have emerged in abundance. To make all of this possible, massive amounts of capital have been invested in urban infrastructure. The rapid changes to the Shanghai landscape in the late 1990s were such that the authorities had to print a new city map every three months on average (Lu, H., 2002, p. 169).

The third Chinese city we consider in this book is Hong Kong. Its global aspirations are nowhere more apparent than in the former Chief Executive Tung Chee Hwa's 1999 Policy Address, in which he talked about the need for Hong Kong to have a long-term development plan that could make Hong Kong 'world class' like London and New York (Tung, 1999, p. 15). In 2000, Hong Kong's Commission on Strategic Development produced a report titled *Bringing the Vision to Life – Hong Kong's Development Needs and Goals*, which crystallized the vision in greater depth and outlined the strategies to realize the vision. Central to achieving Hong Kong's aspiration as 'Asia's World City' is the need for Hong Kong to reinforce its role as a major city in China and establish itself within a fully integrated 'city-region' in the Pearl River Delta (Hong Kong SAR Commission for Strategic Development, 2000, p. 5). The other interrelated themes identified in the report include enhancing Hong Kong's competitiveness, improving the quality of life and reinforcing Hong Kong's identity and image. While the political administration within Hong Kong is convinced that the strengthening of linkages with the mainland is crucial for Hong Kong's climb up the world ranks, some fear Hong Kong could be increasingly overshadowed by its integration into the Pearl River Delta, overtaken by major Chinese cities like Shanghai (Forrest et al., 2004, p. 224) or whittled down to become yet another large provincial city of China (Skeldon, 1997). Global aspirations notwithstanding, the path does not appear clear.

Regardless, Hong Kong's colonial past has allowed it to grow as an international, cosmopolitan centre, well integrated into the world economy. Indeed, the then Chief Secretary for Administration asserted that in the areas of financial services, infrastructure, communications technology and tourism, Hong Kong is considered to have achieved world city status (D. Tsang, 2005), garnering a reputation as a place that works and where deals are secured (V. Fung, 1999). It is certainly working towards higher value-added outputs through innovation and increasing the knowledge content of its economy to sustain its economic development (Tung, 2005). In 2014, it ranked fifth – the highest – among the five cities in the A.T. Kearney Global City Index. Amid the positive assessment, there are also calls for Hong Kong to place greater focus on attracting world-renowned tertiary institutions, improving its environmental quality, enhancing its entertainment facilities and reviewing its immigration laws, all in the bid to attract and retain world-class talent within Hong Kong (Dorfman, 2000).

Singapore, too, has global aspirations to be in the superleague of cities. Indeed, some argue that it can already claim global city status (see Chapter 5), given its connectedness to the rest of the world – through commerce and financial services, air and sea ports, hosting of multinational corporation headquarters, and capital, migrant and tourist flows. In 2014, it featured at number nine in the A.T. Kearney Global City Index. Considering the local politics, Singapore's challenge may be less about proclaiming its global city status – whether discursively or materially – than about addressing its citizens' frustrations about the country's global city characteristics – the high proportion of foreign population, congestion, high cost of living and so forth. The difficulty for Singapore is that it is a city, an island and a state all in one, leaving its residents no retreat from the bustle of city-living. At the same time, the desire of its citizens for a strong sense of local and national identity in the face of large inflows of foreigners shapes their reactions to social and cultural projects where the opportunity presents itself for the sculpting and avowal of identity.

Finally, Taipei might perhaps be described as the younger sibling of the other cities insofar as attaining global city status is concerned. In 2014, it featured at number 40 in the A.T. Kearney Global City Index. Wang Chia-Huang (2003) highlights the Taipei city government's urban policies from the 1990s and how they were strongly influenced by the ambition of becoming a global city, such as building the tallest building in the world (Taipei 101) and creating a new financial district (Xinyi). Perhaps an appropriate descriptor for the city is 'globalizing Taipei' (Kwok, 2005), reflecting the journey rather than the arrival, a journey much mired by domestic and international politics, economic, social and spatial restructuring, competing regional priorities and cultural reorientation.

With the above as reminder of the ambitions of and conditions in the five Asian cities, we turn now to consider what lessons the preceding chapters present to us and what the theoretical implications of their particularities may be.

CULTURAL MONUMENTS, URBAN LANDSCAPES AND GLOBAL CITIES

In the first part of the book, we examined the experience of the five cities in their construction of cultural mega-projects, buoyed by global city aspirations. We examined the vision behind these infrastructural projects and the challenges encountered in delivering them. Further, we drew attention to the continuities and disjunctures between, on the one hand, discursive and material cultural strategies for the making of a global city and, on the other hand, everyday lived experience.

Two main reasons account for why these cities have devoted their resources to the construction of major cultural facilities. The first is the symbolic role played by these facilities. Whereas urban flagships, mega-projects, giant ferris wheels and skyscrapers have been strategies used by cities to boost their development and global prominence, cultural monuments have since joined the category. Not only do they earmark cities as sites of cultural richness and sophistication, they are also icons that celebrate the cities' more wide-ranging achievements, instantiating a city's global standing.

Second, in addition to this emblematic aspect of cultural mega-infrastructure, another impetus for their construction comes from a perception of their pragmatic virtues. The large, new cultural spaces are envisaged as an attraction to well-known international arts groups. This is expected to enhance the quality of cultural life in the cities. At the same time, such international groups, it is believed, will enhance local cultural capital as local groups learn from their interactions with visiting groups. In other words, new cultural facilities can support local cultural development by offering artists and culture workers a creative environment in which to practise their cultural activities.

In reality, as the cases demonstrate, such cultural infrastructure neither straightforwardly enhances a city's status nor does it necessarily spawn productive relationships between international and local arts groups. While these projects do (or may) contribute to the quality of cultural life in the city, this is unevenly achieved across the cities and across segments of the population, and the question of whose quality of life is enhanced becomes a point of contention.

As we demonstrated in earlier chapters, all five cities – Beijing, Shanghai, Hong Kong, Singapore and Taipei – have adopted the strategy of constructing cultural mega-projects as part of their place-oriented strategies to create exciting cities situated in the global urban hierarchy. However, as actually particularized and actualized, there are similarities but also multiple differences across the five cities. We foreground key divergences below, leading to some insights about urban cultural infrastructure and the making of global cities.

Our first line of analysis is focused on the respective cities' motivations for cultural monument development. In all cases, global city aspirations and neoliberal logic are apparent, but in each case there are differing degrees of significance accorded to local and national ambitions and the convergence and divergence between them. There are also different responsibilities assumed by local and central authorities. These differing intersections of local, national and global reflect the different geopolitical and economic situations of the five cities.

In Singapore's case, because it is a city-state, city and national ambitions are convergent. The global city aspiration, anchored in economic imperatives, is at least matched by a desire to rally Singaporeans around urban icons, constructing a shared national identity. Global, national and local objectives are highly convergent.

Hong Kong, on the other hand, as a Special Administrative Region of China, looks outward from China, and may be said to be seeking 'escape' and differentiation from the nation. Its global aspirations are not so much anchored in national goals as they are about economic imperatives and about manifesting its local identity, distinct from that of China. The nation as a frame of reference exists only insofar as it is the 'other'. In fact, Hong Kong recognizes that to remain useful to China, it must stay 'a step ahead' of China's development, rather than become 'just another Chinese city' (*South China Morning Post*, 25 January 1999).

Shanghai's motivations are anchored partly in its desire to regain its former glory and partly in its competition with its rival, Beijing. Its quest for a distinguished city identity is what propels it, rather than a sense of the national, though its rivalry with the national capital keeps the nation in view. That the project of building and maintaining the Shanghai Grand Theatre is a municipal initiative is further emphasized in the fact that the funding comes only from the city government.

In Beijing, the municipal government's construction of its Grand Theatre is a response to the central government's readjustment of political priorities in the post 1990s, shifting culture's mandate from spreading propaganda to constituting an essential ingredient in cultural industrialization strategies, with the ultimate goal of transforming at least some of its cities from Third World to global standing. Beijing received funding directly from state coffers for its Grand Theatre. In that sense, Beijing is like Singapore, where the global, national and local objectives converge. Unlike Singapore, the misalignment came about after the construction, when high operational costs provoked a tussle over whether the central or municipal government would administer and otherwise have responsibility for the facility.

Like Beijing, Taipei's investment in cultural infrastructure was rooted in political and ideological intent prior to the 1990s as a means of demonstrating Taiwan's legitimacy as the true successor to Chinese culture and to facilitate ideological education internally, supporting anti-communism efforts. However, from the 1990s, Taiwan recognized the economic value of its cultural assets and the need for supporting facilities to stay competitive in an increasingly globalized world; it thus began to consider constructing new cultural infrastructure. Yet, party politics, central and local government priorities and regional development strategies made for a protracted process of strategy development and implementation. State-level financial support was lacking; eventually, investment had to be made from municipal sources, while state resources were directed to other cities on account of the then President's policy of balancing development across different regions. The conflicting pulls between national and local objectives delayed Taipei's ability to move swiftly in constructing its New Grand Theatre.

In brief, each city's cultural-urban strategy, while similarly buoyed by global city aspirations and seemingly working to a global neoliberal imperative, relates differently to the nation and national interests, and finds different levels of material support from the central *vis-à-vis* municipal government (with the exception of Singapore, where this distinction does not apply). Because the city's and the nation's goals, outlook and/or responsibilities are variously congruent or divergent, the particularities of each journey in the construction and operation of these cultural monuments differ. We turn to these other dimensions next.

Our second axis of analysis focuses on the making of the cultural monuments. In all instances, international competitions and international architects were involved. Reflecting Beijing's aim to be a global city, the design project was sought through international competition and eventually awarded to French architect Paul Andreu in collaboration with Tsinghua University's Institute of Architecture. The ambition extended to employing state-of-the-art technology from Germany and Japan, and construction firms from Beijing, Hong Kong and Shanghai. The same may be said of the Shanghai Grand Theatre, designed by another French architecture firm, ARTE Charpentier (in collaboration with the East

China Architecture Design Institute). Similarly, the Shanghai Oriental Art Centre boasts world-class architectural design and state-of-the-art technologies, designed by Paul Andreu again (in collaboration with Huadong Architectural Design and Research Institute Co.), though a Chinese company became responsible for its post-construction management. Singapore's Esplanade was designed by London-based Michael Wilford and Singapore's own Vikas Gore from DP Architects. Hong Kong and Taipei's yet-to-be-completed facilities similarly boast the involvement, respectively, of Norman Foster and the Office for Metropolitan Architecture architects Rem Koolhaas and David Gianotten. For the Hong Kong project, Foster and Partners designed the master plan 'City Park', but a range of other facilities drew involvement from numerous Hong Kong architects, such as VPANG Architects and JET Architecture. Taipei's project was undertaken in collaboration with local architecture firm Artech Architects. These cultural infrastructure projects are thus a product of the international division of labour that characterizes globalization.

Given such international involvement in what are essentially projects with strong roots in local/national aspirations, our third axis of analysis is focused on the local response to the projects. Whether it is to make one's city stand out on the world stage or to enhance the quality of local cultural capital, in essence, the motivations and impulses are local and/or national. We thus consider two related angles in our examination of public reactions to the projects. The first is the response to the making of the cultural icons, and the second is the engagement with the completed cultural monuments.

Beijing's National Grand Theatre earned the reputation for being one of China's largest and most controversial turn-of-the-century public projects. Criticisms of the proposed theatre centred on its lack of Chinese characteristics and its disjuncture with the other historic and iconic buildings clustered around Tiananmen Square. The authorities undertook a number of public relations mediation strategies, even temporarily halting the project while they explained their choices, though always with the intention of proceeding. Upon completion, the theatre kicked off to a rousing start, with programme scheduling stretching well ahead even before its first season. However, although the Grand Theatre is unequivocally iconic and its contribution to the city's international imageability is not in doubt, question marks remain over its contribution to the city's cultural development. First, its functionality is called into question: the scale of the investment necessitated that the theatre be managed as an economic entity, and yet it needed to be accessible to the general public. Second, the conflicts over the theatre's identity, function and finances have resulted in and are reinforced by ambiguities in its administration and control structure. Finally, the Grand Theatre contradicts its own mandate to promote local cultural development by operating as an exclusive performing space for top artistes and groups. Its emphasis on 'first-rate only' performances has been criticized as structurally discriminatory, where many local performance groups are excluded given their lack of experience.

The success of the Shanghai Grand Theatre and the Oriental Arts Centre can be assessed by their significant regional and international visibility, with audiences hailing from neighbouring provinces and overseas. They also serve functionally as nodes of cultural exchange. On the other hand, these facilities' accessibility to ordinary citizens (in physical and financial terms) and their role in the enrichment of citizens' cultural lives is doubtful. In other words, while as landmarks and symbols of cultural aspiration they inspire civic pride and a sense of association, as functional performance spaces they restrict participation, accentuate social distinctions and, hence, promote cultural elitism. Further, there is an underutilization of these cultural facilities by local performing artists, particularly small cultural groups and young artists who might be perceived as non-mainstream and less marketable. An additional criticism about these two cultural facilities pertains to the quality of the performances; because these facilities are treated as self-managing economic units, the choice of performances must answer to cost-benefit calculations (and not to quality standards). Finally, the small local market for cultural/artistic consumption lends weight to the view that cultural infrastructure projects (like investments in other physical infrastructure) are deprived from enjoying economies of scale by being forced to compete against one another.

Hong Kong's West Kowloon Cultural District remains to be built and demonstrates a particular moment in post-handover politics, one in which neoliberal economic agendas run into local historical, cultural and political conditions, giving rise to myriad debates about whether the project should proceed, how it should proceed, who it should involve, what it should look like, what uses should be accommodated and what roles it should play. The vociferous protests and debates led to protracted public engagement and consultation exercises totalling seven years over a span of more than a decade, with false starts and seeming abortions along the way. By the time the project is completed, based on the current schedule, it will have been more than 30 years since the idea was first mooted and nearly 30 years since it was officially announced as a project by no less than the Special Administrative Region's chief executive. On the one hand, it may be a success for participatory democracy, giving voice to the people in the making of the city. On the other hand, it may be viewed as a failure of urban governance that the project has been embroiled in such extended debate, so much so that its Asian rival cities (usually seen to be Singapore and, to an extent, Shanghai) have long completed their projects.

In the case of Singapore's Esplanade, early detractors objected to the architecture, which they thought missed an opportunity for local expression. They further argued that the Esplanade did not sufficiently encourage Singapore art and local expression, predicting that it would sacrifice the nurturing of cultural production for economic gain. It was believed that the Esplanade pushed back the schedule for developing small performing spaces in favour of bringing forward large facilities. Further, the encouragement given to large-scale international productions relegates smaller-scale, indigenous acts to the backseat. The clever use of a sun-shading device caused the architecture to resemble the durian and, in the process, earned a feeling of endearment for it. The local architect revealed that there had always been an intention to have some kind of sun-shading device even though it was not apparent from the initial exhibitions of the design that they would be included and what they would look like. Regardless of whether the design element was always intended or a response to the negative feedback, it saved the project somewhat from further criticism that it aped foreign projects. As significantly, conscientious programming brought in local arts groups, while clever use of space brought in local participants, whether for arts and cultural activities or other non-related activities (dining, retail, architecture, environment), thereby enlivening the space and developing a sense of familiarity among the general population.

In recognition of the value of cultural assets in an increasingly competitive and globalized world, and the inadequacy (practically and symbolically) of existing arrangements in the mid-2000s, Taipei's city government approved a proposal for the construction of a new theatre in 2005. It was to be the largest theatre in Taiwan, known as the Taipei New Grand Theatre, in the new Banqiao Central Business District of Taipei County. The project met with many obstacles – a lack of government funds, criticisms over the approach of tendering out the building and political upheavals in Taiwan during the late 2000s. Consequently, the plan never came to fruition. In some ways, this aborted project, which then morphed into the plans put up by a newly elected Taipei mayor in 2008 for the Taipei Performing Arts Centre, was helpful in ensuring that the reception to the plans for the Taipei Performing Arts Centre was positive. There is much anticipation that it will fill the need for a top-quality hall for hosting international performances, and satisfy the needs of local artists and audiences with respect to their cultural activities and cultural life. Yet, persistent issues need to be ironed out: insufficient resources for Taipei to strengthen its cultural facilities; the difficulty of mobilizing the private sector's resources to build new cultural infrastructure; a lack of understanding between the central government and local authorities about relative responsibilities and contributions in the construction and maintenance of cultural facilities; and the balancing of resource allocation across various cultural facilities and activities within Taipei.

In the making of these cultural monuments, numerous factors are at play beyond global city aspirations. Inter-city competition within a national polity features as a motivator (Shanghai) or diverts resources to competitors (Taipei). Party politics (Taipei), political will (Beijing, Singapore) and democratic impulses (Hong Kong) have the effect of speeding up or slowing down the projects. International division of labour is a distinctive feature in all these projects, with the involvement of international 'starchitects' and state-of-the-art (and invariably foreign) technology acting as the very badge of global standards. Yet, the designs produced by foreign architects may not always be well received as reflective of local culture and sources of national pride. More troubling than the production of these projects are their consumption aspects, particularly the extent of local participation of both arts and cultural groups and the local population.

CULTURAL CLUSTERS, URBAN LANDSCAPES AND GLOBAL CITIES

In the second part of the book, we examined a different kind of cultural space – clusters of cultural and creative activity – sometimes organically evolved, sometimes state-initiated, sometimes industry-led. While there are those that emerged in the way Zukin's (1989) loft-living Manhattan and Brooklyn artists did, there are also those that emerged out of municipal authority initiatives (or national government initiatives, in the case of the city-state of Singapore), based on a belief that the creative industry sector can support economic growth and contribute to a thriving city. A particular motivation is the belief that creative industries rely and thrive on clusters for vibrancy and efficiency. This strategy of clustering is adopted in both the official policy for culture-led regeneration and also among private creative enterprises themselves who seek the benefits of clustering and wish to maximize their potential. Policies and initiatives have thus been instituted to promote cluster development in creative industries and knowledge economies. When interrogated, however, their explanatory value, their assumed promise and potential, and certainly their contributions to high-quality and especially indigenously inspired creative and cultural work remain variable at best, and unsubstantiated at worst. Through our ethnographically grounded work on clusters in the five cities, we hope to provide at first hand detailed observations and insights from interviews to cast light on these issues.

Beijing's 798 provides an example of an organic cluster that attracted government attention. In its original formulation, the large spaces and cheap rents presented a draw to artists, and the presence of artistic heavy-weights attracted other artists. There was evidence of the formation of net-works and a sense of community. State intervention was welcome insofar as facilities were improved, but the state's introduction of bureaucratic structures and emphasis on industrialization, consumption and tourism have since turned many artists away. The 798 zone has become more popular, but perhaps less creative.

A similar story is apparent in Shanghai's M50 and Tianzifang, both of which evolved from artists responding to the temporary availability of defunct industrial spaces. Recognizing the initial successes of such clusters, the municipal authorities' enthusiastic implementation of crea-tive parks across the city did not always result in the same outcome, as the study of 1933 shows. The emphasis on the commercial dimensions of the space alienated the creative community, as market competitiveness replaced creative impulse as the key motivation for the existence of the cluster. The result was cultural tourism, with its attendant negative exter-nalities on creative worker habitats. If judged by the proportion of rented space and visitor numbers, 1933 has turned the corner; on a recent wet Saturday morning in July 2014, it drew in crowds for coffee and cakes, corporate events and retail activity. But creative or cultural work was not easily apparent.

Taipei's experience is not dissimilar. State intervention has had the effect of causing costs to rise and an existing, *in situ* creative network (Huashan Park) to disintegrate. The mixed use and signalling in the case of Songshan Cultural Park, with the co-location of a ball park with a cultural park gen-erated ire among the creative community and cultural non-governmental organizations, while the management of Jianguo Brewery Cultural Park by a profit-making enterprise turned it into a place for tourism and leisure rather than a place for creative works. State involvement is not necessarily negative, if confined to making vacated public space available to the crea-tive community and facilitating the transformation of disused spaces. On the other hand, too much state intervention or the setting of multiple goals in cluster development may have unintended detrimental effects.

Rare among the cases examined in this book (and, more generally, in the cities in question) is a cluster entirely organic in origin and evolution. Hong Kong's Fotan succeeds and likely has a sustainable future because of a particular constellation of factors: its genesis (with a core group of artists who already know one another well); its geography (location and physical environment); and its governance (self-organized, with no government intervention). On the other hand, in the government-vaunted Cattle Depot, three lessons are learned. First, clustering in and of itself does not necessarily provide conditions for mutual support and growth among artists. Second, heritage can be a liability rather than an asset if it introduces unwarranted restrictions on use rather than functioning solely as a symbolic resource. Third, governance of culture and urban space is critical in contributing to the sustainability of culture and social life in a cluster. Fractured governance and lack of inter-agency coordination, on the other hand, hinders the potential of a cluster.

Finally, Singapore's cases support and add different perspectives to the preceding observations. The Arts Housing Scheme run by the National Arts Council is similar to, and different from, textbook concepts of the cultural creative cluster. It co-locates artist(e)s and cultural/creative workers based on the belief that clustering produces conditions that enhance collaboration and spark creativity, but differs in that it houses amateur artists and arts groups in need of subsidy rather than creative and cultural businesses where cultural entrepreneurship and consumption are primary. The particular cluster under the scheme examined here (Telok Kurau Studios) demonstrates how the textbook characteristics of clusters do not apply. In particular, the commonly accepted assumption that clusters, by virtue of geographical propinquity, generate trust relationships among constituents is debunked. Instead, the in-fighting, resentments and antipathies are real. Although the artists are culturally productive, they are disengaged from one another; economically, the dependence on subsidies makes the place potentially unsustainable in the long run. Nevertheless, the artists remain in the cluster because of the cheap rents, the reputation effect (on account of well-regarded artists located there) and the quiet and solitude of the environment. On the other hand, Old School, initiated by a group of visionary individuals and managed as a private enterprise, succeeded in drawing on the history, heritage and symbolism of the former school site to create a vibrant cluster of creative production and consumption. Other success factors included an insistence on multi-disciplinarity that stimulated collaboration; a central location in the city, though unique in its siting on a hillock amid canopies of green; and the reputational effect of 'big name' tenants, which drew in other creative workers.

In the making of these cultural and creative clusters, the received wisdom about how they function and thrive is helpful but inadequate. The commonly accepted assumption that clusters, by virtue of geographical propinquity, invariably generate trust relationships among constituents, thus facilitating the building up of social capital, yielding fruitful externalities, creative synergies and tacit knowledge that enhance the work produced (O'Connor, 2004; Turok, 2003), is not invariably borne out. Evidence suggests that such social ties and the resulting social capital are not certain outcomes of spatial proximity. Indeed, empirical analyses suggest that they may develop in cultural clusters under certain conditions that are not related to the fact of geographical propinquity, for example, when there is a need to counter external forces through collective action (for example, at Cattle Depot in Hong Kong). Rather than agglomerating to enjoy productive social relations, evidence suggests that other factors like the reputation effect, the salubrious environment and the affordable rents are more persuasive in attracting and retaining cultural workers.

REFLECTING ON CULTURES AND CITIES

Collectively, we have worked on this book for nearly six years. Our years in the field were mainly concentrated in the late 2000s and early 2010s. In cities as dynamic as the ones featured here, a year can be a long time as forces of globalization bring massive changes, as urban landscapes transform and as culture, economy, politics and society transmute. We are less concerned with the specific details of how particular monuments or clusters may have changed since the bulk of our fieldwork was done. Our concern is with capturing faithfully the dynamics of urban and cultural change as they occurred in a particular historical moment, and with understanding the motivations, visions, strategies, actions and reactions relating to those changes. In so doing, we draw lessons more generally about numerous dimensions of cultures and cities. Ultimately, as cities mature, their identities are rooted not only in their economic trophies but in their cultural capital. The successful production of this cultural capital is factored on a particular mix of conditions: sound urban govern-ance, community engagement, organic evolution, visionary leadership, economic policy, party politics and heritage. In this sense, the making of global cultural cities not only relies on the presence of the arts but remains ultimately an art in itself.

References

Advisory Council on Culture and the Arts (1989), *Report of the Advisory Council on Culture and the Arts*, Singapore: Singapore National Printers.

Amin, Ash and Nigel J. Thrift (1994), *Globalization, Institutions, and Regional Development in Europe*, Oxford and New York: Oxford University Press.

Anderson, Benedict (1991), *Imagined Communities: Reflections on the Origin and Spread of Nationalism*, London: Verso.

Aoyama, Yuko (2007), 'The role of consumption and globalization in a cultural industry: the case of flamenco', *Geoforum*, **38** (1), 103–13.

Artist Magazine (2008), 'Taiwan jianzhu renwen dijingzi tuibian zuotanhui – cong taizhong dadu huige gejuyuan tanqi' ['A forum on the transformation in Taiwan's architecture and cultural landscape'], *Artist Magazine*, **396**, 192–7.

Bailey, Christopher, Steven Miles and Peter Stark (2004), 'Culture-led urban regeneration and the revitalization of identities in Newcastle, Gateshead and the north east of England', *International Journal of Cultural Policy*, **10** (1), 47–65.

Barnes, Kendall, Gordon Waitt, Nicholas Gill and Chris Gibson (2006), 'Community and nostalgia in urban revitalisation: a critique of urban village and creative class as remedies for social problems', *Australian Geographer*, **37** (3), 335–54.

Bassett, Keith (1993), 'Urban cultural strategies and urban cultural regeneration: a case study and critique', *Environment and Planning A*, **25**, 1773–88.

Bassett, Keith, Ron Griffiths and Ian Smith (2002), 'Cultural industries, cultural clusters and the city: the example of natural history filmmaking in Bristol', *Geoforum*, **33**, 165–77.

Baum, Scott (1999), 'Social transformations in the global city: Singapore', *Urban Studies*, **36** (7), 1095–117.

Bayliss, Darrin (2004), 'Denmark's creative potential: the role of culture in Danish urban development strategies', *International Journal of Cultural Policy*, **10** (1), 5–28.

Bayliss, Darrin (2007), 'The rise of the creative city: culture and creative in Copenhagen', *European Planning Studies*, **15** (7), 889–903.

Beaverstock, Jonathan V., Richard J. Smith and Peter J. Taylor (1999), 'A roster of world cities', *Cities*, **16** (6), 445–58.

Beech, Hannah (2000), 'Art rivalry: reviewing an age-old feud, Beijing and Shanghai fight for the title of cultural capital', *Time Asia*, **155** (14), 10 April.

Beijing ribao (2006), 'Wenhua chuangyi chanye jiang chengwei Beijing fazhan xinzeng changdian' ['Creative culture industry will become a new channel for Beijing's economic development'], *Beijing ribao* [*Beijing Daily*], 18 August, available at http://news.china.com /zh_cn/domestic/ 945/20060818/13552498.html (accessed 17 October 2007).

Bianchini, Franco (1993a), 'Culture, conflict and cities: issues and prospects for the 1990s', in Franco Bianchini and Michael Parkinson (eds), *Cultural Policy and Urban Regeneration: The West European Experience*, Manchester and New York: Manchester University Press, pp. 199–213.

Bianchini, Franco (1993b), 'Remaking European cities: the role of cultural politics', in Franco Bianchini and Michael Parkinson (eds), *Cultural Policy and Urban Regeneration: The West European Experience*, Manchester and New York: Manchester University Press, pp. 1–20.

Bianchini, Franco, John Dawson and Richard Evans (1992), 'Flagship projects in urban regeneration', in Patsy Healy et al. (eds), *Rebuilding the City: Property-led Urban Regeneration*, London: E. & F.N. Spon.

Brady, Diane (1995), 'Romancing the arts: Singapore sets stage for cultural tourism', *Wall Street Journal*, 1 December.

Brown, Adam, Justin O'Connor and Sara Cohen (2000), 'Local music policies within a global music industry: cultural quarters in Manchester and Sheffield', *Geoforum*, **31**, 437–52.

Bryan, Jane, Stephen Hill, Max Munday and Annette Roberts (2000), 'Assessing the role of the arts and cultural industries in a local economy', *Environment and Planning A*, **32**, 1391–408.

Cai, Shangwei (2007), 'Chengshi tezhi yu chuangyi chanye luxian xuanze' ['The city's characteristics and the path selection for the development of its creative industry'], available at http://www.scic.gov.cn/creative_ industry/index.htm (accessed 12 September 2007).

Capello, Roberta (1999), 'Spatial transfer of knowledge in high technology milieux: learning versus collective learning processes', *Regional Studies*, **33** (4), 353–65.

Centre for Cultural Policy Research (CCPR) (2005), *A Study on Creativity Index*, Hong Kong: Hong Kong University.

Chan, May, and Barclay Crawford (2006), 'Hui in fresh row with lawmakers', *South China Morning Post*, 28 January, available at http://www.

scmp.com/article/534586/hui-fresh-row-lawmakers (accessed 4 April 2008).

Chang, Sen-dou (1998), 'Beijing: perspectives on preservation, environment, and development', *Cities*, **15** (1), 13–25.

Chau, Sherman (2002), 'Glass dragon builds up for stylish roar', *The Standard*, 16 March, available at http://www.thestandard.com.hk/news_detail.asp?pp_cat=&art_id=14300&sid=&con_type=1&d_str=20020316&sear_year=2002 (accessed 1 April 2008).

Chen, Bingzhao (1999), 'Beijing chengshi jianshe de zhanlüe jueze – zhuazhu jiyu baituo "tan dabing"' ['Strategic choice in Beijing's urban development – seize the opportunity and expand'], *Urban Planning*, **23** (12), 27–39.

Chinese Academy of Social Science and Shanghai Jiaotong University (2002), *China Cultural Industry General Report Bluebook 2001–02* (in Chinese), Beijing: Social Sciences Academic Press.

Chinese Communist Party (2000), *Zhonggong zhongyang guanyu zhiding guomin jingji he shehui fazhan dishige wunianjihuade jianyi* [*The CCP Proposal on Making the Tenth Five-Year Plan of National Economic and Social Development*], available at http://cpc.people.com.cn/GB/64162/71380/71382/71386/4837946.html (accessed 15 July 2014).

Chinese Communist Party (2001), *Wenhua chanye fazhan dishige wunianjihua gangyao* [*Outline of the Development of Cultural Industry, Tenth Five Year Plan*], available at http://www.cnci.gov.cn/content/20001116/news_13601.shtml (accessed 15 July 2014).

Chua, Beng Huat (1993), 'Responding to global challenge: the changing international economy', in Garry Rodan (ed.), *Singapore Changes Guard: Social, Political and Economic Direction in the 1990s*, New York: Longman Cheshire, pp. 101–15.

Chung, Robert T.Y. (2007), *West Kowloon Cultural District (WKCD) Development (WKCD-371)*, available at http://legco.gov.hk/yr04–05/english/hc/sub_com/hs02/papers/hs020106wkcd-371-e.pdf (accessed 18 December 2007).

Clammer, John (2003), 'Globalisation, class, consumption and civil society in south-east Asian cities', *Urban Studies*, **40** (2), 403–19.

Clark, Terry Nichols (2004), 'Urban amenities: lakes, opera, and juice bars – do they drive development?', in Terry Nichols Clark (ed.), *The City as an Entertainment Machine*, Amsterdam: Elsevier, pp. 103–40.

Coe, Neil M. and Jennifer Johns (2004), 'Beyond production clusters: towards a critical political economy of networks in the film and television industries', in Dominic Power and Allen J. Scott (eds), *The Cultural Industries and the Production of Culture*, London and New York: Routledge, pp. 188–204.

Comedia (2003), *Releasing the Cultural Potential of Our Core Cities:*

Culture and the Core Cities, available at http://www.corecities.com/coreDEV/comedia/com_cult.html (accessed 8 June 2008).

Commissioner for Heritage's Office (2013), *Guidelines on the Short-term Lease of Vacant Units and the Open Space at Ex-Ma Tau Kok Animal Quarantine Depot (Cattle Depot)*, available at https://www.heritage.gov.hk/en/doc/conserve/guidelines-lease_at_Cattle_Depot-Mar_2013-Eng.pdf (accessed 8 July 2014).

Cooke, Philip (2002a), *Knowledge Economies: Clusters, Learning and Cooperative Advantage*, London and New York: Routledge.

Cooke, Philip (2002b), 'New media and new economy cluster dynamics', in Leah A. Lievrouw and Sonia M. Livingstone (eds), *The Handbook of New Media*, London: Sage, pp. 287–303.

Creative Clusters Ltd (2010), *Key Concepts: Creative Clusters*, available at http://www.creativeclusters.com/modules/eventsystem/?fct=eventmenus&action=displaypage&id=36 (accessed 23 April 2010).

Culture and Heritage Commission (2003), *Policy Recommendation Report (CB(1)929/04–05(01))*, available at http://www.legco.gov.hk/yr04–05/english/hc/sub_com/hs02/papers/hs020316cb1-wkcd85-e.pdf (accessed 2 April 2008).

De Frantz, Monika (2005), 'From cultural regeneration to discursive governance: constructing the flagship of the "Museums-quartier Vienna" as a plural symbol of change', *International Journal of Urban and Regional Research*, **29** (1), 50–66.

Degolyer, Michael (2001), 'Conditional citizenship versus unconditional love: Hong Kong people's attitudes toward the new motherland', *Citizenship Studies*, **5** (2), 165–83.

Delang, Claudio O. and Yan Ng (2009), 'Urban regeneration and heritage preservation with public participation: the case of the Kai Tak Runway in Hong Kong', *Open Geography Journal*, **2**, 35–64.

Department of Cultural Affairs of Taipei City Government (2007), *A Survey of Cultural Facilities in Taipei* (in Chinese).

Derudder, Ben and Peter J. Taylor (2005), 'The cliquishness of world cities', *Global Networks*, **5** (1), 71–91.

Dhanabalan, Suppiah (1983), 'Widening the cultural horizons of Singaporeans', *Speeches: A Bi-monthly Selection of Ministerial Speeches*, **6** (7), 15–17.

Dicken, Peter, Jamie Peck and Adam Tickell (1997), 'Unpacking the global', in R. Lee and J. Wills (eds), *Geographies of Economies*, London: Arnold, pp. 158–66.

Dorfman, Robert (2000), 'Hong Kong's path to "world city" status', available at http://info.hktdc.com/shippers/vol24_1/vol24_1_annu011.htm (accessed 9 July 2014).

Economic Committee (1986), *Report of the Subcommittee on the Service Sector*, Singapore: Subcommittee on the Service Sector.

Economic Review Committee (2002), *Creative Industries Development Strategy*, Singapore: Ministry of Trade and Industry.

Eisinger, Peter (2000), 'The politics of bread and circuses: building the city for the visitor class', *Urban Affairs Review*, **35** (3), 316–33.

European Urban Knowledge Network (EUKN) (2006), *Urban Renovation of Besòs River Bank – Forum 2004 (Barcelona)*, available at http://www.eukn.org/E_library/Urban_Environment/Urban_Environment/Urban_renovation_of_Bes%C3%B2s_river_bank_Forum_2004_Barcelona (accessed 26 June 2014).

Evans, Graeme (2001), *Cultural Planning: An Urban Rennaissance?* London and New York: Routledge.

Evans, Graeme (2003), 'Hard-branding the cultural city: from Prado to Prada', *International Journal of Urban and Regional Research*, **27** (2), 417–40.

Evans, Graeme (2005), 'Measure for measure: evaluating the evidence of culture's contribution to regeneration', *Urban Studies*, **42** (5/6), 959–83.

Evans, Graeme (2009), 'Creative cities, creative spaces and urban policy', *Urban Studies*, **46** (5/6), 1003–40.

Evans, Graeme, Jo Foord, Phyllida Shaw et al. (2005), *Strategies for Creative Spaces: Phase 1 Report*, London and Toronto: London Development Agency, City of Toronto Economic Development and Culture Divisions and Ontario Ministries of Economic Development and Trade and Culture.

Farrer, James (2005), 'Nationalism pits Shanghai against its global ambition', *YaleGlobal Online*, 29 April, available at http://yaleglobal.yale.edu/content/nationalism-pits-shanghai-against-its-global-ambition (accessed 28 May 2005).

Fenton, A.H. (2004), 'West Kowloon's glass-house effect reflects differing views', *South China Morning Post*, 15 March, available at Lexis-Nexis Academic Universe (accessed 3 April 2008).

Flew, Terry (2005), 'Creative cities and creative clusters', paper presented at Creative Articulations: Creative Research Network Workshop, Brisbane, Australia, 1 October, available at http://eprints.qut.edu.au/2185/1/Creative_cities_and_Creative_Clusters.pdf (accessed 26 June 2014).

Florida, Richard (2002a), *The Rise of the Creative Class: And How It's Transforming Work, Leisure, Community, and Everyday Life*, New York: Basic Books.

Florida, Richard (2002b), 'The rise of the creative class: why cities without gays and rock bands are losing the economic development race', *Washington Monthly*, May, available at http://www.washington monthly.com/features/2001/0205.florida.html.

Florida, Richard (2005), *Cities and the Creative Class*, New York: Routledge.

Forrest, Ray, Adrienne La Grange and Ngai-ming Yip (2004), 'Hong Kong as a global city? Social distance and spatial differentiation', *Urban Studies*, **41** (1), 207–27.

Friedmann, John (1986), 'The world city hypothesis', *Development and Change*, **17**, 69–83.

Friedmann, John (1995), 'Where we stand: a decade of world city research', in Paul L. Knox and Peter J. Taylor (eds), *World Cities in a World-system*, Cambridge: Cambridge University Press, pp. 21–47.

Frith, Simon (1991), 'Knowing one's place: the culture of cultural industries', *Cultural Studies from Birmingham*, **1**, 135–55.

Fukuyama, Francis (1995), 'Social capital and the global economy: a redrawn map of the world', *Foreign Affairs*, **74** (5), 89–103.

Fung, Anthony (2001), 'What makes the local? A brief consideration of the rejuvenation of Hong Kong identity', *Cultural Studies*, **15** (3/4), 591–601.

Fung, Victor (1999), 'Hong Kong: into the new millennium', speech by chairman of Hong Kong Trade Development Council, 4 February, available at http://hong-kong-economy-research.hktdc.com/business-news/vp-article/en/1/1X00HZY5.htm (accessed 8 July 2014).

Gane, Nicholas (2004), *The Future of Social Theory*, London and New York: Continuum.

Gao, Jing (2007), '"2007 Beijing 798 yishujie" yi kaimu' ['Curtains rise on 2007 Beijing 798 Art Festival'], *Artron.net*, 29 April, available at http://news.artron.net/20070429/n25459.html (accessed 17 July 2014).

Gao, Lu-ji (2003), 'Guojia Dajuyuan qiaoqiao fugong' ['The National Theatre quietly returns to work'], *Open Magazine*, June, available at http://www.open.com.hk/old_version/4q.html (accessed 8 July 2014).

Ge, Hongbing, Gao Xian, Xu Chang and Yang Yifei (2014), '2013 niande Shanghai wenhua xiaofei diaoyan baogao' ['A report on Shanghai's 2013 cultural consumption survey'], *Kexue fazhan zazhi*, 17 March, available at http://blog.sina.com.cn/s/blog_473d280c0102eh2g.html (accessed 20 July 2014).

Gereffi, Gary (1996), 'The elusive last lap in the quest for developed-country status', in James H. Mittelman (ed.), *Globalization: Critical Reflections*, London: Lynne Rienner.

Gibson, Chris and Lily Kong (2005), 'Cultural economy: a critical review', *Progress in Human Geography*, **29** (5), 541–61.

Gilmore, Fiona (2004), 'Shanghai: unleashing creative potential', *Journal of Brand Management*, **11** (6), 442–8.

Glaeser, Edward L. (2004), 'Book review of Richard Florida's *The Rise of the Creative Class*', available at http://scholar.harvard.edu/files/glaeser/files/book_review_of_richard_floridas_the_rise_of_the_creative_class.pdf (accessed 16 June 2014).

Gnad, Friedrich (2000), 'Regional promotion strategies for the culture industries in the Ruhr area', in Friedrich Gnad and Jörg Siegmann (eds), *Culture Industries in Europe: Regional Development Concepts for Private-sector Cultural Production and Services*, Duesseldorf, Germany: Ministry for Economics and Business, Technology and Transport of the State of North Rhine-Westphalia and the Ministry for Employment and Social Affairs, pp. 172–7.

Goldsmith, Ben and Thomas O'Regan (2004), 'Locomotives and star-gates: inner-city studio complexes in Sydney, Melbourne and Toronto', *International Journal of Cultural Policy*, **10** (1), 29–45.

Gordon, Ian R. and Philip McCann (2000), 'Industrial clusters: complexes, agglomeration and/or social networks?', *Urban Studies*, **37** (3), 513–37.

Grabher, Gernot (1993), *The Embedded Firm: On the Socio-economics of Industrial Networks*, London: Routledge.

Griffiths, Ron (2006), 'City/culture discourses: evidence from the competition to select the European Capital of Culture 2008', *European Planning Studies*, **14** (4), 415–30.

Grodach, Carl and Anastasia Loukaitou-Sideris (2007), 'Cultural development strategies and urban revitalization: a survey of US cities', *International Journal of Cultural Policy*, **13** (4), 349–70.

Guehenno, Jean-Marie (1995), *The End of the Nation-state*, translated by Victoria Elliott, Minneapolis, MN: University of Minnesota Press.

Haila, Anne (2000), 'Globalising Asian cities: guest editor's introduction', *Urban Studies*, **37** (12), 2141–3.

Hall, Peter (1993), 'Forces shaping urban Europe', *Urban Studies*, **30** (6), 883–98.

Hall, Peter (1997), 'Megacities, world cities and global cities', The First Megacities Lecture, Rotterdam, February.

Hall, Peter (2000), 'Creative cities and economic development', *Urban Studies*, **37** (4), 639–49.

Hamnett, Chris and Noam Shoval (2003), 'Museums as flagships of urban development', in Lily M. Hoffman, Susan S. Fainstein and Dennis R. Judd (eds), *Cities and Visitors: Regulating People, Markets, and City Space*, Malden, MA and Oxford: Blackwell Publishing, pp. 219–37.

Han, Pao-teh and Liu Hsin-yuan (2006), 'A review of unoccupied space

reuse policy', National Policy Foundation, available at http://old.npf.
org.tw/english/Publication/TDP2006.pdf (accessed 13 December 2009).

Han, Pao-teh and Liu Hsin-yuan (2008), 'Manwu mubiaode chuangyi
wenhua yuanqu' ['Aimless cultural park policy'], National Policy
Foundation, available at http://www.npf.org.tw/ post/2/4292 (accessed
13 December 2009).

Harvey, David (1989), *The Urban Experience*, Oxford: Blackwell.

Hill, Michael and Kwen Fee Lian (1995), *The Politics of Nation Building
and Citizenship in Singapore*, London and New York: Routledge.

Hitters, Erik and Greg Richards (2002), 'The creation and management of
cultural clusters', *Creativity and Innovation Management*, **11** (4), 234–47.

Ho, Oscar Hing-kay (2007), 'Comments and suggestions on WKCD by
Oscar Ho Hing-kay (WKCD-405),' available at http://www.legco.gov.
hk/yr04–05/english/hc/sub_com/hs02/papers/hs021009wkcd-405-e.pdf
(accessed 18 December 2007).

Home Affairs Bureau (2005), *Legislative Council Brief: Development of the
West Kowloon Cultural District, the Way Forward*, available at http://
www.legco.gov.hk/yr04–05/english/hc/sub_com/hs02/papers/hs02cb1-
legcobrief-e.pdf (accessed 2 April 2008).

Home Affairs Bureau (2007), *West Kowloon Cultural District Public
Engagement Exercise – Online Discussion Board*, available at http://
wkcddiscussion.hab.gov.hk/forum/topiclist.php (accessed 2 April 2008).

Home Affairs Bureau (2008), *Legislative Council Brief. West Kowloon
Cultural District: The Way Forward and West Kowloon Cultural District
Authority Bill*, available at http://www.legco.gov.hk/yr07–08/english/
bills/brief/b23_brf.pdf (accessed 9 April 2008).

Hong Kong Academy for Performing Arts (2006), *West Kowloon Cultural
District (WKCD-293)*, available at http://legco.gov.hk/yr04–05/english/
hc/sub_com/hs02/papers/hs02cb1-wkcd293-e.pdf (accessed 21 May
2008).

Hong Kong Alternatives (2006), *Re: Latest Independent Poll Resoundingly
Against the WKCD Plan (WKCD-224)*, available at http://legco.gov.
hk/yr04–05/chinese/hc/sub_com/hs02/papers/hs02cb1-wkcd224-ce.pdf
(accessed 21 May 2008).

Hong Kong Arts Administrators' Association (2007), *Submission to
Legco Subcommittee on WKCD 23 October 2007 (WKCD-421)*, available at http://legco.gov.hk/yr04–05/english/hc/sub_com/hs02/papers/
hs021023wkcd-421-e.pdf (accessed 21 May 2008).

Hong Kong Government Information Centre (n.d.), *Asia's World City*,
available at http://www.info.gov.hk/info/sar5/easia.htm (accessed
4 August 2014).

Hong Kong Institute of Architects (2007), *Subcommittee on West Kowloon*

Cultural District Development Meeting on 23 October 2007, available at http://legco.gov.hk/yr04–05/english/hc/sub_com/hs02/papers/hs021023wkcd-431-e.pdf (accessed 21 December 2007).

Hong Kong SAR Commission on Strategic Development (2000), *Bringing the Vision to Life – Hong Kong's Long-term Development Needs and Goals*, Hong Kong: Commission for Strategic Development.

Hong Kong Special Administrative Region (2013), *Hong Kong: The Facts – Creative Industries*, available at http://www.gov.hk/en/about/abouthk/factsheets/docs/creative_industries.pdf (accessed 14 July 2014).

Hsia, Chu-Joe (2006), 'A preliminary observation on the conservation of industrial heritage in Taiwan: a critical reflection', *Journal of Building and Planning National Taiwan University*, **13**, 91–106.

Hsing, Woan-Chian and Tsu-Lung Chou (2003), *Quanqiuhua qushi xia wenhua chanye yuanqu fazhan celüe zhi yanjiu [A Study of Cultural Parks' Development Strategies Under the Trend of Globalization]*, Taipei: National Development Council.

Huang, Shu-Yuan (2007), 'Dushi wenhua yuanqu jiangou zhi zhiduhua – yi Huashan wenhua yuanqu, boer yishu tequ weili' ['The Institutionalization of Urban Cultural Quarter Construction – the Cases of Huashan Culture Park and the Pier-2 Art District'], Master's degree thesis, Graduate Institute of Urban Planning, Taipei University.

Huashan Creative Park (2005–09), *What's the Story?*, available at http://www.huashan1914. com/en/story.html (accessed 26 March 2010).

Hui, Sylvia (2004a), 'Caution raised at canopy', *The Standard*, 2 June, available at http://www.thestandard.com.hk/news_detail.asp?pp_cat=&art_id=5504&sid=&con_type=1&d_str=20040602&Asear_year=2004 (accessed 1 April 2008).

Hui, Sylvia (2004b), 'A cultural revolution', *The Standard*, 8 July, available at http://www.thestandard.com.hk/news_detail.asp?pp_cat=&art_id=6915&sid=&con_type=1&d_str=20040708&sear_year=2004 (accessed 1 April 2008).

Hui, Sylvia (2004c), 'Culture zone plan "helps developers"', *The Standard*, 15 November, available at http://www.thestandard.com.hk/news_detail.asp?pp_cat=&art_id=13357&sid=&con_type=1&d_str=20041115&sear_year=2004 (accessed 1 April 2008).

Hung, Denise and Olga Wong (2007), 'Developers will not be let loose on waterfront; official places the emphasis on open space for public in repackaging of arts hub', *South China Morning Post*, 13 September, available at Lexis-Nexis Academic Universe (accessed 4 April 2008).

Hutton, Thomas A. (2004), 'The new economy of the inner city', *Cities*, **21** (2), 89–108.

Hymer, Stephen (1972), 'The multinational corporation and the law of uneven development', in Jagdish N. Bhagwati (ed.), *Economics and World Order from the 1970s to the 1990s*, New York: Collier-MacMillan, pp. 113–40.

Iau, Robert (1988), *Report of Committee on Performing Arts*, Singapore: Committee on Performing Arts.

International Association of Art Critics – Hong Kong (2007), *Submission by The International Association of Art Critics – Hong Kong (AICA-HK) to The Consultative Committee on the Core Arts and Cultural Facilities of the West Kowloon Cultural District (WKCD-422)*, available at http://legco.gov.hk/yr04–05/english/hc/sub_com/hs02/papers/hs021023wkcd-422-e.pdf (accessed 21 May 2008).

Jacobs, Jane M. (1996), *Edge of Empire: Postcolonialism and the City*, London: Routledge.

James, Al (2005), 'Demystifying the role of culture in innovative regional economies', *Regional Studies*, **39**, 1197–216.

Johnson, P. and B. Thomas (2001), 'Assessing the economic impact of the arts', in Sara Selwood and Geoffrey Brown (eds), *The UK Cultural Sector*, London: Policy Studies Institute, pp. 202–16.

Keane, Michael (2011), *China's New Creative Clusters: Governance, Human Capital and Investment*, London and New York: Routledge.

King, Anthony D. (1990), *Urbanism, Colonialism and the World-economy, Cultural and Spatial Foundations of the World Urban System*, London: Routledge.

Knox, Paul L. and Peter J. Taylor (1995), *World Cities in a World-system*, Cambridge: Cambridge University Press.

Kong, Lily (2000a), 'Cultural policy in Singapore: negotiating economic and socio-cultural agendas', *Geoforum*, **31**, 409–24.

Kong, Lily (2000b), 'Introduction: culture, economy, policy: trends and developments', *Geoforum*, **31** (4), 385–90.

Kong, Lily (2005), 'The sociality of cultural industries: Hong Kong's cultural policy and film industry', *International Journal of Cultural Policy*, **11** (1), 61–76.

Kong, Lily (2007), 'Cultural icons and urban development in Asia: economic imperative, national identity, and global city status', *Political Geography*, **26** (4), 383–404.

Kong, Lily (2008), 'Review of *The Art of City Making* by Charles Landry', *European Planning Studies*, **16** (9), 1325–7.

Kong, Lily (2009a), 'Beyond networks and relations: towards rethinking creative cluster theory', in Lily Kong and Justin O'Connor (eds), *Creative Economies, Creative Cities: Asian-European Perspectives*, Dordrecht, the Netherlands: Springer, pp. 61–75.

Kong, Lily (2009b), 'The making of sustainable creative/cultural space:

cultural indigeneity, social inclusion and environmental sustainability', *Geographical Review*, **99** (1), 1–22.

Kong, Lily (2011), 'Sustainable cultural spaces in the global city: cultural clusters in heritage sites, Hong Kong and Singapore', in Gary Bridge and Sophie Watson (eds), *The New Blackwell Companion to the City*, Malden, MA: Wiley-Blackwell, pp. 452–62.

Kong, Lily (2012a), 'Ambitions of a global city: arts, culture and creative economy in "post-crisis" Singapore', *International Journal of Cultural Policy*, **18** (3), 279–94.

Kong, Lily (2012b), 'Conceptualising cultural and creative spaces', *Bunkakeizaigaku (Cultural economics)*, **9** (1), 12–22.

Kong, Lily (forthcoming), 'Singapore's creative industries: policy directions', in Terence Chong (ed.), *A History of Cultural Policy in Singapore*, Singapore: Institute of Policy Studies.

Kong, Lily and Brenda Yeoh (2003), *The Politics of Landscapes in Singapore: Constructions of 'Nation'*, Syracuse, NY: Syracuse University Press.

Kong, Lily, Chris Gibson, Louisa-May Khoo and Anne-Louise Semple (2006), 'Knowledges of the creative economy: towards a regional geography of diffusion and adaptation in Asia', *Asia Pacific Viewpoint*, **47** (2), 173–94.

Konstadakopulos, Dimitrios (2000), 'Learning behavior and cooperation of small high technology firms in the ASEAN region', *ASEAN Economic Bulletin*, **17** (1), 48–59.

Kwok, Reginald Yin-Wang (2005), *Globalizing Taipei: The Political Economy of Spatial Development*, New York: Routledge.

Lai, Chloe (2005a), 'Bidders press case for dropping canopy', *South China Morning Post*, 4 July, available at Lexis-Nexis Academic Universe (accessed 3 April 2008).

Lai, Chloe (2005b), 'Hub's development model "may vary"; legislators and artists could help run the project, says official', *South China Morning Post*, 24 March, available at Lexis-Nexis Academic Universe (accessed 3 April 2008).

Lam, Anita (2006), 'We won't budge on hub, says minister', *South China Morning Post*, 9 January, available at *South China Morning Post* (accessed 4 April 2008).

Lam, Wai-man (2004), *Understanding the Political Culture of Hong Kong: The Paradox of Activism and Depoliticization*, Armonk, NY: M.E. Sharpe.

Landry, Charles (2000), *The Creative City*, London: Comedia.

Landry, Charles (2006), *The Art of City Making*, Trowbridge: Cromwell Press.

Landry, Charles and Phil Wood (2003), *Harnessing and Exploiting the Power of Culture for Competitive Advantage: A Report by Comedia for the Liverpool City Council and the Core Cities Group*, London: Comedia.

Leaf, Michael (1995), 'Inner city redevelopment in China: implications for the city of Beijing', *Cities*, **12** (3), 149–62.

Lee, Khoon Choy (1967), 'The role of the Singapore Arts Council', speech delivered at the Rotary Club, Singapore, 12 October.

Lee, Kwang-Suk (2007), 'Questioning a neoliberal urban regeneration policy: the rhetoric of "cities of culture" and the city of Gwangju, Korea', *International Journal of Cultural Policy*, **13** (4), 335–47.

Legislative Council (2005), *Concept Plan Competition for the Development of an Integrated Arts, Cultural and Entertainment District at the West Kowloon Reclamation, Hong Kong: Report of the Jury (WKCD-119)*, available at http://www.legco.gov.hk/yr04–05/english/hc/sub_com/hs02/papers/hs020422cb1-wkcd119-e.pdf (accessed 2 April 2008).

Legislative Council (2007), *Paper for the House Committee Meeting on 9 March 2007: Progress Report of the Subcommittee on West Kowloon Cultural District Development (CB(1)1085/06–07)*, available at http://www.legco.gov.hk/yr06–07/english/hc/papers/hc0309cb1-1085-e.pdf (accessed 18 December 2007).

Leyshon, Andrew (2001), 'Time–space (and digital) compression: software formats, musical networks, and the reorganisation of the music industry', *Environment and Planning A*, **32**, 49–77.

Li, Wuwei (2006), 'Shanghai fazhan chuangyi zhanyede zhongyao yiyi' ['The important meanings for Shanghai developing its creative industry'], available at http://www.scic.gov.cn/ creative_industry/index.htm (accessed 12 September 2007).

Liang, Caiheng (2007), 'Cong Shanghai Dajuyuan dao Guojia Dajuyuan' ['From the Shanghai Grand Theatre to the National Grand Theatre'], *Renminwang (People)*, 11 October, available at http://mnc.people.com.cn/GB/54849/69894/104887/104897/6365728.html (accessed 14 October 2009).

Lianhe Shibao (n.d.), 'Gaojia yanchuling baixing quebu, weiyuan jianyi: jiyu yi jiben guanli chengben wei jizunde caizheng butie' ['High ticket prices prohibit audience attendance: cultural practitioners recommend government subsidies'], available at http://shszx.eastday.com/node2/node4810/node4851/mssd/u1ai61258.html (accessed 14 July 2014).

Liberty Times Net (2011), '"Taibeidu hui" Taipei yishu zhongxin rongru yeshi wenhua' ['Taipei Arts Centre integrates night market culture'], 18 June, available at http://news.ltn.com.tw/news/local/ paper/501614 (accessed 15 July 2014).

Lim, Lan Yuan and Malone-Lee Lai Choo (1995), 'Singapore as a global city: strategies and key issues', *Urban Futures*, **19**, 90–6.

Lo, Fu-Chen and Peter J. Marcotullio (2000), 'Globalisation and urban transformations in the Asia-Pacific region: a review', *Urban Studies*, **37** (1), 77–111.

Logan, William S. (2001), *The Disappearing Asian City: Protecting Asia's Heritage Townscapes in the Face of Economic and Cultural Globalization*, Oxford: Oxford University Press.

Loh, Christine (2004), 'Cultural icon or just a big roof?', *The Standard*, 3 December, available at http://www.thestandard.com.hk/news_detail.asp?pp_cat=&art_id=14594&sid=&con_type=1&d_str=20041203&sear_year=2004 (accessed 1 April 2008).

Lu, Hanchao (2002), 'Nostalgia for the future: the resurgence of an alienated culture in China', *Pacific Affairs*, **75** (2), 169–86.

Lu, Jun (2007), *Beijingshi zhongxin chengqu wenhua chuangyi chanye fazhan yanjiu* [*A Study on the Development of the Creative Cultural Industry in Beijing's Central Districts*], Beijing: Peking University.

Lui, Tai-lok (2008), 'City branding without content: Hong Kong's aborted West Kowloon mega-project, 1998–2006', *IDPR*, **30** (3), 215–26.

Lui, Win-Ting (2004), 'Huashan yiwen tequ zhi yiwen shengtai ji shehui guanxi tanxi' ['The ecology of performing arts and social relationship of Huashan Art District'], Master's degree thesis, Department of Sociology, Soochow University.

Ma, Rongrong (2007), 'Guojiade Dajuyuan' ['National Grand Theatre'], *Shenhuo zhoukan* [*Lifeweek*], **460**, 16 December, available at http://magazine.sina.com/bg/lifeweek/460/2007-12-16/ba44619.html (accessed 3 February 2008).

Markusen, Ann (1996), 'Sticky places in slippery space: a typology of industrial districts', *Economic Geography*, **72** (8), 293–313.

Markusen, Ann (2007), 'The urban core as cultural sticky place', in Dietrich Henckel, Elke Pahl-Weber and Benjamin Herkommer (eds), *Time Space Places*, Berlin: Peter Lang Verlag, pp. 173–87.

Martin, Ron and Peter Sunley (2003), 'Deconstructing clusters: chaotic concept or policy panacea?', *Journal of Economic Geography*, **3** (1), 5–35.

McCann, Eugene J. (2007), 'Inequality and politics in the creative city-region: questions of liveability and state strategy', *International Journal of Urban and Regional Research*, **31** (1), 188–96.

Miles, Steven and Ronan Paddison (2005), 'Introduction: the rise and rise of culture-led urban regeneration', *Urban Studies*, **42** (5–6), 833–39.

Ministry of Information and the Arts (MITA) (1988), *Report of the Committee on Performing Arts*, Singapore: Ministry of Information and the Arts.

MITA (2000), *Renaissance City Report: Culture and the Arts in Renaissance Singapore*, Singapore: Ministry of Information and the Arts.

MITA (2002), *Investing in Singapore's Cultural Capital*, Singapore: Ministry of Information and the Arts.

Mitter, Rana (2004), *A Bitter Revolution: China's Struggle with the Modern World*, Oxford: Oxford University Press.

Mommaas, Hans (2004), 'Cultural clusters and the post-industrial city: towards the remapping of urban cultural policy', *Urban Studies*, **41** (3), 507–32.

Museum of Site (2006), *The Building-up of a New Communication Space: Provisional WKCD Council Prior to the Establishment of a Statutory Body for the West Kowloon Cultural District (WKCD-291)*, available at http://legco.gov.hk/yr04–05/english/hc/sub_com/hs02/papers/hs02cb1-wkcd291-e.pdf (accessed 21 May 2008).

National Arts Council (2010), *New Framework for Arts Spaces*, Singapore: National Arts Council.

National Arts Council (2014), *Arts Spaces: Little India Arts Belt*, available at https://www.nac.gov.sg/arts-spaces/arts-housing-scheme/little-india-arts-belt (accessed 8 July 2014).

National Theatre and Concert Hall (n.d.), *Guanyu liang tingyuan* [*About the Two Concert Halls*], available at http://npac-ntch.org/about/show?categoryName=introduction&lang=zh (accessed 14 July 2014).

Ng, Kang-chung (2007), 'Canopy may yet be built at cultural hub', *South China Morning Post*, 21 September, available at Lexis-Nexis Academic Universe (accessed 4 April 2008).

Ng, Kang-chung (2007), 'Women weishenme qianglie fandui guojia Dajuyuan fangan?' ['Why do we strongly oppose the National Grand Theatre design?'], available at http://news.sina.com.cn/china/2000–08–11/116414.html.

Ng, Mee Kam (2008), 'From government to governance? Politics of planning in the first decade of the Hong Kong Special Administrative Region', *Planning Theory & Practice*, **9** (2), 165–85.

Ng, Mee Kam (2010), 'Place-making battlefields: three empty reclaimed sites in Victoria Harbour', *disP – The Planning Review*, **180** (1), 8–17.

Ng, Mee Kam (2011), 'Power and rationality: the politics of harbor reclamation in Hong Kong', *Environment and Planning C*, **29**, 677–92.

Ng, Mee Kam and Peter Hills (2003), 'World cities or great cities? A comparative study of five Asian metropolises', *Cities*, **20** (3), 151–65.

Ng, Mee Kam, Wing Shing Tang, Joanna W.Y. Lee and Darwin Leung (2010), 'Spatial practice, conceived space and lived space: Hong Kong's "piers saga" through the Lefebvrian lens', *Planning Perspectives*, **25** (4), 411–31.

O'Connor, Justin (2004), '"A special kind of city knowledge": innovative clusters, tacit knowledge and the "creative city"', *Media International Australia*, **112**, 131–49.

O'Connor, Justin and Gu Xin (2006), 'A new modernity? The arrival of creative industries in China', *International Journal of Cultural Policy*, **9** (3), 271–83.

Ohmae, Kenichi (1995), *The End of the Nation State: The Rise of Regional Economies*, London: Harper Collins.

Paul, Darel E. (2004), 'World cities as hegemonic projects: the politics of global imagineering in Montreal', *Political Geography*, **23**, 571–96.

Peng, Peigen (2007), *Ershiyi shiji de zhongguo jianzhu: ruhe chengxianqihou jinru shijieyiliude hanglie* [*Chinese Architecture in the Twenty-first Century: Striving Towards World-class*], Beijing: Tsinghua University.

People's Panel on West Kowloon (2005), *People's Panel on West Kowloon: Views on WKCD Development (WKCD-181)*, available at http://legco.gov.hk/yr04–05/english/hc/sub_com/hs02/papers/hs020913cb1-wkcd181-e.pdf (accessed 21 May 2008).

Plaza, Beatriz (2000), 'Evaluating the influence of a large cultural artifact in the attraction of tourism: the Guggenheim Museum Bilbao case', *Urban Affairs Review*, **36** (2), 264–74.

Ponzini, Davide and Ugo Rossi (2010), 'Becoming a creative city: the entrepreneurial mayor, network politics and the promise of an urban renaissance', *Urban Studies*, **47** (5), 1037–57.

Porter, Michael E. (1995), 'The competitive advantage of the inner city', *Harvard Business Review*, **73**, May–June, 55–71.

Porter, Michael E. (1998), 'Cluster and the new economics of competition', *Harvard Business Review*, **76** (6), 77–90.

Porter, Michael E. (2000), 'Location, competition, and economic development: local clusters in a global economy', *Economic Development Quarterly*, **1**, 15–34.

Porter, Michael E. (2003), 'The economic performance of regions', *Regional Studies*, **37**, 549–78.

Porter, Michael E., Christian Ketels and Mercedes Delgado (2007), 'The microeconomic foundations of prosperity: findings from the Business Competitiveness Index', in Michael E. Porter, Xavier Sala-i-Martin and Klaus Schwab (eds), *World Economic Forum: The Global Competitiveness Report 2007–2008*, New York: Palgrave Macmillan, pp. 51–81, available at http://www.labconvergencia.org:16080/sitio1/MEL/HTML_nva_version-bckp2011/ana_estra_ind/Documentos/U1/The_Microeconomic_Foundations.pdf (accessed 9 June 2014).

Potts, Jason and Michael Keane (2011), 'Creative clusters and innovation', in Jason Potts (ed.), *Creative Industries and Economic Evolution*, Northampton, MA, USA and Cheltenham, UK: Edward Elgar, pp. 152–61.

Power, Dominic (2002), 'Cultural industries in Sweden: an assessment of their place in the Swedish economy', *Economic Geography*, **78** (2), 103–27.

Pratt, Andy C. (1996), 'Cultural industries in the digital age: technological convergence, globalization and innovation', summary paper for the Regional Studies Association annual conference Art and Sport in Local and Regional Economic Development, West Yorkshire Playhouse, Leeds, 14 November.

Pratt, Andy C. (1997), 'The cultural industries production system: a case study of employment change in Britain, 1984–91', *Environment and Planning A*, **29** (11), 1953–74.

Pratt, Andy C. (2000a), 'Cultural tourism as an urban cultural industry: a critical appraisal', in *Cultural Tourism*, Barcelona: Interarts and Turisme de Catalunya, Diputacio de Barcelona, pp. 33–45.

Pratt, Andy C. (2000b), 'New media, the new economy and new spaces', *Geoforum*, **31** (4), 425–36.

Pratt, Andy C. (2004a), 'Cultural industries: beyond the cluster paradigm', mimeo, available from the author.

Pratt, Andy C. (2004b), 'Creative clusters: towards the governance of the creative industries production system?', *Media International Australia*, **112**, 50–66.

Pratt, Andy C. (2006), 'Inside and across clusters: production and peer respect networks', paper presented at the Cultural Creative Spaces Conference, Beijing, 19–21 October.

Pratt, Andy C. (2008), 'Creative cities: the cultural industries and the creative class', *Geografiska Annaler: Series B, Human Geography*, **90** (2), 107–17.

Pratt, Andy C. (2011), 'Microclustering of the media industries in London', in Charlie Karlsson and Robert G. Picard (eds), *Media Clusters: Spatial Agglomeration and Content Capabilities*, Northampton, MA, USA and Cheltenham, UK: Edward Elgar, pp. 120–35.

Raco, Mike and Katherine Gilliam (2012), 'Geographies of abstraction, urban entrepreneurialism, and the production of new cultural spaces: the West Kowloon Cultural District, Hong Kong', *Environment and Planning A*, **44**, 1425–42.

Reed, Howard Curtis (1981), *The Preeminence of International Financial Centers*, New York: Praeger.

Renaissance City Plan III (2008), Singapore: Ministry of Information, Communications and the Arts.

Riding, Alan (2004), 'Barcelona tried cultural forum to encourage urban renewal', *New York Times*, 26 July, available at http://www.nytimes.com/2004/07/26/arts/barcelona-tries-cultural-forum-to-encourage-urban-renewal.html (accessed 13 June 2014).

Robinson, William I. (2009), 'Saskia Sassen and the sociology of globalization: a critical appraisal', *Sociological Analysis*, **3** (1), 5–29.

Sabapathy, T.K. (1995), 'Reflections', in The Substation (ed.), *Art vs Art: Conflict and Convergence – the Substation Conference*, Singapore: The Substation, pp. 15–20.

Sally, Razeen (2014), 'Challenges of the global city', *Straits Times*, 31 May.

Sassen, Saskia (1988), *The Mobility of Capital and Labor: A Study in International Investment and Labor Flow*, Cambridge: Cambridge University Press.

Sassen, Saskia (1991), *The Global City*, Princeton, NJ: Princeton University Press.

Sassen, Saskia (1994), *Cities in a World Economy*, London: Pine Forge Press.

Sassen, Saskia (1995a), 'On concentration and centrality in the global city', in P.L. Knox and P. Taylor (eds), *World Cities in a World-system*, Cambridge: Cambridge University Press, pp. 63–75.

Sassen, Saskia (1995b), 'Urban impacts of economic globalisation', in J. Brotchie et al. (eds), *Cities in Competition*, Melbourne, VIC: Longman Australia, pp. 36–57.

Sassen, Saskia (2000), 'Analytical borderlands: economy and culture in the global city', in Gary Bridge and Sophie Watson (eds), *A Companion to the City*, Malden, MA: Blackwell, pp. 168–80.

Scheff, Josef (2001), *Learning Regions: Regional Networks as an Answer to Global Challenges*, New York: Peter Lang.

Scott, Allen J. (1996), 'Regional motors of the global economy', *Futures*, **28** (5), 391–411.

Scott, Allen J. (1997), 'The cultural economy of cities', *International Journal of Urban and Regional Researches*, **21** (2), 323–39.

Scott, Allen J. (1999), 'The cultural economy: geography and the creative field', *Media, Culture & Society*, **21**, 807–17.

Scott, Allen J. (2000a), *The Cultural Economy of Cities*, London: Sage.

Scott, Allen J. (2000b), 'The cultural economy of Paris', *International Journal of Urban and Regional Research*, **24** (3), 567–82.

Scott, Allen J. (2001), *Global City-regions: Trends, Theory, Policy*, Oxford: Oxford University Press.

Scott, Allen J. (2004), 'Cultural products industries and urban economic development: prospects for growth and market contestation in global context', *Urban Affairs Review*, **39** (4), 461–90.

Scott, Allen J. (2006), 'Creative cities: conceptual issues and policy questions', *Journal of Urban Affairs*, **28** (1), 1–17.

Scott, Allen J. (2014), 'Beyond the creative city: cognitive-cultural capitalism and the new urbanism', *Regional Studies*, **48** (4), 565–78.

Shanghai City Government (2004), *Shanghaishi chengshi zongti guihua (1999–2020) zhong, jingqi jianshe xingdong jihua* [*Shanghai City Master Plan (1999–2020) Short- and Medium-term Construction Plan*], available at http://www.shanghai.gov.cn/shanghai/node2314/node12959/node12967/userobject21ai50955.html (accessed 14 July 2014).

Shanghai Creative Industries Centre (2006), *Shanghai chuangyi chanye fazhan baogao – peiyu fazhan chuangyi chanyede tansuo yu shijian* [*2006 Shanghai Creative Industries Development Report*], Shanghai: Shanghai Scientific and Technological Literature Publishing House.

Shanghai Creative Industries Centre (2007), *Shanghai chuangyi chanye fazhan baogao* [*Shanghai Creative Industries Development Report*], Shanghai: SCIC.

Shanghai Grand Theatre (2014), *Guanyuwomen* [*About Us*], available at http://www.shgtheatre.com/jsp/portal/center.jsp?branchID=1000002152 (accessed 14 July 2014).

Shanghai Oriental Art Centre (2014), *Gaikuang* [*Summary*], available at http://www.shoac.com.cn/NewsInfo.aspx?NewsID=7466 (accessed 14 July 2014).

Shin, Kyoung-Ho and Michael Timberlake (2000), 'World cities in Asia: cliques, centrality and connectedness', *Urban Studies*, **37** (12), 2257–85.

Simmie, James (2004), 'Innovation and clustering in the globalised international economy', *Urban Studies*, **41** (5/6), 1095–112.

Sinema (2009), *Sinema Old School*, available at http://www.sinema.sg/about/oldschool/ (accessed 8 July 2014).

Singapore Advisory Council on Culture and the Arts (1989), *Report of the Advisory Council on Culture and the Arts*, Singapore: Singapore National Printers.

Singapore Tourist Promotion Board (1995), *Singapore, Global City for the Arts*, Singapore: Singapore Tourist Promotion Board.

Skeldon, Ronald (1997), 'Hong Kong: colonial city to global city to provincial city?', *Cities*, **14** (5), 265–71.

Smith, David A. and Michael Timberlake (1995), 'Conceptualising and mapping the structure of the world systems city system', *Urban Studies*, **32** (2), 287–302.

So, Una (2007), 'Let's talk, for arts' sake!', *The Standard*, 13 September, available at http://www.thestandard.com.hk/news_detail.asp?pp_cat=

12&art_id=53380&sid=15358568&con_type=3&d_str=20070913& sear_year=2007 (accessed 6 August 2014).

The Standard (2003), 'Developers split over cultural job', 7 October, available at http://www.thestandard.com.hk/news_detail.asp?pp_cat=&art_ id=28973&sid=&con_type=1&d_str=20031007&sear_year=2003 (accessed 1 April 2008).

Stevenson, Deborah (2004), '"Civic gold" rush: cultural planning and the politics of the third way', *International Journal of Cultural Policy*, **10**, 119–31.

Stolarick, Kevin M. and Richard Florida (2006), 'Creativity, connections and innovation: a study of linkages in the Montreal region', *Environment and Planning A*, **38**, 1799–817.

Storper, Michael (1997), *The Regional World: Territorial Development in a Global Economy*, New York: Guilford Press.

Strom, Elizabeth (2002), 'Converting pork into porcelain: cultural institutions and downtown development', *Urban Affairs Review*, **38** (1), 3–21.

Subcommittee on West Kowloon Cultural District Development (2005a), *Land Use and Planning (WKCD-91)*, available at http://www.legco.gov. hk/yr04–05/english/hc/sub_com/hs02/papers/hs020221cb1-wkcd91-e. pdf (accessed 14 April 2008).

Subcommittee on West Kowloon Cultural District Development (2005b), *Shortfall and Long-term Needs in the Development of Arts and Culture in Hong Kong (WKCD 110)*, available at http://www.legco.gov.hk/ yr04–05/english/hc/sub_com/hs02/papers/hs020408cb1-wkcd-110-e.pdf (accessed 2 April 2008).

Subcommittee on West Kowloon Cultural District Development (2005c), *West Kowloon Cultural District Development Updated Background Brief (LC Paper No. CB(1) 848/04–05(01))*, available at http://www.legco. gov.hk/yr04–05/english/hc/sub_com/hs02/papers/hs020204cb1–848–1e. pdf (accessed 2 April 2008).

Subcommittee on West Kowloon Cultural District Development (2007a), *Recommendation Report of Consultative Committee on the Core Arts and Cultural Facilities of the West Kowloon Cultural District (WKCD-398)*, available at http://www.hab.gov.hk/wkcd/pe/eng/report4.htm (accessed 2 April 2008).

Subcommittee on West Kowloon Cultural District Development (2007b), *Summary of Views of Various Organizations and Individuals Expressed at the Meetings on 9 and 23 October 2007 (WKCD-450)*, available at http://www.legco.gov.hk/yr04–05/english/hc/sub_com/hs02/papers/ hs021129wkcd-450-e.pdf (accessed 23 April 2008).

Subcommittee on West Kowloon Cultural District Development (2008), *Major Findings of the Public Engagement Exercise and Follow-up Work for the WKCD Project*, available at http://www.legco.gov.hk/yr07–08/ english/bills/brief/b23_brf.pdf (accessed 9 April 2008).

Substation (ed.) (1995), *Art vs Art: Conflict and Convergence – The Substation Conference*, Singapore: The Substation.

Taipei New Horizon (2013), *About Us* (in Chinese), available at http:// www.taipeinewhorizon.com.tw/TNH/AboutUs (accessed 24 July 2014).

Taiwan Design Center (2009), *About TDC*, available at http://www.tdc. org.tw/en_about01.htm (accessed 8 July 2014).

Tamney, Joseph B. (1996), *The Struggle Over Singapore's Soul: Western Modernization and Asian Culture*, Berlin and New York: Walter de Gruyter.

Tan, Chengwen and Li Guoping (2001), 'Zhongguo shouduquan fazhande san dazhanlüe' ['Three development strategies of China's capital belt'], *Science of Geography*, **21** (1), 12–18.

Tan, Kenneth Paul (ed.) (2007), *Renaissance Singapore? Economy, Culture and Politics*, Singapore: NUS Press.

Taoho Design Architects and Hong Kong Tourist Association (1999), *Study on the Feasibility of a New Performance Venue in Hong Kong: Executive Summary (WKCD-96)*, available at http://www.legco.gov. hk/yr04–05/english/hc/sub_com/hs02/papers/hs020316cb1-wkcd96-e-scan.pdf (accessed 2 April 2008).

Taylor, Peter J. (1997), 'Hierarchical tendencies among world cities: a global research proposal', *Cities*, **14** (6), 323–32.

Taylor, Peter J. (2000), 'World cities and territorial states under conditions of contemporary globalization', *Political Geography*, **19**, 5–32.

Taylor, Peter J. (2001), 'Specification of world city network', *Geographical Analysis*, **33** (2), 181–94.

Taylor, Peter J. (2004), *World City Network: A Global Urban Analysis*, London: Routledge.

Taylor, Peter J., Gilda Catalano and David R.F. Walker (2002), 'Measurement of the world city network', *Urban Studies*, **39** (13), 2367–76.

Telok Kurau Studios (TKS) (2007), *Telok Kurau Studios: Commemorating a Decade*, Singapore: Telok Kurau Studios.

Tsang, Donald (2003), 'Statement by Mr Donald Tsang, Chief Secretary for Administration, at a press conference held on 5 September 2003, announcing the invitation for proposals for development of the West Kowloon Cultural District, Hong Kong'.

Tsang, Donald (2004), 'Statement on West Kowloon Cultural District project', available at http://www.info.gov.hk/gia/general/200411/10/1110252.htm (accessed 14 April 2008).

Tsang, Donald (2005), 'Government shares vision with community', speech as Chief Secretary for Administration, 18 March, available at http://

archive.news.gov.hk/isd/ebulletin/en/category/ontherecord/050319/ html/050319en11001.htm (accessed 8 July 2014).

Tsang, Stephen, Margarett Burnett, Peter Hills and Richard Welford (2009), 'Trust public participation and environmental governance in Hong Kong', *Environmental Policy and Governance*, **19**, 99–114.

Tung, Chee Hwa (1999), 'The 1999 policy address: quality people, quality home – positioning Hong Kong for the 21st century', available at http:// www.policyaddress.gov.hk/pa99/english/espeech.pdf (accessed 8 July 2014).

Tung, Chee Hwa (2005), 'The 2005 policy address: working together for economic development and social harmony', available at http://www. policyaddress.gov.hk/2005/eng/pdf/ speech.pdf (accessed 8 July 2014).

Turok, Ivan (2003), 'Cities, clusters and creative industries: the case of film and television in Scotland', *European Planning Studies*, **11** (5), 549–65.

van Heur, Bas (2009), 'The clustering of creative networks: between myth and reality', *Urban Studies*, **46** (8), 1531–52.

Wang, Chia-Huang (2003), 'Taipei as a global city: a theoretical and empirical examination', *Urban Studies*, **40** (2), 309–34.

Wang, Feng (2013), 'Beijing as a globally fluent city', Brookings-Tsinghua Center for Public Policy and Global Cities Initiative, available at http:// www.brookings.edu/~/media/research/files/papers/2013/10/14%20 beijing%20as%20a%20globally%20fluent%20city/beijing%20as%20 a%20globally%20fluent%20city (accessed 8 July 2014).

Wang, Jici and Wang Jixian (1998), 'An analysis of new-tech agglomeration in Beijing: a new industrial district in the making?', *Environment and Planning A*, **30**, 681–701.

Wang, Jing (2003), 'Framing policy research on Chinese "cultural industry": cultural goods, market-state relations, and the international free trade regime', paper presented at the Critical Policy Studies of China International Workshop, Policy Cultural Project, Harvard Asia Center, 15–16 November.

Wang, Jing (2004), 'The global reach of a new discourse: how far can "creative industries" travel?', *International Journal of Cultural Studies*, **7** (1), 9–19.

Wang, Ping (2009), 'Huashan "xin Taiwan yiwen zhi xing" zhi zhengce xingcheng yu zhixing' ['The policy formation of Huashan Creative and Cultural Park'], Master's degree thesis, Graduate Institute of Building and Planning, Taiwan University.

Wang, Weijia (2006), *Investigation Report on 798 Art Zone*, Beijing: Policy and Regulation Division of Beijing Tourism Bureau.

Wang, Zhangling (1993), *Dalu wenhua sichao* [*Cultural Trends in the Mainland*], Taipei: Mainland Affairs Council.

Ward, Kevin (2007), 'Creating a personality for downtown: business improvement districts in Milwaukee', *Urban Geography*, **28** (8), 781–808.

Watkins, Helen and David Herbert (2003), 'Cultural policy and place promotion: Swansea and Dylan Thomas', *Geoforum*, **34** (2), 249–66.

World Economic Forum (WEF) (2008–2009), *The Global Competitiveness Report 2008–2009*, available at http://www.weforum.org/pdf/GCR08/GCR08.pdf (accessed 11 June 2014).

WEF (2013–2014), *The Global Competitiveness Report 2013–2014*, available at http://www3.weforum.org/docs/WEF_GlobalCompetitivenessReport_2013–14.pdf (accessed 10 June 2014).

Wei, Shaonong (2006), 'Chuangyi Shanghai, fuwu Shibo' ['Creative Shanghai and servicing World Expo'], available at http://www.scic.gov.cn/creative_industry/index.htm (accessed 12 September 2007).

Whitt, J. Allen (1987), 'Mozart in the metropolis: the arts coalition and the urban growth machine', *Urban Affairs Quarterly*, **23** (1), 15–36.

Wikipedia (Chinese) (n.d.), *Da Taibei xinjuyuan* [*Taipei Grand New Theatre*], available at http://zh.wikipedia.org/wiki/%E5%A4%A7%E5%8F%B0%E5%8C%97%E6%96%B0%E5%8A%87%E9%99%A2 (accessed 15 July 2014).

Wojan, Timothy R., Dayton M. Lambert and David A. McGranahan (2007), 'Emoting with their feet: bohemian attraction to creative milieu', *Journal of Economic Geography*, **7** (6), 711–36.

Wong, Martin (2004), 'Kowloon canopy a must: Suen', *South China Morning Post*, available at Lexis-Nexis Academic Universe (accessed 3 April 2008).

Wong, Olga (2008), 'Arts hub bill to be tabled amid fears on autonomy, financing', *South China Morning Post*, 20 February, available at Lexis-Nexis Academic Universe (accessed 2 April 2008).

Wong, Olga and Denise Hung (2007), 'New vision unveiled for cultural hub; arts project changes direction', *South China Morning Post*, 13 September, available at Lexis-Nexis Academic Universe (accessed 4 April 2008).

Wu, Chin-Tao (2002), *Privatising Culture: Corporate Art Intervention since the 1980s*, London and New York: Verso.

Wu, Fulong (2000), 'The global and local dimensions of place-making: remaking Shanghai as a world city', *Urban Studies*, **37** (8), 1359–77.

Wu, Helen (2007), 'Only 2 venues at cultural hub will break even', *South China Morning Post*, 14 September, available at Lexis-Nexis Academic Universe (accessed 4 April 2008).

Wu, Liangyong (2006), 'Xinxingshixia Beijing guihua jianshe zhanlüede sikao' ['Thoughts on Beijing's strategic planning and development under new circumstances'], in China Urban Development Report

Committee (ed.), *Zhongguo chengshi fazhan baogao 2006* [*China Urban Development Report 2006*], Beijing: China City Publishing House.

Wu, Meisen (2006), 'Tianzifangde fazhan zhi lu' ['The path of the Tianzifang development'], in Shanghai Creative Industries Centre (ed.), *Shanghai peiyu fazhan chuangyi chanyede tansuo shijian* [*The Exploration and Practice of Cultivating Shanghai's Creative Industry*], Shanghai: Shanghai Scientific and Technological Literature Publishing House, pp. 95–9.

Wu, Weiping (2005), *Dynamic Cities and Creative Clusters*, World Bank Research Working Paper 3509, February.

Xie Rui (2005), 'Poxi Shanghai Dajuyuan de yunying he guanli' ['The operation and management of Shanghai Grand Theatre'], Cultural Industry Section of the Cultural Department, available at http://www.cassrccp.com/plus/view.php?aid=707 (accessed 6 August 2014).

Xu, Peng (2004), 'Beijing "798" dangdai yishuqu mianlin "shengsi jueze"' ['"798" Art Zone in Beijing facing life or death situation'], *Xinhua Net*, 22 December, available at http://news.xinhuanet.com/news center/2004–12/22/content_2366756.htm (accessed 7 November 2007).

Xu, Yujun and Huang Fuqi (2008), 'Da Taibei Xinjuyuan an' ['The case of Taipei New Grand Theatre'], 4 March, available at http://ccindustry.pixnet.net/blog/post/15016189-%E5%A4%A7%E5%8F%B0%E5%8C%97%E6%96%B0%E5%8A%87%E9%99%A2%E6%A1%88-%E9%81%8E%E9%97%9C- (accessed 15 July 2014).

Xue, Xiufang (2004), 'Gaobie weiquan, Zhongshantang kaimen' ['Leaving authority, the opening of Zhongshan Hall'], *Shuxiang yuanfu*, **14**, 26–9.

Yang, Margaret (2007), 'Missing ingredient', *South China Morning Post*, 20 September, available at Lexis-Nexis Academic Universe (accessed 21 December 2007).

Yang, Yifeng and Yixuan Zhang (2007), 'Shenmi 798 daodi shenme yang' ['What does the mysterious 798 look like?'], *People's Daily* (overseas edition), 9 April, available at http://big5.xinhuanet.com/gate/big5/news.xinhuanet.com/travel/2007–04/09/content_5952089.htm (accessed 17 June 2014).

Yatsko, Pamela (2001), *New Shanghai: The Rocky Rebirth of China's Legendary City*, New York: John Wiley & Sons.

Yeo, George Yong Boon (1991), 'Building in a market test for the arts', *Speeches: A Bi-monthly Selection of Ministerial Speeches*, **15**, 54–7.

Yeo, George Yong Boon (1993), 'An international market for the arts', *Speeches: A Bi-monthly Selection of Ministerial Speeches*, **17**, 62–6.

Yeoh, Brenda (1999), 'Global/globalizing cities', *Progress in Human Geography*, **23** (4), 607–16.

Yeoh, Brenda (2005), 'The global cultural city? Spatial imagineering and politics in the (multi)cultural marketplaces of south-east Asia', *Urban Studies*, **42** (5/6), 945–58.

Yeung, Chris (2005), 'Tsang faces tough role in cultural hub drama', *South China Morning Post*, 12 January, available at Lexis-Nexis Academic Universe (accessed 2 April 2008).

Yi, Ming (2006), '798 yishuqu yu zhuanxing chuangyi chanyeyuan' ['798 Art Zone to turn into a creative industry park'], *Xinhua Net*, 9 March, available at http://www.chahua.org/art/news/hr/2006–03/114. html (accessed 16 July 2014).

Yusuf, Shahid and Kaoru Nabeshima (2005), 'Creative industries in East Asia', *Cities*, **22** (2), 109–22.

Yusuf, Shahid and Wu Weiping (2002), 'Pathways to a world city: Shanghai rising in an era of globalization', *Urban Studies*, **39** (7), 1213–40.

Zhang, Chun (2006), 'Qiangzhan xianji youshi mingxian, Beijing wenhua chuangyi chanye dayoukeyi' ['Seizing opportunities, exhibiting advantages, creative culture will have a great future in Beijing'], *Xinhua Net*, 25 April, available at http://news3.xinhuanet.com/ent/2006–04/25/ content_4471639.htm (accessed 7 November 2007).

Zhang, Jingcheng (2007), *Zhongguo chuangyi chanye baogao* [*China Creative Industry Development Report*], Beijing: China Economies Publisher.

Zhang, Jingqiu (2004), 'Beijingshi wenhua sheshi kongjian fenbu yu wenhua gongneng yanjiu' ['Study on the distribution and cultural functions of Beijing's cultural spaces and facilities'], *Beijing Social Science*, **2**, 53–60.

Zhongguo, Jingjiwang (2013), 'Yanchu piaojia gaoyin wenhua yishujie weiyuan reyi changdi zujin gao daozhi' ['Cultural practitioners point to high rentals as cause of high ticket prices'], 6 March, available at http://big5.ce.cn/gate/big5/www.ce.cn/celt/wyry/201303/06/t20130306_ 24170752.shtml (accessed 14 July 2014).

Zhou, Hongyu (2006), 'Inspiration comes from 798', *New Economic Weekly*, **113**, available at http://nisuwang.net/report/b194.htm (accessed 17 June 2014).

Zhou, Yixing (1996), 'Beijingde jiaoquhua ji yinfade sikao' ['Thoughts on the suburban expansion in Beijing'], *Science of Geography*, **3**, 198–206.

Zhou, Yu (2005), 'The making of an innovative region from a centrally planned economy: institutional evolution in Zhongguancun Science Park in Beijing', *Environment and Planning A*, **37**, 1113–34.

Zhou, Yu and Tong Xin (2003), 'An innovative region in China: interaction between multinational corporations and local firms in a high-tech cluster in Beijing', *Economic Geography*, **79** (2), 129–52.

Zimmerman, Paul (2007), 'Too tied to one idea', *South China Morning*

Post, 21 September, available at Lexis-Nexis Academic Universe (accessed 21 December 2007).

Zonta Club (2005a), *Response to the Subcommittee on West Kowloon Cultural District Development's 'Invitation of Views on the Way Forward for the WKCD Project' (WKCD-216)*, available at http://legco.gov.hk/yr04–05/english/hc/sub_com/hs02/papers/hs02cb1-wkcd216-e.pdf (accessed 21 May 2008).

Zonta Club (2005b), *Submission on the Proposals to the West Kowloon Cultural District (WKCD-116)*, available at http://legco.gov.hk/yr04–05/english/hc/sub_com/hs02/papers/hs02cb1-wkcd116-e.pdf (accessed 21 May 2008).

Zonta Club (2005c), *Submission to the Legco Subcommittee on West Kowloon Cultural District Development by the Zonta Club of Hong Kong (WKCD-189)*, available at http://legco.gov.hk/yr04–05/english/hc/sub_com/hs02/papers/hs020913cb1-wkcd189-e.pdf (accessed 21 May 2008).

Zukin, Sharon (1982), 'Loft living as "historic compromise" in the urban core: the New York experience', *International Journal of Urban and Regional Research*, **6** (2), 256–76.

Zukin, Sharon (1989), *Loft Living: Culture and Capital in Urban Change*, New Brunswick, NJ: Rutgers University Press.

Zukin, Sharon (1995), *The Cultures of Cities*, Oxford: Blackwell Publishers.

Index